Android™ Development Patterns

Android™ Development Patterns

Best Practices for Professional Developers

Phil Dutson

⋏⋏ Addison-Wesley

Boston • Columbus • Indianapolis • New York • San Francisco • Amsterdam • Cape Town
Dubai • London • Madrid • Milan • Munich • Paris • Montreal • Toronto • Delhi
Mexico City • São Paulo • Sidney • Hong Kong • Seoul • Singapore • Taipei • Tokyo

For information about buying this title in bulk quantities, or for special sales opportunities (which may include electronic versions; custom cover designs; and content particular to your business, training goals, marketing focus, or branding interests), please contact our corporate sales department at corpsales@pearsoned.com or (800) 382-3419.

For government sales inquiries, please contact governmentsales@pearsoned.com.

For questions about sales outside the U.S., please contact intlcs@pearson.com.

Visit us on the Web: informit.com/aw

Library of Congress Control Number: 2015958569

ISBN-13: 978-0-133-92368-1
ISBN-10: 0-133-92368-1

Text printed in the United States on recycled paper at RR Donnelley in Crawfordsville, Indiana.

First printing: February 2016

Editor-in-Chief
Mark Taub

Executive Editor
Laura Lewin

Development Editor
Sheri Replin

Managing Editor
Kristy Hart

Project Editor
Elaine Wiley

Copy Editor
Bart Reed

Indexer
Tim Wright

Proofreader
Laura Hernandez

Technical Reviewers
Romin Irani
Douglas Jones
Raymond Rischpater

Editorial Assistant
Olivia Basegio

Cover Designer
Chuti Prasertsith

Compositor
Nonie Ratcliff

To all of those who believe in magic,
especially the digital kind.

Contents

x   Contents

Preface

The growth of Android since the launch of Cupcake has been astonishing. Today, Android powers more than just mobile phones; it has become the go-to solution for manufacturers of audio equipment, tablets, televisions, cars, and more.

As the use of Android becomes more prevalent, the demand for developers who are familiar with using it has also scaled. Developers who understand how the system can be built, leveraged, and used are necessary to provide the next wave of amazing and must-have applications.

Many people around the world are being introduced to Android for the first time, and we as developers need to make sure to provide them with a first-class experience that will put a smile on their face and help them understand how truly amazing the Android system is.

Why Development Patterns?

In the fast-paced world of development, patterns are the time-saving solutions that developers use and access to maximize their output and minimize time wasted creating a solution that will ultimately fail.

Android development is a special place that is both familiar and foreign to many Java and object-oriented programmers. The relationship it has with the Java language and structure helps to bring in developers who have experience and get them up to speed in an almost effortless manner. However, there are some optimizations and memory-handling techniques that are not optimal for the seasoned Java developer.

This particular book is the bridge that helps seasoned developers understand the Android way of building and thinking. It is written so that those new to Android development gain a foundation for the platform and how to work with the many facets and intricacies that Android brings to the table while giving some in-depth hints and strategies that advanced developers will need to make their app a success.

Who Should Read This Book?

Anyone interested in how Android development works should find this book enjoyable and helpful. Those just beginning their Android journey may not find this as complete of a volume, but some development experience will help; however, those who are tenacious and don't mind getting elbows-deep should find this to be an acceptable companion on their quest toward their perfect app.

Those who are interested in seeing only theoretical development patterns with large explanations about individual bit-shifting and hand-tuning memory management will be disappointed in that this book instead focuses on how Android works together piece-by-piece with example snippets that help solidify how things should be accomplished in a best-practices manner.

Getting Started

For those new to developing Android applications, the minimum requirement is a computer running either OS X, Windows, or Linux. On these systems, you should download Android Studio from http://developer.android.com/sdk/. Android Studio comes with the Android SDK.

Full use of the Android SDK requires downloads of the version and sample code for which you want to develop. Although you can certainly download only a specific version of Android, you should download all versions of Android on which you want your app to work.

You should also use the Android SDK to download system images of emulators or Android Virtual Device (AVD) files. These system images allow you to test your app without actually having an Android device.

It is highly recommended that you acquire at least one Android device for testing, with a preference of having multiple devices in many form-factors so that you can accurately test, monitor, and experience your app as your users will.

Visit the following websites to keep up on Android and see when new features are introduced and how to use them:

- **StackOverflow:** http://www.stackoverflow.com/
- **Official Android Developer Site:** http://developer.android.com/
- **Android Developers Blog:** http://android-developers.blogspot.com/
- **Google Developers on YouTube:** https://www.youtube.com/user/androiddevelopers
- **Android Source Code (AOSP):** http://source.android.com/

Book Structure

This book starts with the basics of Android development, including how to set up an environment. It takes you through the importance of creating a proper development flow and adding testing to your app to make sure your code performs and behaves the way you expect.

It continues step by step through the various pieces and parts that make up the Android framework. This includes how applications are structured, using widgets and components, and learning how to use and create views.

You are then introduced to application design paradigms and learn how to make sure you are creating an app that you can manage and update easily. This includes adding media and network connections that will not end up wasting precious battery power and giving users the most accurate and up-to-date information possible.

Optional hardware components, Android Wear, and Android TV are also covered later in this book to expose you to taking your app to the next level and exploring new opportunities. As Android finds itself being included in more devices, you'll understand how and why it is in your best interest to provide apps to users who invest in these platforms.

Finally, you learn about some key optimization strategies as well as how to package your app for distribution through enterprise systems, email, and the Google Play Store.

When you are finished with this book, you will have an understanding of how the Android system works and, more importantly, how to craft an app that is optimized, distributed, and enjoyed by what will hopefully be millions of users.

Register your copy of *Android Development Patterns* at informit.com for convenient access to downloads, updates, and corrections as they become available. To start the registration process, go to **informit.com/register** and log in or create an account. Enter the product ISBN **9780133923681** and click **Submit**. Once the process is complete, you will find any available bonus content under "Registered Products."

Acknowledgments

Creating a book is a monumental effort that is never accomplished without the help, effort, guidance, and diligence of a small band of heroes. I could never have completed this work without the correction of three of the greatest technical editors in the field today. Massive thanks, a hat-tip, and cheers go to Romin Irani, Douglas Jones, and Ray Rischpater for each bringing a personal penchant of perfection to the book and making sure I didn't stray too far off the established path.

I also give an enthusiastic thanks to my development editor, Sheri Replin. Sheri has been great to work with, and she tolerates the brief moments of madness I have where I am certain that the words I have chosen make complete sentences when they are actually the inane babble of a caffeine-deprived developer. Also, credit is due to my amazing copy editor, Bart Reed. He miraculously managed to properly apply a clever and intelligent sheen to my stark ravings, making the book read as it originally sounded in my head, as well as making it clear to the reader.

As always, the world-class team at Pearson deserves more thanks than I believe they get. Specifically, I would like to call out Laura Lewin, Olivia Basegio, Elaine Wiley, Kristy Hart, Mark Taub, and the entire production staff. The steps that are taken to create these volumes of technical instruction do not happen overnight, and these fine folks have undergone hours of meetings, emails, phone calls, and more to make sure that you get the greatest-and-latest book possible.

I want to thank my family for letting me disappear almost every night and every weekend for the past year. It has been an epic struggle keeping the book on schedule, working a sometimes more-than-full-time job, and also making sure that I attend the activities that matter most with them. I believe that it is all of you who have let me keep a pretty good work-life-book balance.

Finally, I thank you! Thank you for picking up this book and giving it a place on your shelf (digital or otherwise). With all the amazing people I have had the opportunity to work with, I believe we have crafted a book that will get you on the best path to creating Android applications that will be used for years to come.

About the Author

Phil Dutson is a Solution Architect over client-side and mobile implementation for one of the world's largest e-commerce retailers in fitness equipment. He has been collecting and developing for mobile devices since he got his hands on a US Robotics Pilot 5000. He is the author of *Sams Teach Yourself jQuery Mobile in 24 Hours* (Sams, July 2012), *jQuery, jQuery UI, and jQuery Mobile: Recipes and Examples* (Pearson, November 2012), *Android Developer's Cookbook, Second Edition* (Pearson, July 2013), and *Responsive Mobile Design* (Addison-Wesley Professional, September 2014).

1

Development Tools

The toolset of choice for Android development has changed over the last few years. Once, the Eclipse IDE was the integrated development environment (IDE) of choice, but we now stand at the changing of the guard where the now fully support Android Studio is the current weapon of choice for developers. In this chapter, you learn about Android Studio, how to get the stand-alone SDK tools, various Android emulators, and version-control systems that are used with Android development.

Android Studio

Many Android developers have used or have had some experience with the Android Development Tools (ADT) bundle. This package, provided by the Android team, consisted of the Android SDK and the Eclipse IDE, which was used to help developers create rich Android applications on software that many Java developers were already using.

On May 15th, 2013, at the Google I/O developer conference, Android Studio was announced. This new toolset is composed of several additions aimed at making Android development easier, faster, and better than the ADT bundle that it replaced. Initially, it was released as a beta project but is now the officially supported platform from Google for Android development.

Android Studio is based on the JetBrains IntelliJ IDEA platform. This IDE has many new-and-improved features that the Android team feels better suits the development of Android applications. Features such as auto-save on every keystroke, the ability to separate the build process from the application, and smart auto-complete and import help developers create their applications faster and make them less reliant on complicated workspace setups and less worried about potential data loss.

Android Studio also comes as an installation instead of a packed file. This allows closer ties to the operating system on which it is installed, making it easier for developers to install without having to manually unpack and manage the SDK and IDE on their file system.

The new Gradle build system allows for a much easier build process that gives control back to developers and makes project collaboration much easier. On the surface, it appeared that any

Android project could be exported or checked into a code repository without any problems. However, when another developer checked out the project, there were occasions when different versions of the support library, SDK tools, or even the project build target would include different .jar files, making the project fail to compile and bringing development to a complete halt.

With the new Gradle-based build system, compiled .jar files are created and included as needed from the installed SDK. This greatly speeds up team collaboration because projects can now be passed through a code repository without worrying about specific versions of the compiled support .jar files or similar .jar files being sent separately to the developer to allow the project to be built.

Installing Android Studio

Android Studio is available for Windows, Linux, and OS X. You can download the current version of Android Studio from http://developer.android.com/sdk/. The website attempts to detect your currently installed operating system and give you a downloadable installation file. If you are using a different computer than the one on which you plan on running your install, you can download different versions of the Android Studio installation file under the Other Download Options section of the site.

Once you have selected to download Android Studio, you are moved to a new page asking you to read the terms and conditions of the download. After reading the terms thoroughly and checking the Agree box, you are then allowed to download the installation file. When the download is complete, you can run or execute the file to begin installation.

Note

If you are on a metered or cellular connection, you should find a broadband connection before attempting your download because the installation file may be over 200MB. Even if you manage to download the executable when Android Studio is installed, it will check for and install updates as well as portions of the Android SDK, which can add more than 2GB of data.

Unlike in previous installations where an application was uncompressed to your file system, Figure 1.1 shows the execution of the Android Studio installation file when executed on OS X.

During either the installation process (Windows) or when you open Android Studio for the first time (OS X), you will be walked through the SDK wizard. Because Android requires Java, you will be asked for the path to the Java 7 or higher Java Development Kit (JDK). Currently Java 7 is the preferred version of Java used with Android development, so you should download the latest version 7 release possible. Note that you must have the JDK installed and not the Java Runtime Environment (JRE). The JDK does contain the JRE, but it also contains extra components that are used by Android Studio for compiling Java code and resources. The currently installed JDK will attempt to be located automatically by the installation process, but if it is not found you may download the JDK by visiting http://www.oracle.com/technetwork/java/javase/downloads/.

Figure 1.1   Android Studio is now installed like a standard application in OS X. You just drag the application to your Applications folder.

Once you install the proper JDK, you can continue through the setup process. Most developers should be fine with the default installation options; however, if you want to know exactly where and what is being installed on your system, you may opt for the Custom installation. The Custom installation path allows you to choose to install the Android SDK, the Intel HAXM emulation enhancement, and an optimized Android Virtual Device (AVD). You are also given the option to change the installation path of the Android SDK on your system. The standard installation installs the SDK, the Intel HAXM, and the AVD.

The wizard asks you to accept more terms and conditions and then begins downloading the necessary components to give you a fully functional workbench that you will use to get your Android application started.

Note

If you have been using the ADT Bundle as your main development IDE, you should migrate your current project as soon as possible by following the migration guides available at http://developer.android.com/sdk/. You can still use the ADT bundle if you want, but it is no longer under official support, and if you run into problems you will be on your own.

For the official migration instruction visit http://developer.android.com/sdk/installing/migrate.html.

When the wizard finishes the download, you are shown the Welcome screen of Android Studio. You should now be able to start using Android Studio.

Using Android Studio

Unlike with the ADT Bundle, when Android Studio is launched, you are not taken to a workbench; instead, you are shown a Welcome screen. Figure 1.2 shows the Welcome screen.

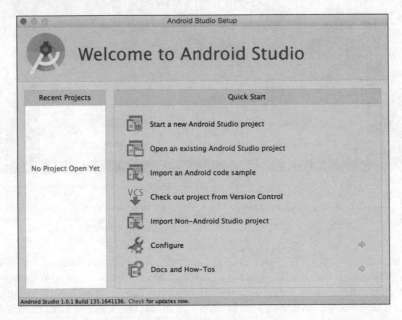

Figure 1.2   The Welcome screen of Android Studio v1.0.1. Even newer versions such as 1.4 have remained the same.

As you begin to develop a project, the Recent Projects list populates and you can choose a project to begin working on it. To begin a new project, you can use the Start a New Android Studio Project button in the Quick Start section.

Occasionally, you may find that some projects are not listed in the Recent Projects list. When this happens you should use the Open an Existing Android Studio Project button to locate the project and open it.

If you are new to Android development or if you want to see some examples on specific portions of Android development, you can click Import an Android Code Sample. This starts a download that will grab a list of sample projects that you can open to look at to help with understanding how different pieces of the Android system interact and are used for application building.

If you have a project that was created using ADT, you can attempt to import it by choosing Import Non-Android Studio Project and choosing the project folder. Android Studio will then attempt to convert the project into an Android Studio project. If your migration runs into issues, you may need to export the project from ADT or generate a `build.gradle` file before attempting to import.

If you need to update your SDK tools, you can do so through the SDK Manager. This is accessible by clicking the Configure button and choosing SDK Manager on the pane that slides in. If you are already working inside a project, you can open this by clicking Tools, Android, SDK in the menu. This launches a new window that checks for updates for the Android SDK. If any are found, you are prompted to update and install them. Figure 1.3 shows the Android SDK Manager window with some packages ready to be installed.

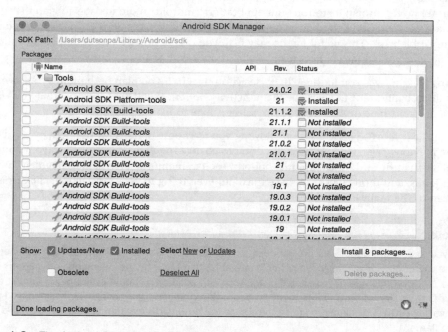

Figure 1.3   The Android SDK Manager is used to install and update components of the Android SDK.

Many extra components and packages can be installed by using the Android SDK Manager. If you find that you cannot create or open some projects, it may be due to missing packages. This is a good place to start when trying to troubleshoot problems with compiling, importing, or opening projects.

Starting a New Project

Clicking the Start a New Android Studio Project button starts the new project wizard. The first page lets you configure the initial settings of your project. The name of your application is set here as well as your package name. In order to help you create packages properly, Android Studio has you enter a company domain. This helps ensure that applications do not overlap and cause potential conflicts due to having the same package name. If you have a specific location that you want to save your project, you can also change the default location.

Clicking the Next button allows you to choose what your application will target. Note that you are not limited to creating an app that will only work on a watch, TV, or mobile device. If you want your application to work on multiple devices, you should check the box next to the platform you wish to support. When you check a platform, you will then be able to choose which API level you require to run your application. Android Studio updates to grab the current Android fragmentation lists to give you a percentage of how many devices your application will be compatible with. This useful metric may help you decide how you will build your application and give you an idea of how many Android users will be able to run your application.

Clicking Next moves you to the Activity-selection screen. If you plan on building your own UI, you will probably want to select the Blank Activity option. If you already know that you will need a different type of Activity, you can select it here to have it added for you.

Clicking Next moves you to a screen allowing you to choose options for the Activity you chose on the previous page. Options here allow you to change the Activity name, the layout name, as well as the title and other potential options, such as menu resource names, fragment names, object kinds, and more. Once you have filled out everything to your satisfaction, click Finish to be taken to the main IDE screen.

> **Note**
>
> If you see errors about your project being unable to build, Gradle having missing components, or another similar message, you should see an option to "retry the operation." If you retry and the process fails again, you should check your JDK build path. Some systems will default to the first version of Java that is found on your system. If you are working with Lollipop, you must have Java JDK 7 or higher; pointing the IDE to the newer JDK location should fix your build problems.

When the project opens you will be shown your activity .xml file. Figure 1.4 shows the Design view of `activity_main.xml`, which is the main layout file that was created as a new project using the Blank Activity option.

The Design view is used for drag-and-drop development. A list of layouts, widgets, and various components can be dragged on to the Android device, and the view will be updated to show what will happen when they are added. Even if you decide not to use the drag-and-drop interface and instead code in all of your components, they will be rendered in this view so that you can see how your project will look.

Figure 1.4   The `activity_main.xml` file is open in the Design view.

The right side of the Design view gives you a component tree of the components that have been added to the activity as well as a Properties section. The Properties section can be used to adjust components by tweaking various settings. Note that some properties can be changed to use hard-coded values rather than the ones created in a resources file such as `strings.xml`. This may not seem to be an issue at first, but it can snowball into a massive update effort when you decide to take your application global and need to localize all the text used in your application.

The middle section will initially be set to show you a default device based on what your application is targeted for. If you are developing a phone or tablet application, then a phone will displayed. This can be changed by using the option buttons above the device. A drop-down will list the current "skin" and will allow you to change to another device. This is extremely useful to see how different devices will handle the layout of your components. You can also change and modify the AppTheme as well as which Activity you want to view and the API level.

> **Note**
>
> The Design view is a preview of what your application will probably look like when run on an Android device. However, it may not always be 100% accurate, especially on every Android device. Whenever possible, test on as many actual devices as you can, as well as on software emulators.

After you are done playing with the visual aspects of your Activity, click the Text tab at the bottom of the window. This changes the view to let you view the actual nodes and elements that make up your Activity XML file. As a reminder, you do not have to use the Design mode; if you are comfortable, you can code the entire Activity directly into the XML. A Preview pane is available to show you what is happening when you add and remove code to and from the Activity XML. Figure 1.5 shows a button that has been added to the Text view and is rendered in the Preview pane.

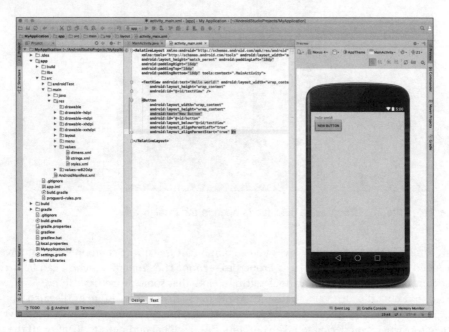

Figure 1.5   A button has been added and is displayed in the Preview pane.

Android Studio extends the IntelliJ platform, giving you the features you may already be used to as well as several new options, including the following:

- Auto-save functionality
- Customizable panel and pane arrangement
- Code linting
- Syntax highlighting
- Automatic imports for classes
- ADB integration
- LogCat integration

- Maven and Gradle build options
- File Commander
- Event Log
- Memory Monitor
- GitHub integration
- Bookmarks and breakpoints

You can learn more about the features of the IDE by reading the documentation for IntelliJ IDEA at https://www.jetbrains.com/idea/documentation/.

This is done by going to the application menu and clicking File, Close Project. This immediately closes the project you are working on as well as the IDE and displays the Welcome to Android Studio window.

If you decide that you do not need Android Studio or are only interested in some of the tools bundled in the Android SDK, you may be interested in downloading and using the standalone SDK tools.

Standalone SDK Tools

You are not required to use Android Studio to develop Android applications. Other IDEs are available, and some IDEs offer an Android plugin that will handle compiling and publishing an application, provided it has access to the Android SDK.

If you find that you only need the Android SDK, you can download it as a compressed file from the download page at http://developer.android.com/sdk/. The download will be labeled as SDK Tools Only or as Other Download Option on the page.

If you are using Windows for development, you should still download the executable installation file instead of a compressed .zip file. The installation will give you easier access to the Android SDK Manager and other tools that you will need to use to keep your installation up to date. Be sure to take note of where you install the tools on your system so that you can add them to your system path, or reference them when using the command-line tools.

The standalone Android SDK Tools does not contain a complete tools install. It contains only a few folders, a readme file, and a Tools directory that you will use to download the pieces of the Android SDK that you want to work with.

To get started developing, you must download a version of Android as well as the Platform-tools. You can complete this by navigating into the Tools directory that's executing the Android program.

> **Note**
>
> The entire Android SDK is several gigabytes in file size. To cut back on how much a developer needs to download in order to get started developing, the downloads have been separated into sections. These sections will help you reduce how much bandwidth you need to get started, but an Internet connection will be needed during development as patches, samples, and updates are posted to the download repository.

When you execute the `android` command, the Android SDK Manager will be launched. If you get an error message or nothing appears, you need to make sure you have Java installed. Linux users may need to install Java through a package manager (such as apt-get). Figure 1.6 shows the Android SDK Manager window launched on OS X via the `android` command.

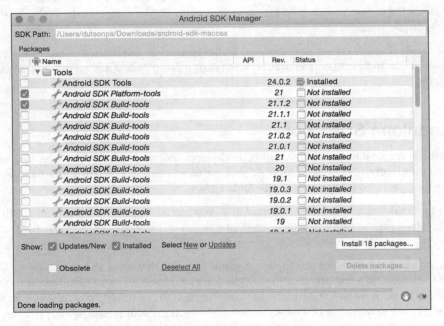

Figure 1.6   The Android SDK Manager is used to update the SDK as well as offer new packages.

After you download all the components and packages that you selected, you are ready to start using the Android SDK. Note that using the standalone SDK is best suited to advanced developers who are already familiar with building projects or ones who need specific tools such as `adb` and `dmtracedump`.

Android Device Emulation

It would be practically impossible for any developer to have every device that Android runs on in their office to use for live device testing. This is where an Android emulator can come into play.

Emulators allow developers to get a rough idea and feel for how an application is going to behave on a specific version of Android. As a developer, it gives you the opportunity to tune, tweak, and alter device settings such as system memory, screen size, screen dpi, and even some sensor information. Using an emulator is no excuse for skipping live device testing, but it certainly can be a boost to developers who would otherwise be unable to test their applications on device models that they do not actually have.

Android Virtual Device

The Android Virtual Device (AVD) is the emulator available through the Android SDK. AVDs are managed through the AVD Manager, which can be launched directly from Android Studio by finding the icon for AVD Manager. Alternatively, you can launch it from the command line by navigating to the "tools" directory of your Android SDK and executing `android avd`.

Note that when you use the `android avd` command, the manager launched will be different from the AVD Manager launched from Android Studio. To launch the AVD Manager from Android Studio, you can either click the AVD Manager button or select Tools, Android, AVD Manager.

By launching the AVD Manager from Android Studio, you can see what virtual devices are currently available for use. If you have not created a virtual device yet or if a default virtual device is not available, you need to click the Create Virtual Device button to launch the configuration wizard. The wizard will allow you to create a virtual phone, tablet, Wear device, or TV. After selecting the type of device you would like to emulate, you can then choose to create a new hardware profile, import a hardware profile, clone a device, or continue the setup.

Cloning a device creates a copy of the basic settings and allows you to change the device skin. If you choose a device that already exists and click the Next button, you are given the option of choosing the version of Android as well as the chip architecture that the emulator will run on. Clicking the Next button shows you a page that allows you to name the AVD, shows you a summary of the device settings, lets you adjust the scale of the device, and gives you the choice of either using your GPU to help with processing or creating a snapshot of the device that will be used for a faster boot time. You can only use one of these settings at a time, so you need to decide whether having a fast boot or having potentially better performance while using the emulator is more important to you. You can always edit the AVD later to use the other option if you find that one option is not working out for you.

> **Note**
>
> Scaling the device can be useful for developers who are working on laptops or smaller screen devices that may not be able to accurately demonstrate the raw pixel resolution of modern Android devices. If you select "Auto" for scale, your emulator will adjust itself as best as it can to fit your screen.

When you finish modifying your AVD, you can click the Finish button to complete the wizard and wait while the AVD is created and stored. To start an AVD, click the Play button, and the emulator window will appear with a skinned AVD. Figure 1.7 shows an AVD of a Nexus 6 running.

Figure 1.7   The AVD has scaled the displayed resolution to fit my screen and has been skinned to match a Nexus 6.

GenyMotion

GenyMotion is another Android emulator that uses Oracle VM VirtualBox as a platform for launching and controlling Android images. When using GenyMotion, the first thing you might notice is how fast the emulator is. By leveraging a different VM process than AVD, you are given an emulator that achieves a near real-time response.

To get started with GenyMotion, you should first download Oracle VM VirtualBox by visiting https://www.virtualbox.org/wiki/Downloads and downloading the binary package for your system. After downloading and installing the package, you can then get the GenyMotion installation file from https://www.genymotion.com/.

GenyMotion is available for developers under various license agreements. If you are just going to try GenyMotion, you can use the Free license, which grants you access to a limited emulator that lets you launch an application but will not grant you priority support and will not give you the right to use the emulator for commercial projects.

The Business license will give you many more options, such as multi-touch, screen-casting, Java API access, and priority support. This is not a fixed cost, but is sold as a subscription.

There is also an Indie license that is available for developers who want to use all of the features of GenyMotion but do not have a company or business to reimburse the cost and who only have one or two developers.

When trying GenyMotion, you should start with the Free license to get a taste and then move to either an Indie or Business license, as your situation allows. You should also know that GenyMotion has plugins for both IntelliJ and Eclipse, allowing you to use it inside of Android Studio as your emulator of choice.

After you have installed Oracle VM VirtualBox and GenyMotion, you can launch the GenyMotion application. When it launches for the first time, you will be asked if you would like to download an emulator. If you want to download one of the pre-built and tuned emulators, you should click the Yes button. You will then be prompted for a login. GenyMotion does require that you register with them in order to download emulators. Note that registration is easy and is required when managing your license.

After entering in your user information, you will be able to choose what emulator you would like to download. To help you quickly get the one you want, you can use the sorting options for API level and device type. Continuing through the emulator-creation wizard will start a download of the device you have picked. When the image download has completed, you can launch your emulator by selecting it and clicking the Start button.

GenyMotion is definitely worth checking out, especially if you need to have a fast emulator that will run as fast as a physical device.

Xamarin Android Player

Xamarin is typically thought of as the framework used for cross-platform or as the go-to solution for writing Android applications with C#. Xamarin has also released an emulator that can pair with any IDE or development solution that uses adb.

The Xamarin Android Player is not as full featured as other emulation options; however, it is under active development, with features being added as development continues. It currently runs in a similar fashion to GenyMotion, which means that it requires Oracle VM VirtualBox installed for use. Unlike with GenyMotion, if Oracle VM VirtualBox is not already installed on your system, it will be downloaded and the installation started for you. For information about the installation process and using the program, you should visit the Xamarin Android Player documentation page at http://developer.xamarin.com/guides/android/getting_started/installation/android-player/.

Because Android Player is a solution from Xamarin, you must have an active Xamarin. Android trial or subscription in order to use it. Windows (both 32- and 64-bit) and OS X (10.7+) are both supported. You can learn more about the Xamarin Android Player by visiting https://xamarin.com/android-player.

Version-Control Systems

The need for using a code repository should seem pretty straightforward, but for some developers it may take a hard-drive failure or an accident for them to realize why having a code storage solution is a must when developing.

Many types of code repositories are available, including CVS, SVN, Git, Mercurial, and others. The following is breakdown of a few code repository solutions that are available for use with your Android development.

Subversion

Subversion (https://subversion.apache.org/) is still a fairly common version-control system that is compatible with several different clients. It was created in 2000 by CollabNet and is managed by the Apache Foundation today. There are plugins for Eclipse, IntelliJ, and even plugins that incorporate into the system shell. Subversion is commonly referred to as SVN and creates "shadow" copies of every file that enters revision control. These files are used for comparison and recovery; however, they take the same space as the actual file. This means that on your system you will need twice as much space for your project when using SVN.

There are several options for using SVN; some solutions are available through cloud storage whereas others are available as an enterprise or in-house solution. Although SVN is generally installed on a Linux server, there are some distributions, such as VisualSVN, that allow for your SVN server to run in a Windows environment.

Subversion offers the following features:

- Ignore file list managed with an .svnignore file
- Branches
- Versioning
- Merge tracking
- Tagging
- Command-line and client access

Git

Git (http://git-scm.com/) takes a different approach to version-control systems. Instead of being reliant on having a centralized code repository, it distributes itself to each user. It was initially created in 2005 by Linus Torvalds for Linux kernel development. In the time since, it has become one of the most popular code repository systems.

Although there is still a centralized location, each user creates a local "clone" of the remote repository and works against the local version. This means that changes are committed locally and when ready are "pushed" to the remote resource. The benefit is that users are able to work abstractly and then send "pull requests" to the remote system when a fix or change is ready to be added to the main repository.

Git is available for free through the GNU General Public License version 2; however, you can find online hosts that will offer personal storage with public projects or private hosting for a fee.

Git offers the following features:

- Distributed repositories through cloning
- Command-line and client access
- Forking projects
- Ignore file list through .git configuration
- Context switching
- Branching

Mercurial

Another option for your version-control system is Mercurial (http://mercurial.selenic.com/). Mercurial runs quite similarly to Git in that each developer is given a local copy of the repository to work with, only sending changes up to the remote location when branches or merges are final.

Mercurial is written in Python and has a client available for Windows, Linux, and OS X. Being written in Python also makes the system extensible through plugins, which can be found on the Mercurial wiki site or by writing your own.

Mercurial offers the following features:

- Distributed repositories
- Branching
- Merging
- Workflows

Summary

This chapter introduced you to the tools you need to start developing Android applications. You learned about Android Studio, the supported platform from the Android team that is based on IntelliJ IDEA Community Edition. You learned about installing the standalone SDK tools for use with your own IDE or build tools. You also learned that version-control systems can be leveraged to help you keep your code in a safe state for recovery and sharing.

2

Testing and Debugging

Testing and debugging are two important parts of developing for Android. These procedures revolve around making sure that your application is trustworthy, dependable, and maintainable. By using various methods of testing, you can make sure that you are working with code that does what you believe it should. By debugging your application, you can determine problems that may exist in your code, as well as get a glimpse into what is happening on the device while your application is running.

In this chapter, you learn about unit testing, integration testing, and using the debugging tools that are available with Android Studio. This will give you an understanding of why testing is important and how you can use it with your own applications.

Unit Testing

To some developers, unit testing is not just a suggestion; it is a vital part of the development process. Without testing your code and knowing exactly what it will do and is capable of, you are not be able to trust it.

Generally, unit tests are written for specific modules of your code. Modules may include entire classes or they may be as simple as testing a single function. You will be the one writing the actual unit tests against your code, so you will probably want to adopt some of the creeds of test-driven design. The following list of questions helps you get the most out of your unit testing:

- What is the purpose of this module?
- What types of input will the module support?
- What happens when invalid data is sent to the module?
- Does this module return any data or objects?
- Does the returned data or object require validation?
- How can the result be reached in the simplest manner?

Unit testing goes further than just making sure that your code does what you believe it should. It is a useful tool in validating your code when collaborating and working with others.

When working on team projects, you may have a module that you know works but every time you submit a pull request, synchronize, or otherwise check your code into your code repository, you are informed from another team member that your module is broken and that you need to fix it before it will be added to the master or main branch of your code repository.

Even if you are absolutely sure that your module is fine, without running tests to prove that your module works correctly, you may find yourself in an endless argument with other members of your team that will waste your time and cause your project to be delayed while the problem is resolved. By providing a test with your code, you can let other developers see exactly how you have tested your module, and allow them an opportunity to provide a test of their own that will help explain what they are expecting your module to be able to handle.

To begin writing tests in your project, you need to make a few modifications to your project. If your project does not already contain testing folders, you will need to create them in the following path: `app/src/test/java`. This folder contains your test code, whereas the code you want to perform the testing on should reside in the `app/src/main/java` folder.

Having confirmed or created the folder structure, you can then modify the `gradle.build` file of your app module to add support for JUnit. This can be done as follows:

```
dependencies {
  // other dependencies
  testCompile 'junit:junit:4.12'
}
```

With the folder structure and dependencies taken care of, you can now write your test classes. Test classes use annotations to declare test methods as well as to perform special processing. The following shows a sample class with imports for JUnit as well as a method that uses the `@Test` annotation to designate the method as a testing method:

```
import org.junit.Test;
import java.util.regex.Pattern;
import static org.junit.Assert.assertFalse;
import static org.junit.Assert.assertTrue;

public class EmailValidatorTest {

  // use @Test to specify a testing method

  @Test
  public void emailValidator_CorrectEmail_ReturnsTrue() {
    // using assertThat() to perform validation of email address
    assertThat(EmailValidator.isValidEmail("myemail@address.com"), is(true));
  }
```

```
// other testing methods and logic would continue here

}
```

Other annotations that you may be interested in using for testing are shown in Table 2.1.

Table 2.1   **JUnit Annotations**

@Before	Used to specify code that's used to set up test operations that are invoked at the beginning of each test. Note that multiple @Before blocks may exist but may not be processed in specific order.
@After	Used to specify code that will be run at the end of every test. This is used for cleanup purposes and should be where any resources that were loaded into memory are released.
@BeforeClass	Used to specify static methods that are used once per test class. This should be used when performing expensive operations such as connecting to databases.
@AfterClass	Used to specify static methods that should be used after all other tests have been performed. If you previously used the @BeforeClass annotation to define and use resources, you should use @AfterClass to release the definitions and resources that were used.
@Test	Used to specify a method that's used for testing. You may have multiple test methods in your test class, with each having the @Test annotation.
@Test(timeout=<milliseconds>)	Used to specify a timeout period where the test may be considered to fail once the timeout has been reached. If the timeout is reached and the method has not returned yet, a failure will automatically be returned.

After you create your test classes and methods, you can run them from Android Studio by opening the Build Variants window. This can be done by using the quick access menu on the left side of the screen, or by using the Build, Select Build Variant... menu. Once the window is displayed, make sure that Test Artifact has the Unit Tests option selected. Your tests will then be listed and can be executed by right-clicking the class or method you would like to run and then selecting Run.

When the test has completed running, the results will be displayed in the Run window. If you require a full project that demonstrates how to integrate and use automated testing, you can visit the official testing sample from Google via GitHub at https://github.com/googlesamples/android-testing.

There are still other options for testing that can be leveraged to round out and complete your testing strategy. The Robotium automation framework (https://code.google.com/p/robotium/) is a well-tested and trusted framework that can be leveraged as a stand-alone component or as an addition to your testing suite.

Another option that you want to consider is Appium (http://appium.io/). Appium is a cross-platform product that is closer to a set of automation libraries that can be used for native, hybrid, and web applications. Appium is based on Selenium WebDriver and allows you to use the language you are comfortable with to create and run tests, including Ruby, .NET, Java, Python, JavaScript, Swift, Objective C, and more. If you are already comfortable with how Selenium WebDriver works, this is definitely an option you will want to check out.

Integration Testing

After unit testing has been completed, integration testing takes things further by testing an entire sequence of events, testing the user interface (UI) components, and potentially working with various service providers for end-to-end testing.

One of the ways you can perform integration testing is with monkeyrunner. The monkey-runner app is a tool that executes Python scripts that can open or install an application on an Android device through an ADB connection and then send keyboard and touch events as well as take screenshots of the mayhem it creates while running. This can be a valuable tool in creating an application that can stand programmatic stress testing and that will self-document results through imagery. Listing 2.1 shows a sample Python script that you can create that opens an application and sends button presses to it.

Listing 2.1   **Python Script That Can Be Used with `monkeyrunner`**

```python
from com.android.monkeyrunner import MonkeyRunner, MonkeyDevice
import commands
import sys
import os

print "** MonkeyRunner Start"

# Determine if screenshot directory exists, make if not
# Note, this is made where this script is executed from
if not os.path.exists("screenshots"):
  print "creating the screenshots directory"
  os.makedirs("screenshots")

# Connect MonkeyRunner to the device
device = MonkeyRunner.waitForConnection()

# What app are we testing, install if not found
apk_path = device.shell('pm path com.dutsonpa.debugexample')
```

```
if apk_path.startswith('package:'):
  print "App Found."
else:
  print "Installing App"
  device.installPackage('com.dutsonpa.debugexample.apk')

print "Starting MainActivity"
device.startActivity(component='com.dutsonpa.debugexample/com.dutsonpa.
➡debugexample.MainActivity')

# Take a Screenshot
MonkeyRunner.sleep(1)
result = device.takeSnapshot()
result.writeToFile('./screenshots/monkeyrunner_ss.png','png')
print "Screenshot Taken"

#sending an event which simulate a click on the menu button
device.press('KEYCODE_MENU', MonkeyDevice.DOWN_AND_UP)

print "** MonkeyRunner Finish"
```

> **Note**
>
> You must have Python installed on your system and have it in your system path so that the script can be executed. You should also have the Android SDK in your system path so that monkeyrunner can be executed from your command line or terminal.

Another testing tool you may find useful is the UI/Application Exerciser Monkey (Monkey). Monkey runs similarly to monkeyrunner, but instead of being a Python script it is a command-line application that you can configure and run on either an emulator or on a device.

Monkey can simulate touch, click, gesture, directional, trackball, and similar device events. When the application crashes, performs a permission error, or runs into an Application Not Responding (ANR) notice, Monkey will stop sending events to the device or emulator. If you really want to drive your device or emulator to the limit, you can override these default settings and Monkey will continue to throw random events.

Using Monkey can be as simple as the following line:

```
adb shell monkey -p com.dutsonpa.debugexample -v 300
```

Here, I have an emulator launched and accessible via adb. This means that adb is processed first. The shell command is then passed to open a remote shell on the target device. Next comes the call for monkey as well as an argument option of p. The -p argument acts as a constraint that will force Monkey to only work in the package that is specified immediately after it. The com.dutsonpa.debugexample is the package name that Monkey will be constrained in. The argument of -v is used to show verbose logging to the terminal. You can omit the argument, but very little information will be shown when it is omitted. The 300 at the end of the line is used as the number of events that should be used. In this case, 300 random events will be sent to the emulator. The output of running a command with 100 events from the terminal is shown in Figure 2.1.

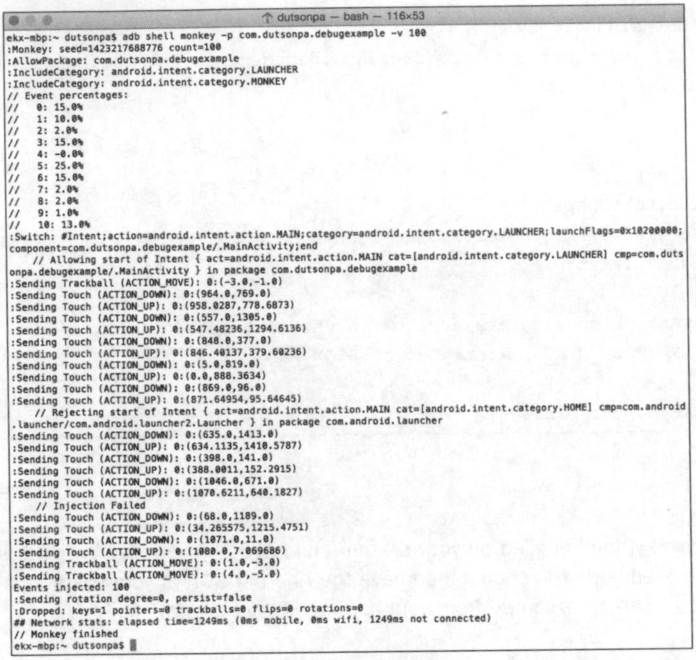

Figure 2.1   With the verbose argument passed, the terminal displays information about the events sent to the emulator.

Monkey can also be somewhat tuned to act in a more controlled manner. By using different arguments, you can control how fast the input events are triggered as well as how many of them will be touch, motion, trackball, gesture, and other input events. Another wonderful feature is that when an error does occur with the test, a full stack trace is printed to your terminal, including application memory usage, the packages that were running at the time of the crash, the type of crash, the exact point during the testing when the application crashed, and thread traces.

Using Monkey is a great way to get a quick evaluation on your application. It may seem like sending random events is overkill, but in reality it gives you a way to evaluate the responsiveness of your application under heavy stress. When working with applications that need to do rapid screen updates or even handle many input events at the same time (such as a game), Monkey can generate random and mass input. Monkey also has the benefit of doing things that may interrupt your application. By pulling down the status bar and pressing the back, home, and menu keys, Monkey gives your application a chance to work on the `OnPause()`, `OnResume()`, and other methods.

Monkey may not always be the solution that solves all of your problems, but it should be part of your testing strategy because it is easy to run, comes with the Android SDK, and gives instant feedback on how your device will handle your application.

Another tool that you should consider using during your integration testing is user interface (UI) testing. This can be done with another tool that is bundled with the Android SDK. The UI Automator Viewer is run from the command line or terminal window from the Tools directory of your SDK installation.

> **Note**
>
> If you installed Android Studio and do not know where the Android SDK has been installed on your system, you can find out by opening Android Studio and then clicking the SDK Manager icon, or by using the menu to select Tools, Android, SDK Manager. This will launch the SDK Manager, which will list the path on your system to the SDK in a text field at the top of the window.

To start using the UI Automator Viewer, open your command shell and navigate to the tools directory of your Android SDK installation location. Note that if the tools directory is in your system path, you do not need to navigate to the directory; instead, you may simply run the command to start using the UI Automator Viewer. Once you have located the proper path, run the following:

```
./uiautomatorviewer
```

Note that Windows users should not need the `./` and can just type in `uiautomatorviewer` to start the application. When the application starts, you will be greeted with a fairly sparse interface that is ready to be used.

Before you go any further, make sure that you have connected an actual Android device to your computer and that you have USB debugging enabled.

> **Tip**
>
> You can make sure that you have a device connected and ready to go either by checking the Android DDMS window of Android Studio and looking for your device to be listed or by using the `adb` command to list devices attached to your computer. Typing `adb devices` into your command line should return a list of devices that are connected and ready to be debugged. If nothing is returned, check your connections and make sure that you have USB debugging turned on for your device.

Once you have your device connected and the application that you want to test open, you can click the Device Screenshot icon near the top of the UI Automator Viewer window. This starts a process of taking a UI XML snapshot. This grabs the current screen and displays it on the left side of the window. Here, you can drag your mouse over various elements and inspect them. As you mouse over various elements, a window on the right side will move through the layout and show you where it belongs in the view hierarchy.

When you click an element, layout, or widget, a red border appears and the details of that item are displayed, including class, package, and property information. Figure 2.2 shows a button selected with the property information being displayed inside of the UI Automator Viewer.

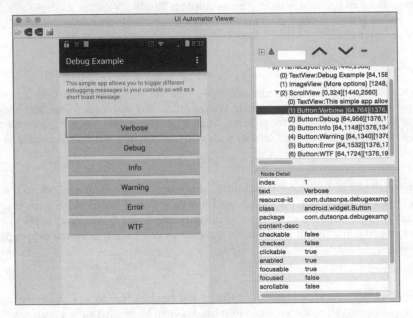

Figure 2.2   On the left, the button being inspected has a border applied while various properties of the button are displayed on the right.

You may find that some items are not displayed on the screen but are present in your application. For these items you can browse through the hierarchy and select the item. A dashed border is applied to the item and the item properties are still listed below. Using this information, you can determine if the item is where it should be, or it will give you a clue as to where the item went when the application was loaded.

> **Note**
>
> One of the best features of the UI Automator Viewer is that you can see what will be shown, displayed, or read to a user when the accessibility mode of the device has been enabled. If you notice that "content-desc" has no value, you should address this immediately by adding a proper value. Keep in mind, though, that not everything needs a value—for example, you wouldn't want the device to announce "scroll view" or "frame layout" to a user using your app. You would, however, want buttons and navigation options announced.

Using the UI Automator Viewer can help you spot potential layout problems, find "missing" components, widgets, and elements, and help you get a great view of how the layout is put together when rendered on an Android device.

Debugging

Many developers devote a good portion of their time to writing unit tests and testing scripts in order to ship applications that are stable, working, and run with near 100% certainty. At times, especially with Android development, a test works on some devices but will behave differently on others. In this case, the best way to find the problem and fix it is with debugging. Debugging on Android can be broken down into profiling, tracing, and messaging.

Profiling

When working with an application, it is good to know how much memory is available and how much your application is using. Due to the flexibility that Android brings to the table, many manufacturers have modified the general UI of Android, giving it special effects, new applications, and extended functionality. However, this customization comes with a cost attached. As manufacturers add on special features and "built-in" functionality, they change the amount of system memory available and add or extend many of the built-in functions of the device.

More than just being aware of system memory, you should also be looking at the amount of CPU that your application is using and how much is available. Something that many developers overlook is how many CPU cycles are being used by their application. This may not seem like something to worry about, but using the device CPU is not free. Every task you perform and process that you start uses power. The more power-hungry your application, the greater chance your user has of not using and eventually uninstalling your application.

To get started profiling your application, you need to either start your emulator or connect an Android device to your computer with USB Debugging enabled.

> **Tip**
>
> To enable "Developer mode" on your Android device, open Settings, then find About Device or About Phone, then tap Build Number until a toast (notification) appears telling you that you are a developer. Note that some devices or phones may have a Software Information menu option that contains the Build Number option. This will unlock the Developer Options, and you can enable USB Debugging and many other options that will help you develop and debug your applications.

Once your device is connected, you are ready to start the Android Device Monitor. This can be launched either from a command line or from Android Studio. To launch from a command line, you need to navigate to the Tools directory of your Android SDK installation, or have that folder added to your system path. You then need to find and run `monitor`. Note that Linux and similar systems will need to run `./monitor` in order to start the application.

If you want to start the Android Device Monitor from Android Studio, you can do so by clicking the Tools menu and then Android and Android Device Manager. Regardless of how you start it, a splash screen will appear and then the Android Device Monitor window will appear. Figure 2.3 shows what the Android Device Monitor window looks like.

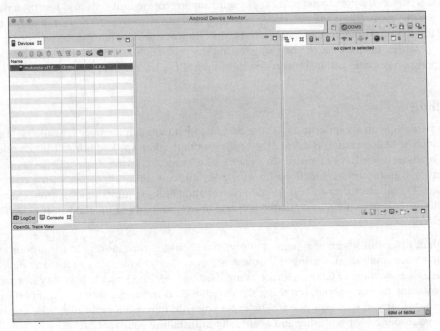

Figure 2.3   The Android Device Monitor may look plain when getting started, but will show you a wealth of information.

Your device should be listed in the Android Device Monitor. Listed beneath it are any running packages that can be profiled. By clicking one of these packages, you can start profiling the package by clicking Update Heap; the icon should look like a cylinder that is partially colored green. Before any information is shown, you will also need to click the trashcan icon for garbage collection to run. You can then click the Head tab that is located on the right side of the Android Device Monitor to view collected information. Figure 2.4 shows data that has been collected from one of the packages running on my phone.

By capturing a heap dump, I was able to see that my application was allocated a heap size of just under 35MB and that I was using 27MB of it, leaving 7% free. As Figure 2.4 shows, all the objects created by my application are listed and how much memory they take. This allows me to quickly see what is using the most memory, and can give me a clue into what I should be looking at to trim back any objects that may be inefficiently created.

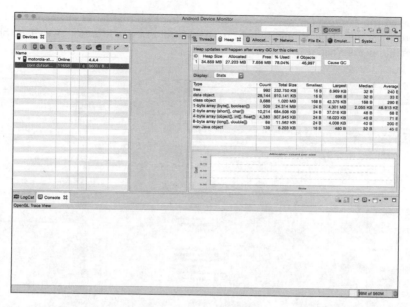

Figure 2.4   Many areas of the Android Device Monitor can be resized, which allows you to view information easier.

It should be noted that depending on your application, the version of Android you are targeting, and the device you are using, you will see different results. This is one of the reasons why it is best to test your applications on as many physical devices as possible so that you can see real results.

Another helpful stat is at the bottom of the Android Device Monitor window. It shows me the amount of memory available on my device and where the current usage is. This can be helpful in establishing a baseline of memory available on a device, and can be right-clicked to toggle options for showing the max heap level.

Another portion of the Android Device Monitor that you may find helpful while profiling is the System Information tab. This window shows you the current CPU load, memory usage, and frame render time of your device. Keep in mind that when polling the CPU and memory, it will poll your entire device, not just a particular package.

Now that you know how to get some basic profiling information, it is time to learn how to add tracing to your code to help you analyze and optimize your code.

Tracing

For tracing what your code is doing, you can use a system-wide tracing utility called Systrace that polls your device for running applications, memory usage, and more. When Systrace completes, it generates an HTML report that can be viewed in a web browser. To launch

Systrace, open the Android Device Monitor and click the icon that looks like green and red bars. Figure 2.5 shows the icon highlighted in the Android Device Monitor as well as the option window that appears when it is clicked.

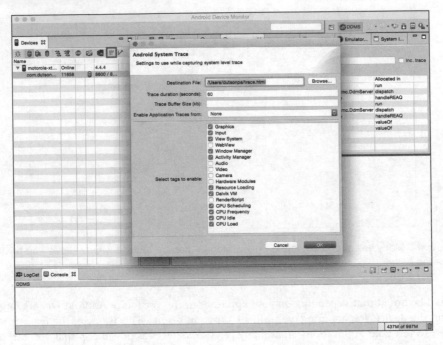

Figure 2.5   When the Systrace icon is clicked, a window appears, allowing you to set your desired tracing options.

The window that appears allows you to choose the following options:

- Where to save the report
- How long to run the trace
- Size limit of the trace (in KB)
- What application to trace (select "None" for all applications)
- Specific tags to collect data on

The Systrace tool is powerful, and reviewing the report it generates will give you a great insight into what your application and device are doing. If you generate a report and find it difficult to read, try turning on only the specific tags you need data for.

Another method of debugging your code involves putting messages into a debug output when the application is running.

Messaging

It seems that every language has a way to print values to the console or into a debug log that can be viewed as a program runs. For web developers, this used to mean using the `alert()` method, and recently the `console.log()` method. For Java developers, this was occasionally the `System.out.println()` method when not using a system of breakpoints and stepping through with a debugger.

In Android, you have access to the `Log` class, which in turn allows you to leave yourself messages that can be viewed by LogCat. To use LogCat from the command line, you should first connect a device or emulator and have it visible to `adb`. You can then type `adb logcat`, and information should start flowing into your console window. You can also pass some options to the command-line call to control the output. Table 2.2 lists the options and what they do.

Table 2.2 **The adb `logcat` Options**

`-c`	Clears the log and exits.
`-d`	Dumps the log to the command line and then exits.
`-f <filename>`	Allows you to specify a file to save the output to.
`-g`	Displays information about the log buffer and then exits.
`-n <number>`	Sets how many rotated logs to keep. The default is 4 and requires the use of the `-r` option.
`-r <kbytes>`	Sets the size value for a log before it is rotated.
`-s`	Filters the log to the silent level.
`-v <format>`	Sets the format used for log output. The default is `"brief"`. Other options are `"process"`, `"tag"`, `"raw"`, `"time"`, `"threadtime"`, and `"long"`.

LogCat is also integrated into Android Studio as part of the Dalvik Debug Monitor Server (DDMS). It is visible through the Android tool window. If that window is not currently visible inside of Android Studio, you can open it by clicking View, then Tool Windows, and then Android.

The LogCat window consists of an output area, a log level select box, a search input, and a filter select box. Figure 2.6 shows an image of these areas.

Because LogCat shows the system log, it can display lots of system information. This is good because it allows you to see what is going on your device, but it can also make it difficult to find a specific log message. This is what the search, filter, and log-level options are for.

Figure 2.6   The output area (1) shows the log; the log level selector (2) allows fine tuning of the log shown; the search area (3) allows you to filter based on a query; the Filters selector (4) allows you to switch between viewing the global, custom, and application-specific logs.

By typing a query into the search field, you can filter by package or application name and only messages that refer to that search query will be shown. By adjusting the log level, you can restrict what is shown to only messages that are logged at that particular level. By using a filter, you can view messages that are generated by the system, your application, or by a custom filter that you can create.

You can mix and match these options to help you narrow down and find the messages you want quickly and efficiently. As mentioned before, you can use log levels to view only some messages. These can be set in your application by using the Log class.

To set log levels in your application, you need to import the Log class. This is done by including `import android.util.Log;` in the import section of your class file. You can then start logging messages in your code by using the following:

```
Log.v("MainActivity", "This is a verbose log message.");
```

Note that two arguments are passed to the `Log.v()` method. The first is a string that you should set to the class you are currently in. This will help you identify where this particular message was triggered from. If you do not wish to pass a string in this manner, you can declare a variable in your class and use the variable instead. Doing so would look like the following:

```
private static final String TAG = "MainActivity";

Log.v(TAG, "This is a verbose log message.");
```

There are several levels of logging. Table 2.3 shows the levels available that you can use in your code.

Table 2.3   **Available Methods for Logging**

`Log.v(String tag, String msg)`	Verbose
`Log.d(String tag, String msg)`	Debug
`Log.i(String tag, String msg)`	Info

Log.w(String tag, String msg)	Warn
Log.e(String tag, String msg)	Error
Log.wtf(String tag, String msg)	Assert, What a Terrible Failure (WTF)

Each of these levels is called in the same manner, with the differences being on when each message appears when filtered in the logs. As an example, I have an application that has buttons tied to trigger a log message when clicked. When I am filtering my LogCat console with the Verbose level, the following is displayed:

```
02-01 09:42:01.168  16414-16414/com.dutsonpa.debugexample V/MainActivity :
Verbose button has been clicked.
02-01 09:42:01.856  16414-16414/com.dutsonpa.debugexample D/MainActivity :
Debug button has been clicked.
02-01 09:42:02.665  16414-16414/com.dutsonpa.debugexample I/MainActivity :
Info button has been clicked.
02-01 09:42:03.471  16414-16414/com.dutsonpa.debugexample W/MainActivity :
Warning button has been clicked.
02-01 09:42:04.277  16414-16414/com.dutsonpa.debugexample E/MainActivity :
Error button has been clicked.
02-01 09:42:05.151  16414-16414/com.dutsonpa.debugexample A/MainActivity :
WTF button has been clicked.
```

The messages generated by the log contain a timestamp, the application that the message was generated from, the level of log used (V, D, I, W, E, or A), with the tag that was used, and then the message that was passed to be shown.

Note that when using LogCat inside of DDMS, if I change my level to Warn, the LogCat console only displays the following:

```
02-01 09:42:03.471  16414-16414/com.dutsonpa.debugexample W/MainActivity :
Warning button has been clicked.
02-01 09:42:04.277  16414-16414/com.dutsonpa.debugexample E/MainActivity :
Error button has been clicked.
02-01 09:42:05.151  16414-16414/com.dutsonpa.debugexample A/MainActivity :
WTF button has been clicked.
```

This is because of the order of severity of these messages. Verbose will show all Verbose and above log messages. Because Verbose is the bottom level of severity, all log messages will be shown. When I changed the log level to Warn, only the Warn, Error, and WTF log messages were shown.

> **Note**
>
> The WTF tag is reserved for errors or sections of code that should *never* fail. It is also listed as being an Assert, which is the highest level of logging. Code logged at the Assert level will always be visible in LogCat because it has been signified as being of extreme or dire importance.

Logging files does not replace the benefits or merits of profiling, tracing, or even using break-points. It does, however, give you, the developer, a way to see values and variables as they change in real time without pausing threads and rummaging through a stack.

Note that although they are very helpful while developing your app, they are not something you will want to leave in the final build of your application. Leaving them in will cause more memory usage, overhead, and potentially more file space to be used if any external logging libraries are packed into your APK.

Summary

In this chapter, you learned about various methods and ways you can test and debug your Android applications. You learned writing tests for your applications is important, and that when collaborating with others, tests help you confirm that your code does what you believe it will.

You learned about the importance of automated testing tools to help you identify, control, fix problems with rapid user input and layout problems. You also know that you have tools that are built into the Android SDK that you can use from the command line to help you achieve testing success.

You learned how to monitor your Android device or emulator for memory and CPU usage, and how to create reports to understand what is using your system resources so that you can optimize your code. You also learned that not every manufacturer ships the same Android experience, which gives you the opportunity to either extend new functionality or to be aware that it is there when you are writing your own application.

Lastly, you learned about the logging process and how you can log messages to the console and view them either with the command-line `logcat` tool or by using the Android tool window in Android Studio and adjusting the LogCat output filters.

3

Application Structure

With the decision to change the supported development platform from the ADT bundle to Android Studio also came the decision to start using Gradle as the build system. This opened the door for many developers to start assembling Android applications in a more collaborative way and changed the file structure with which prior projects were built.

In this chapter, you learn the new file system structure as well as the types of files you can include in your project, including where XML files are located, where image assets are stored, and where the Gradle build files are stored.

When you create an application in Android Studio, you find that the project is divided into an App folder and Gradle scripts. Figure 3.1 shows this structure.

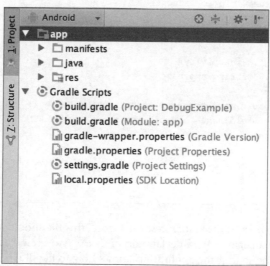

Figure 3.1　The App folder and the Grade Scripts section are visible in the Project window.

The App folder contains three subfolders that house the files and resources that make up your application. They are divided so that it should be fairly easy to determine which assets go in which folder; however, those new to application development or those looking to migrate from the older Eclipse-based development model might not be certain where files should go. To make this easier, I walk you through each folder and what it contains.

Manifests

The manifests folder lives up to its name. This is where you would put your manifest files. Depending on your target, you may have only one manifest file, or you may have several. You may have several manifest files due to application versioning, or even for supporting specific hardware.

A manifest file is generated by Android Studio when you create a project. Listing 3.1 shows a generated manifest file.

Listing 3.1   **Contents of a Generated Manifest File from Android Studio**

```xml
<?xml version="1.0" encoding="utf-8"?>
<manifest xmlns:android="http://schemas.android.com/apk/res/android"
    package="com.dutsonpa.helloandroid" >

    <application
      android:allowBackup="true"
      android:icon="@drawable/ic_launcher"
      android:label="@string/app_name"
      android:theme="@style/AppTheme" >
      <activity
        android:name=".MainActivity"
        android:label="@string/app_name" >
        <intent-filter>
          <action android:name="android.intent.action.MAIN" />
          <category android:name="android.intent.category.LAUNCHER" />
        </intent-filter>
      </activity>
    </application>

</manifest>
```

If you have worked with an Android manifest file before, this file should look familiar. It is an XML file and as such begins with a declaration of `<?xml version="1.0" encoding="utf-8"?>`. This is done so that the application knows how to handle the information contained within the file. Because it has been declared as an XML file, you will find that options and settings inside this file consist of elements that may contain attributes. The next element after the declaration is a prime example.

The <manifest> element contains some attributes: the XML namespace for Android and the package name for your application. The package name is the one you created when you started the project. The <manifest> element can also contain child elements.

In Listing 3.1, there is only one child element: the <application> element. This contains more attributes that will affect how your application is displayed as well as if the user is allowed to have the application be backed up. Other child elements may include any Activities, Intents, Providers, Receivers, Services, and so on, that the application will need to use.

Your manifest may also contain other elements, such as the <uses-permission> element. This element is both the bane and balm of the application developer. By allowing your application some access to system functionality, you can create applications that appear to be pure magic, giving users access to everything they want when they want it. This unfortunately can also cause some very scary messages to be displayed to the user when they install your application. A user is much more likely to install your application if you ask for only what you absolutely need in order to accomplish a task rather than requesting the keys to the kingdom and promising that you won't compromise the user or their personal data.

> ### Note
> You may have previously used <compatible-screens> elements to target specific screen sizes for your application. This is no longer an encouraged method of creating applications. Instead, you should use different layout resources to allow as many users as possible to enjoy and use your application.

Due to the nature of XML, the order in which you add or remove elements does not matter as much as the child-parent relationship. However, note that the official documentation lists that the following elements be ordered as shown in the following pseudo-code:

```
<manifest>
  <uses-permission />
  <permission />
  <permission-tree />
  <permission-group />
  <instrumentation />
  <uses-sdk />
  <uses-configuration />
  <uses-feature />
  <supports-screens />
  <compatible-screens />
  <supports-gl-texture />
  <application>
    <activity>
      <intent-filter>
        <action />
```

```
          <category />
          <data />
      </intent-filter>
      <meta-data />
    </activity>
    <activity-alias>
      <intent-filter></intent-filter>
      <meta-data />
    </activity-alias>
    <service>
      <intent-filter></intent-filter>
      <meta-data/>
    </service>
    <receiver>
      <intent-filter></intent-filter>
      <meta-data />
    </receiver>
    <provider>
      <grant-uri-permission />
      <meta-data />
      <path-permission />
    </provider>
    <uses-library />
  </application>
</manifest>
```

You may be tempted to invent and add your own elements; however, you should know that the manifest is parsed for a specific set of elements and when custom elements are found it will cause an error. This is also true when using custom attributes inside of elements.

Java

The java folder is self-explanatory. This is the folder in your project where you will be storing all of the Java files you use to create and work with your application.

All of your classes will be available here, and Android Studio will even bundle together the package path so that you can work with the files without having to drill down through the folders that make up your package.

You are not limited to keeping your classes inside of the package root. Just like when working with other Java applications, you are free to create subdirectories that make sense and place your classes inside of them.

For example, if you were working with database connections and wanted all of your data classes to reside in an easy-to-use storage location, you could create a "data" folder and place your classes inside.

Depending on how you are creating your application, you may be able to import your classes for use inside of your `MainActivity`. If I had created a class for database work named `MyDB` and placed it in the "data" folder, I would use the following import to use it inside of my `MainActivity`:

```
import com.dutsonpa.HelloAndroid.data.MyDB;
```

When working with your own project, you need to change the domain (`dutsonpa`) and application name (`HelloAndroid`) to match.

Res (Resources)

The manifest and java folders have so far held the essential portions of the application that allow it to be installed and the logical portion of your application. The "res" folder switches things up a little bit by controlling the layout, media, and constants that will be used in your application. The folder is thus named due to it containing all of the resources that your app relies on. It contains folders that help you separate and sort the resources of your application.

When you use Android Studio to create a new application, some folders will be automatically generated for you. However, these folders are not the only ones you can use in your project. The following are the folders that can be used inside of the res folder.

Drawable

The drawable folder contains all the visual media and resources that your application will need to use. Table 3.1 shows drawable types that you can place and use inside of this folder.

Table 3.1   **Resource Files for Drawable Folder**

Drawable Resource	File Type
Bitmap	Images files (such as .jpg, .png, and .gif).
Clip Drawable	An XML file consisting of points that is used in conjunction with another drawable to create a clipped object.
Insert Drawable	An XML file that is used to place one drawable inside the bounds of another drawable.
Layer List	An XML file that contains an array made up of other drawables. Note that items will be drawn in order based on location in the array placing item [0] on the bottom layer.
Level List	An XML file that is used to display other drawables that can be accessed based on the level requested through `setImageLevel()`.
Nine-Patch	A PNG image file that can stretch specific portions to scale based on content size.

Drawable Resource	File Type
Scale Drawable	An XML file that contains a drawable that changes the dimension value of another drawable based on its current value.
Shape Drawable	An XML file that contains the values of geometric shape, color, size, and similar attributes.
State List	An XML file that is used for images that have multiple or different states of appearance.
Transition Drawable	An XML file that contains a drawable that can be transitioned between two items.

When working with Android Studio, be aware that not all folders may be shown for your resources. On your file system, you may have separate drawable, drawable-hdpi, drawable-mdpi, and drawable-xhdpi folders, with each containing a resource that is named the same but that is to be used specifically for a different display density. In Android Studio this resource will be shown in the drawable folder as a folder that can be expanded, with the resource it will be used with in parentheses. Figure 3.2 shows how Android Studio displays resources with the same name in folders that are pixel density dependent.

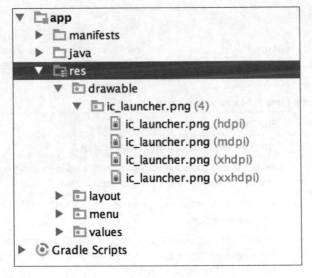

Figure 3.2   The `ic_launcher.png` file is several folders, but is displayed as a single resource with density-specific versions shown when the main resource is expanded.

Layout

The layout folder houses the XML files used for your layouts. The default layout file is named after your Activity, which if you created a new project in Android Studio and selected the default settings would be `activity_main.xml`.

This file is used to set up the layout for your Activity and is used for basic alignment of your layouts, components, widgets, and similar assets that are used for the UI of your application.

Similar to the drawables folder, you may have multiple layout folders to handle different devices. This can be helpful when working with layouts that need to be adjusted for devices with more or less screen space available. Developers who are used to working with Fragments to change the layout of the page will be pleased that they can now use a separate layout file that will automatically be used rather than having to work with a Fragment.

To use a separate layout based on screen size, you need to specify the layout based on the dp unit width or height of the device and place it as the filename. The dp unit stands for density independent pixel. This unit allows you to use relative measurements that will not be off when used on devices with different physical pixel resolutions. For example, tablets that are 7" and larger will generally have a width of 600dp units; this allows you to create a folder named layout-sw600dp and place your layout XML file there. When the application is opened, it will check to see which layout should be used and display the layout appropriate for the device.

Layouts can also be supported based on screen density based on dots-per-inch (dpi) by using folders that are named based on the density, as listed:

- **ldpi**: Used with screens that have ~120dpi.
- **mdpi**: Used with screens that have ~160dpi.
- **hdpi**: Used with screens that have ~240dpi.
- **xhdpi**: Used with screens that have 320dpi.
- **xxhdpi**: Used with screens that have ~480dpi.
- **xxxhdpi**: Used with screens that have ~640dpi.
- **nodpi**: Resources here will be used on all densities.
- **tvdpi**: Used on screens sized between mdpi and hdpi, approximately 213dpi.

Menu

If you opted to create or add a menu to your application, the XML that defines your menu resides in this folder. You have the option of creating whatever name you would like for your menu, but if you created a new project in Android Studio and used the default options, you will find that your menu have been named `menu_main.xml`.

This naming convention is actually quite helpful because it identifies what the XML file is for "menu" and what activity is assigned to "main."

Values

The values folder is used to keep track of the values you will be using in your application. To create applications with an easier maintenance cycle, it is highly recommended to no longer hard-code values into your code. Instead, place values in XML files inside of the values folder.

Here's an example of this:

```
// Hard-coding a resource
<TextView
  android:text="Hello Android!"
  android:layout_width="wrap_content"
  android:layout_height="wrap_content" />


// Using a value from /res/values/strings.xml
<TextView
  android:text="@string/hello_android"
  android:layout_width="wrap_content"
  android:layout_height="wrap_content" />
```

In the previous example, the value shown in the TextView would change based on the string entered into strings.xml. The following is an example of a strings.xml file:

```
<?xml version="1.0" encoding="utf-8"?>
<resources>
  <string name="hello_android">Hello Android!</string>
</resources>
```

When you create a new project with Android Studio, the following XML files will be generated automatically:

- dimens.xml
- stings.xml
- styles.xml

By looking at these files, you'll notice that each of them is an XML file with a parent element of <resources>. This may lead you to think that you could put all of your values in one XML file and use it inside your application. Although this is something you can do, for the sake of maintaining your application and knowing exactly where your data is, it is strongly recommended that you break your values into multiple files. The following list of files may be used in your application to help keep different values separated:

- arrays.xml
- colors.xml
- dimens.xml
- strings.xml
- styles.xml

Each file is clearly named so that you know exactly what you are dealing with. Also, each file is named after the element that would be placed in a parent `<resource>` element. For example, color values would reside in a `<color>` element that is a child of the `<resource>` element.

Other Resources

You can create other folders for other resources in your application. Table 3.2 lists each folder name as well as what should be stored in that folder.

Table 3.2 **Application Resource Folders**

Folder Name	Folder Contents
animator	XML files for property animations
anim	XML files for tween animations
color	XML files for color state lists
raw	Stores files that will be read with an AssetManager
xml	Any XML files that you will be using in your application with the `Resources.getXML()` method

> **Tip**
>
> You may be wondering where to place audio files that your application uses. You can store them in `/res/raw` and access them with `R.raw.audio_file`. This eliminates the need for any other project-level folders and keeps your res folder organized.

Gradle

With Android Studio, the decision was made to leave ant for project building and move to Gradle. To help you manage your build files, Android Studio adds a section named Gradle Scripts to your project. When expanded, Gradle Scripts will show you your build configuration file, properties, and setting files.

When you are migrating a project created with Android Studio, you may find that you need to adjust some of these settings to match newer versions of Gradle or of the build tools used. You can see the current settings by viewing the `build.gradle` file in your app folder. Listing 3.2 shows a sample build file.

Listing 3.2   **A `build.gradle` File for an Android Application**

```
apply plugin: 'com.android.application'

android {
  compileSdkVersion 21
  buildToolsVersion "21.1.2"

  defaultConfig {
    applicationId "com.dutsonpa.helloandroid"
    minSdkVersion 15
    targetSdkVersion 21
    versionCode 1
    versionName "1.0"
  }
  buildTypes {
    release {
      minifyEnabled false
      proguardFiles getDefaultProguardFile('proguard-android.txt'),
        'proguard-rules.pro'
    }
  }
}

dependencies {
  compile fileTree(dir: 'libs', include: ['*.jar'])
  compile 'com.android.support:appcompat-v7:21.0.3'
}
```

When you're migrating or upgrading your application, the lines you need to pay the most attention to are the `compileSdkVersion`, `buildToolsVersion`, `minSdkVersion`, and `targetSdkVersion`. If these numbers do not match what you have installed on your system, you will see compilation errors and your application will fail to launch on an emulator or device, or even compile.

The other Gradle files should be managed by Android Studio and will be updated as need when your project is built and compiled. If you want to learn more about Gradle, visit the official website: https://gradle.org/.

Summary

In this chapter, you learned about the components that make up an Android application. You learned that with the change from Eclipse with the ADT plugin to Android Studio as the development IDE, the project structure and application assets are stored in different locations.

You learned about the application manifest and the various elements that can be included, such as the security elements that allow your application to access system resources to further extend the functionality of your application.

You also learned that you can use folders that contain assets for specific devices based on the device screen density. This allows you to create specific layouts for multiple devices without having to resort to using Fragments for layout changes.

Finally, you learned that Android Studio uses the Gradle build system and that some problems can be avoided by making sure that it has been configured for your environment.

4

Components

When you're developing an Android application, having an understanding of the components that make up the application will accelerate the development as well as simplify the process. Knowing how pieces of the architecture work with each other can turn creating an impossible application into an attainable one.

In this chapter, you are introduced to the components that are used by the Android system to pass information and display data to the user. Specifically, you learn about Intents, Activities, and Fragments.

Intents

When it comes to application components, the Intent component is one that is aptly named. You use an Intent to inform the system that you want to start something. You can think of it exactly as it sounds: letting the system know what your intent is.

When using an Intent, you can send two types: an explicit Intent and an implicit Intent. These mostly differ in how you would like the Intent to be interpreted.

An explicit Intent requires that you specify the component you want by using a fully qualified class name. For example, you can use an Intent that calls `com.mycompany.MyActivity`. This allows specific Activities or services to be called. There are times, however, when you will want other applications to be able to listen to and process your Intent. This is when you would use an implicit Intent.

> ### Note
>
> To keep your application secure, always make sure you are using an explicit Intent. You should also avoid setting up Intent filters that expose your services. This is crucial because any explicit Intents will be processed regardless of any Intent filters you have in place for your application. If another developer were to decompile your code, they would see your services and may end up using them for their own nefarious purposes. To help protect you from making this mistake, Android 5.0+ throws an exception whenever there's an attempt to use `bindService()` with an implicit Intent. This serves as a reminder to use an explicit Intent.

If you create an application that processes photos, shares data, or even allows a form of text messaging, you may want to allow the user to decide how this is handled. For the example of processing photos, you can use an implicit Intent to tell the Android system that you would like to use the camera on the device. This would then fire up the basic needs of previewing an image, taking it, and saving it to memory. The image would then be passed back to your application, where you would do your processing and saving. For sharing data or messages, you may want to use an implicit Intent to allow the user to choose from a list of applications they already have installed to complete the sharing process.

Allowing users to choose to use their own applications is potentially a great idea because it may save you in having to develop code that handles connecting to third-party APIs, dealing with developer agreements, and compatibility issues, but allows users to use applications that they are already familiar with and efficient at using. You need to keep in mind, however, that the user may not have any applications installed that will respond to the Intent you are attempting to use. Because it is always wise to have a contingency plan, you should always perform a check to see if the system has an application registered to read your Intent.

To build your Intent, you need to name it, instantiate it, and, then, if making it explicit, give the Intent the information required for the service or Activity to start. The following shows the creation of an explicit Intent:

```
Intent serviceIntent = new Intent(this, MyApplication.class);
```

To create an implicit Intent, you can leave out the specific call to the qualified domain class:

```
Intent shareIntent = new Intent();
```

Whenever you use an implicit Intent, check with the system to make sure there is an application that can handle your request. This can be done as follows:

```
if (shareIntent.resolveActivity(getPackageManager()) != null) {
  startActivity(shareIntent);
}
```

Intent Filters

Intent filters are created by adding an `<intent-filter>` element to your application manifest file. You must include `<action>`, `<data>`, and `<category>` elements as child elements in the `<intent-filter>`.

The following is a sample Activity that would be included inside of your application manifest XML:

```
<activity android:name="SharingActivity">
  <intent-filter>
    <action android:name="android.intent.action.SEND"/>
    <category android:name="android.intent.category.DEFAULT"/>
    <data android:mimetype="text/plain"/>
  </intent-filter>
</activity>
```

By declaring the Intent filter, you are allowing your application (and in turn your Activities or services) to be available to other applications. It is recommended that you do not use Intent filters for calls from your own application; as mentioned previously, this will expose your services and may be a security concern for your application.

Broadcast Receivers

When an Intent is created and sent, your application needs a way to retrieve it. This is done by creating a broadcast receiver. This is a two-part process: You first create a `BroadcastReceiver` in a class file and then register the class file inside of your manifest XML with a `<receiver>` that contains a child `<intent-filter>` element.

The following demonstrates a Java class that listens for an Intent and displays a toast message when invoked:

```
public class MyBroadcastReceiver extends BroadcastReceiver {
  @Override
  public void onReceive(Context context, Intent intent) {
    Toast.makeText(context, "Broadcast Received!", Toast.LENGTH_SHORT).show();
  }
}
```

To complete the broadcast receiver, the following demonstrates a `<receiver>` element that is a child element inside of the `<application>` element in the manifest XML that invokes the `onReceive()` method:

```
<receiver android:name=".MyBroadcastReceiver">
  <intent-filter>
    <action android:name="com.dutsonpa.helloandroid.MyBroadcastReceiver" />
  </intent-filter>
</receiver>
```

Note that in the `<action>` element, the name is set to the value that is set when the Intent is created. If it is not added when initialized, the name can be set with the `setAction()` method that is used on the Intent object.

Broadcast receivers can also be created and destroyed dynamically, as needed, during your application lifecycle. This can be done by using `registerReceiver()` and `unregisterReceiver()`. By using these methods, you can make services or activities available only when you need them. Another place you may want to use them is during the `onResume()` and `onPause()` methods of your application. The following demonstrates using `registerReceiver()` in the `onResume()` method and `unregisterReceiver()` in the `onPause()` method:

```
@Override
protected void onResume() {
  super.onResume();
  registerReceiver(new MyBroadcastReceiver(),
```

```
            new IntentFilter(com.dutsonpa.helloandroid.MyBroadcastReceiver));
}

@Override
protected void onPause() {
  super.onPause();
  unregisterReceiver(MyBroadcastReceiver);
}
```

Choosing between creating broadcast receivers when needed versus adding them to your manifest XML may come down to your personal preference; however, when starting out it may be more beneficial to add any broadcast receivers to your manifest first so that you have a list of the ones you are using in your application. The system Intents you plan on accessing will also be a factor when choosing to use dynamic versus static broadcast receivers.

Another component that is heavily used in the creation of Android applications is an Activity.

Activities

An Activity can be simply described as one of the screens of your application. The main screen of your application would be one Activity and an options screen would be another Activity. Each Activity is essentially a combination of a layout, widgets, and application components that run when active.

An application can consist of multiple Activities, but can only have one Activity in focus at a time. When an Activity is running and a new Activity is called, the Activity that was running is stopped and placed into the back stack. If a third Activity is called, then the second Activity is also placed into the back stack on top of the first Activity. Activities are stacked this way so that when a user presses the "back" button on their device, the application knows which Activity to display.

Creating an Activity

Creating an Activity is a two-step process: You create a subclass of `Activity` and then add the Activity to your application manifest. Creating a subclass is generally done by extending `Activity` or `ActionBarActivity`. This can be done as follows in your Activity class file:

```
public class MainActivity extends Activity {
  // Overrides, variables, callbacks, and methods go here
}
```

If your application uses an action bar, you will want to change the class to extend `ActionBarActivity`, like so:

```
public class MainActivity extends ActionBarActivity {
  // Overrides, variables, callbacks, and methods go here
}
```

The second step to making your Activity work in your application is to add your Activity to the application manifest. To achieve this, you need to add an `<activity>` element as a child to the `<application>` element. If you are adding a new Activity to a project that already has an Activity, you may only need to add an element that specifies the name of your new Activity. In the following example, an Activity named `OptionsActivity` was created and has been added to the manifest:

```
<application
  android:allowBackup="true"
  android:icon="@mipmap/ic_launcher"
  android:label="@string/app_name"
  android:theme="@style/AppTheme" >
  <activity
    android:name=".MainActivity"
    android:label="@string/app_name" >
    <intent-filter>
      <action android:name="android.intent.action.MAIN" />
      <category android:name="android.intent.category.LAUNCHER" />
    </intent-filter>
  </activity>
  <activity android:name=".OptionsActivity"/>
</application>
```

The original Activity, named `MainActivity`, is listed first and has additional options, such as an Intent filter added to it. You can see from the example that if your Activity does not use any Intent filters, it doesn't need to list them in the application manifest.

I briefly mentioned that Activities follow a lifecycle. This lifecycle helps keep the entire Android system running smoothly and also helps you, as a developer, to ready, write, and maintain data integrity while providing the user the experience they expect.

Activity Lifecycle

The Activity lifecycle is the process that all Activities use in order to be called, run logic, and finish in a structured and reliable manner. This helps the system maintain stability and manage system resources. Some methods, such as `finish()`, can be called in your Activity to force the Activity to close; however, it is recommended that you allow the Android system to manage when to finish or destroy an Activity.

Every stage of the Activity lifecycle has callback methods that do not all need to be implemented inside of your Activity logic. With that said, the `onCreate()` callback method is required, and the `onPause()` method should also be implemented so that you can save data or perform last-minute operations before the Activity is destroyed.

To help you visualize how the Activity lifecycle process works, Figure 4.1 shows the Activity lifecycle.

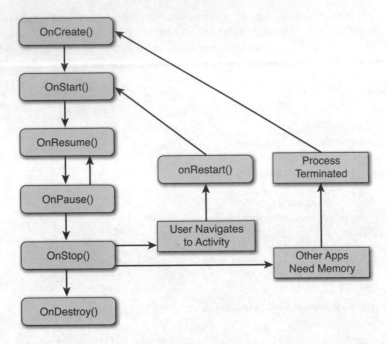

Figure 4.1   When an Activity starts, it follows the cycle demonstrated in this diagram. You can override these methods to perform logic in the various states an Activity cycles through.

Listing 4.1 shows the logic from an Activity that contains the usable Activity lifecycle callback methods along with comments on what each callback does.

Listing 4.1   **Activity Callback Methods**

```
public class MainActivity extends ActionBarActivity {

  @Override
  protected void onCreate(Bundle savedInstanceState) {
    super.onCreate(savedInstanceState);
    /* This activity is called whenever the application is started
     * any variables you need as well as static assets should be
     * created in this method
     */
    setContentView(R.layout.activity_main);
  }
  @Override
  protected void onStart() {
```

```java
    super.onStart();
    // This method runs either before onStop() or onResume()
  }
  @Override
  protected void onResume() {
    super.onResume();
    // This method happens right before the activity is officially running
  }
  @Override
  protected void onPause() {
    super.onPause();
    /* This method runs when the application is about to be terminated for
     * memory, or when the activity is changed or interrupted by another
     * activity such as a phone call. This is the method to use to save
     * data and changes
     */
  }
  @Override
  protected void onStop() {
    super.onStop();
    // This method runs when the activity is stopped but not yet destroyed
  }
  @Override
  protected void onDestroy() {
    super.onDestroy();
    // Last call before the activity and any data it has will be destroyed
  }
}
```

It is important to note from Listing 4.1 that each callback method uses a `super` method to extend the implementation. Failing to use the `super` method results in an error and causes your application to fail when it is compiled. As documented in each method in the listing, each callback has a different purpose and allows you to perform different actions.

> **Tip**
>
> Although it may be tempting to do your final save or processing of data in the `onDestroy()` method, this is not a suitable method for doing final work. Depending on the resources needed by the system, this method may be executed and finished before your operations and will leave your application in a broken state. Stick to getting your data-saving work done in the `onPause()` callback.

Another component that extends the functionality of an Activity is a Fragment.

Fragments

When the first Android tablets started to appear on the market with Android 3.0 (Honeycomb), developers were given their first glance at how Fragments can be used to change the layout and structure of an application. Users were finally given devices that had displays large enough to allow more than a single-line list item or line of text to be shown. Email apps could now have a list of emails on one-third of the screen with a large preview window taking up the other two-thirds. The most amazing part was that the same application could be run on a smaller device, with the list taking up the full screen and the preview being shown when tapped.

When working with Fragments, you will get the greatest benefit by thinking of your Activities as reusable modules. This allows you to focus on creating complete Fragments that don't require or rely on the functionality of other Fragments in order to work. This also has the added benefit of making sure that each Fragment will behave as expected on a device that only supports viewing one Fragment at a time.

Creating a Fragment

Creating a Fragment is similar to creating an Activity, although there are a couple of subtle differences. You first need to create a subclass that extends the `Fragment` class. Note that you do not need to create separate class files. If you have an Activity that uses a Fragment, you can place the Fragment code within the same class file You will then need to implement at least a couple of the Fragment lifecycle methods. Finally, if you want your Fragment to have a UI, you will need to return a `View`.

As with Activities, Fragments have a lifecycle with callback methods. The following lists the methods that can be included in your Fragment:

- `onAttach()`: The first stage of Fragment initialization.
- `onCreate()`: When the Fragment is created, the logic here will be processed.
- `onCreateView()`: When the Activity that the Fragment has been included in returns from the Activity stack, the logic here is run as part of the resuming process.
- `onActivityCreated()`: The Activity the Fragment is in has been fully created or resumed.
- `onStart()`: Called when the Fragment has been started.
- `onResume()`: This will run when the Fragment resumes, and is the last point for logic changed before the Fragment is considered active.
- `onPause()`: As the Fragment is placed into the back stack, the logic here is processed.
- `onStop()`: The Fragment is going to be destroyed soon, so the logic can be run here.
- `onDestroyView()`: The current view is going to either load the Fragment back to the Activity cycle through `onCreateView()` or be destroyed.

- **onDestroy()**: The Fragment is going to be destroyed; this is the last chance for the logic to be run before the Fragment is destroyed and detached from the view.

- **onDetach()**: As the Fragment is removed, this is the last method you can work with as part of the Fragment-destroy process.

Fragments also contain a lifecycle. Figure 4.2 shows how the fragment lifecycle works.

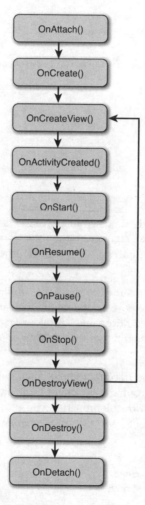

Figure 4.2   Fragments have a lifecycle as well as methods that can be overridden, similar to Activities. However, the flow differs in Fragments moving to the bottom or top of the stack.

As when working with Activities, you are not required to use all of the lifecycle callbacks, but it is encouraged that you include at least one of the `create` and `onPause()` methods. The following shows a sample Fragment class:

```
public class PlaceholderFragment extends Fragment {

  public PlaceholderFragment() {
  }

  @Override
  public View onCreateView(LayoutInflater inflater, ViewGroup container,
   Bundle savedInstanceState) {
    View rootView = inflater.inflate(R.layout.fragment_main, container, false);
    return rootView;
  }

  @Override
  public void onPause() {
    super.onPause();
    // logic should go here for handling the fragment data
  }
}
```

Inside of the `onCreateView()` method, a `LayoutInflater` is used along with a `ViewGroup`. This is done to add the UI from the Fragment to the final layout. This happens when `return rootView` executes, as the layout requires a View to be returned in order to properly add the Fragment as part of the layout.

The `onPause()` method has been included to show the similarity between the Fragment and Activity logic. Just as you should be putting any saving logic inside of the `onPause()` callback method in an Activity, you should do the same with your Fragment. This way, the logic will have time and be certain to finish rather then relying on the `onDestroyView()` or `onDestroy()` callback method.

After you create your Fragment, you need to add the Fragment to the Activity layout XML file. Depending on your chosen layout and Fragment implementation, this can be as simple as adding a `<fragment>` element with the properties you want set inside of your layout. The following is an example of the layout XML with two Fragments:

```
<LinearLayout xmlns:android="http://schemas.android.com/apk/res/android"
  android:orientation="horizontal"
  android:layout_width="match_parent"
  android:layout_height="match_parent">

<fragment android:name="com.cookbook.fragments.ItemFragment"
  android:id="@+id/item_fragment"
  android:layout_weight="1"
  android:layout_width="0dp"
  android:layout_height="match_parent" />
```

```
<fragment android:name="com.cookbook.fragments.TextFragment"
   android:id="@+id/text_fragment"
   android:layout_weight="2"
   android:layout_width="0dp"
   android:layout_height="match_parent" />

</LinearLayout>
```

Communicating with Fragments

Even though Fragments should be created and treated as individual modules, they will probably need to pass data to the Activity that is loading the Fragment. Fragments can access objects in the Activity by using the getActivity() method. Views can be accessed by chaining the findViewById() method to the getActivity() method. For example, a ListView that exists in the Activity could be accessed from the Fragment with the following code inside the Fragment:

```
View listView = getActivity().findViewById(R.id.list);
```

If you need to pass data from a Fragment to an Activity, you will need to create a callback method via a public interface inside your Fragment. After you create the interface, you can extend your Activity to include it.

The following shows a sample public interface from inside of a Fragment class:

```
public interface OnItemSelectedListener {
   public void onItemSelected(int position);
}
```

Now that the interface has been created, it can be added to an Activity and then accessed by instantiating it. The following shows sample code from an Activity that adds the interface and sets up an object to use it:

```
public class MainActivity extends FragmentActivity
     implements ItemFragment.OnItemSelectedListener {

   //...
   ItemFragment firstFragment = new ItemFragment();
   //...

   @Override
   public void onAttach(Activity activity) {
     super.onAttach(activity);
     try {
       mListener = (OnItemSelectedListener) activity;
     } catch (ClassCastException e) {
```

```
        throw new ClassCastException(activity.toString() + " must implement
OnItemSelectedListener");
    }
  }

}
```

Note that in the previous code, the ItemFragment should be called from inside of an Activity lifecycle callback method such as onCreate(). It should also be noted that the onAttach() callback method has been added. In the onAttach() method, a try/catch statement is used to help detect whether the interface has been implemented. Because this pseudo-code example is short, it would be fairly easy to spot if the interface has not been implemented. In your code, however, there may be hundreds of lines of code and you may not be sure if you have implemented the interface. The try/catch will come in handy because you will get an exception that tells you which Activity and which interface it is that was missed. If the interface was properly implemented, the mListener is defined so that it can be used to pass events from the Fragment to the Activity.

Another way to load data into either a Fragment or an Activity is to use a Loader.

Loaders

The Loader is a wonderful component that can be used on both Activities and Fragments. A Loader has the ability to asynchronously collect data and deliver it. It also has the ability to monitor for changes, which makes it great to use in Fragments because it can poll for a change.

Because many Loaders may be used, a LoaderManager is used to manage the ones in your Activity or Fragment. This is most easily accomplished by using getLoaderManager() and then using initLoader() to make sure that the Loader has been created, and if it has previously been created, to reuse it. In order to determine whether the Loader has been created, an ID is passed to the initLoader() method. The following line shows these methods in use:

```
getLoaderManager().initLoader(0, null, this);
```

Here, 0 is the ID of the loader, the null value is passed in lieu of additional arguments, and this is used because the third argument of initLoader() needs a LoaderManager.LoaderCallbacks implementation.

There may be occasions when you reuse the Loader but want to discard the data that was previously used with it. This can be accomplished by using restartLoader() in one of your state-change methods. This would appear as follows:

```
getLoaderManager().restartLoader(0, null, this);
```

Implementation of LoaderCallbacks is generally done with a Cursor. The following is an example of implementing on a Fragment class:

```
public class MyFragment extends Fragment
    implements LoaderCallbacks<Cursor> {
```

```
  // fragment class code
}
```

To manage connections, data, and cleanup, you need to implement three methods that are part of LoaderCallbacks: onCreateLoader(), onLoadFinished(), and onLoaderReset(). When initLoader() is called, onCreateLoader() is called automatically. Because the previous example used a CursorLoader, the following demonstrates how the onCreateLoader() is used with a CursorLoader:

```
public Loader<Cursor> onCreateLoader(int id, Bundle args) {
  CursorLoader loader = new CursorLoader(
    this.getActivity(),
    CONTENT_URI,
    projection,
    selection,
    selectionArgs,
    sortOrder);
  return loader;
}
```

In the previous example, the CursorLoader object is created, populated, and then returned. Some developers find it easier to instead create the variables separately and then return and declare the new object at the same time. This is programmer preference, and you should follow the method that fits your coding standard and style.

The onLoadFinished() method is called when a load is finished. It is guaranteed to execute and is a good place to do data management. However, you should not close the cursor here because the Loader will handle that by itself. The following is an example of swapping data without closing the cursor:

```
SimpleCursorAdapter myAdapter;

public void onLoadFinished(Loader<Cursor> loader, Cursor data) {
  myAdapter.swapCursor(data);
}
```

The onLoaderReset() callback method is used when a previously created Loader is reset rather than being reused. Using this method is fairly straightforward because it relies on only having access to the adapter being used to hold data, and then calling the swapCursor() method on it and passing a null value. The following shows an example of a SimpleCursorAdapter being reset:

```
SimpleCursorAdapter myAdapter;

public void onLoaderReset(Loader<Cursor> loader) {
  myAdapter.swapCursor(null);
}
```

Summary

In this chapter, you learned about Intents and how they are used to start various processes and communicate with the Android system. You learned that there are implicit and explicit forms of Intents and that each has a benefit to being used. You learned that Intent filters allow your application to answer Intent calls from other applications. This is especially helpful when allowing the user to use functionality that they may be used to using inside of another application.

You also learned about Activities and how each Activity can be thought of as a display screen inside of your application. You learned that Activities are created by using Java and by adding them to your application manifest XML. You also learned that Activities have a lifecycle that is used to manage how they are interacted with and that this lifecycle can be accessed via callback methods. These methods allow you to make sure that data integrity is maintained and that users have a seamless experience.

You then learned about Fragments and how they are used to create applications that take full advantage of available screen space by combining what would otherwise be Activities into a shared Activity. You also learned that, like Activities, Fragments follow a lifecycle with callback methods that you can use. You also learned that Fragments can communicate with each other and pass events back and forth.

Finally, you learned about Loaders and the role they play in asynchronously getting data that can be used in either Activities or Fragments. You learned how they are created, reused, and even reset.

5

Views

Of all the pieces of the Android system, views are probably the most used. Views are the core building block on which almost every piece of the UI is built. They are versatile and, as such, are used as the foundation for widgets. In this chapter, you learn how to use and how to create your own view.

The `View` Class

A view is a rather generic term for just about anything that is used in the UI and that has a specific task. Adding something as simple as a button is adding a view. Some widgets, including `Button`, `TextView`, and `EditText` widgets, are all different views.

Looking at the following line of code, it should stand out that a button is a view:

```
Button btnSend = (Button) findViewById(R.id.button);
```

You can see that the `Button` object is defined and then set to a view defined in the application layout XML file. The `findViewById()` method is used to locate the exact view that is being used as a view. This snippet is looking for a view that has been given an `id` of `button`. The following shows the element from the layout XML where the button was created:

```
<Button
  android:layout_width="wrap_content"
  android:layout_height="wrap_content"
  android:text="@string/button_text"
  android:id="@+id/button"
  android:layout_below="@+id/textView"
  android:layout_centerHorizontal="true" />
```

Even though the element in the XML is `<Button>`, it is still considered a view. This is because `Button` is what is called an indirect subclass of `View`. In total, there are more than 80 indirect subclasses of `View` as of API level 21. There are 11 direct subclasses of `View`: `AnalogClock`, `ImageView`, `KeyboardView`, `MediaRouteButton`, `ProgressBar`, `Space`, `SurfaceView`, `TextView`, `TextureView`, `ViewGroup`, and `ViewStub`.

The `AnalogClock` Subclass

The `AnalogClock` is a complex view that shows an analog clock with a minute-hand and an hour-hand to display the current time.

Adding this view to your layout XML is done with the following element:

```
<AnalogClock
  android:layout_width="wrap_content"
  android:layout_height="wrap_content"
  android:id="@+id/analogClock"
  android:layout_centerVertical="true"
  android:layout_centerHorizontal="true" />
```

This view can be attached to a surface by using the `onDraw(Canvas canvas)` method, and it can be sized to scale to the screen it is being displayed on via the following method:

`onMeasure(int widthMeasureSpec, int heightMeasureSpec)`

It should be noted that if you decide to override the `onMeasure()` method, you must call `setMeasuredDimension(int, int)`. Otherwise, an `IllegalStateException` error will be thrown.

The `ImageView` Subclass

The `ImageView` is a handy view that can be used to display images. It is smart enough to do some simple math to figure out dimensions of the image it is displaying, which in turn allows it to be used with any layout manager. It also allows for color adjustments and scaling the image.

Adding an `ImageView` to your layout XML requires the following:

```
<ImageView
  android:layout_width="wrap_content"
  android:layout_height="wrap_content"
  android:id="@+id/imageView"
  android:src="@drawable/car"
  android:layout_centerVertical="true"
  android:layout_centerHorizontal="true" />
```

To show multiple figures, you can use multiple `ImageViews` within a layout. Similar to other views, you can attach events such as a click event to trigger other behavior. Depending on the application you are building, this may be advantageous versus requiring the user to click a button or use another widget to complete an action.

The `KeyboardView` Subclass

The `KeyboardView` is one of the most interesting views that exist. This is one of the true double-edged components of the Android system. Using the `KeyboardView` allows you to create your own keyboard. Several keyboards exist in the Play store that you can download right now and use on your Android device that are based on using the KeyboardView.

The problem is that using an application with a custom keyboard means that all data entry must pass through it. Every "keystroke" is passed through the application, and that alone tends to send shivers down the spine of those who are security conscious. However, if you are an enterprise developer and need a custom keyboard to help with data entry, then this view may be exactly what you are looking for.

> **Note**
>
> The KeyboardView requires creating a new input type for your device, and the keyboard you create will be accessible in all programs. This also means that users may opt to not use your keyboard, and may even disable it as an option.

Creating your own keyboard is an involved process. You need to do the following:

- Create a service in your application manifest.
- Create a class for the keyboard service.
- Add an XML file for the keyboard.
- Edit your strings.xml file.
- Create the keyboard layout XML file.
- Create a preview TextView.
- Create your keyboard layout and assign values.

The KeyboardView has several methods you can override to add functionality to your keyboard:

- onKey()
- onPress()
- onRelease()
- onText()
- swipeDown()
- swipeUp()
- swipeLeft()
- swipeRight()

You do not need to override all of these methods; you may find that you only need to use the onKey() method.

The `MediaRouteButton` Subclass

The `MediaRouteButton` that is part of the compatibility library is generally used when working with the Cast API. This is where you need to redirect media to a wireless display or ChromeCast device. This view is the button that is used to allow the user to select where to send the media.

Note that per Cast design guidelines, the button must be considered "top level." This means that you can create the button as part of the menu or as part of the ActionBar. After you create the button, you must also use the `.setRouteSelector()` method; otherwise, an exception will be thrown.

First, you need to add an `<item>` to your menu XML file. The following is a sample `<item>` inside of the `<menu>` element:

```
<item
android:id="@+id/mediaroutebutton_cast"
android:actionProviderClass="android.support.v7.app.MediaRouteActionProvider"
android:actionViewClass="android.support.v7.app.MediaRouteButton"
android:showAsAction="always"
android:visible="false"
android:title="@string/mediaroutebutton"/>
```

Now that you have a menu item created, you need to open your `MainActivity` class and use the following import:

```
import android.support.v7.app.MediaRouteButton;
```

Next, you need to declare it in your `MainActivity` class:

```
private MediaRouteButton myMediaRouteButton;
```

Finally, add the code for the `MediaRouteButton` to the menu of the `onCreateOptionsMenu()` method. Remember that you must also use `setRouteSelector()` on the `MediaRouteButton`. The following demonstrates how this is accomplished:

```
@Override
public boolean onCreateOptionsMenu(Menu menu) {
  super.onCreateOptionsMenu(menu);
  getMenuInflater().inflate(R.menu.main, menu);

  myMediaRouteItem = menu.findItem(R.id.mediaroutebutton_cast);
  myMediaRouteButton = (MediaRouteButton) myMediaRouteItem.getActionView();
  myMediaRouteButton.setRouteSelector(myMediaRouteSelector);
  return true;
}
```

The `ProgressBar` Subclass

The progress bar is a familiar UI element. It is used to indicate that something is happening and how far along this process is. It is not always possible to determine how long an action will take; luckily, the ProgressBar can be used in indeterminate mode. This allows an animated circle to appear that shows movement without giving a precise measurement of the status of the load.

To add a ProgressBar, you need to add the view to your layout XML. The following shows adding a "normal" ProgressBar:

```
<ProgressBar
   android:layout_width="wrap_content"
   android:layout_height="wrap_content"
   android:id="@+id/progressBar"
   android:layout_centerVertical="true"
   android:layout_centerHorizontal="true" />
```

Other styles of ProgressBar may also be used. To change the style, you need to add a property to the <ProgressBar> element. The following styles may be used:

```
Widget.ProgressBar.Horizontal
Widget.ProgressBar.Small
Widget.ProgressBar.Large
Widget.ProgressBar.Inverse
Widget.ProgressBar.Small.Inverse
Widget.ProgressBar.Large.Inverse
```

Depending on your implementation, you may apply the style either with your styles.xml or from your attrs.xml. For the styles from styles.xml, you would use the following:

```
style="@android:style/Widget.ProgressBar.Small"
```

If you have styles inside your attrs.xml file that you want applied to the progress bar, use the following property in the <ProgressBar> element:

```
style="?android:attr/progressBarStyleSmall"
```

If you are planning on using the indeterminate mode, you need to pass a property of android:indeterminate into the <ProgressBar> element. You may also specify the loading animation by setting the android:indeterminateDrawable to a resource of your choosing.

A ProgressBar that is determinate requires updates to be passed to it via the setProgress() or incrementProgressBy() method. These methods should be called from a worker thread. The following shows an example of a thread that uses a Handler and an int for keeping the progress value, and a ProgressBar has been initialized:

```
new Thread(new Runnable() {
  public void run() {
    while (myProgress < 100) {
      myProgress = doWork();
      myHandler.post(new Runnable() {
        public void run() {
          myProgressBar.setProgress(myProgress);
        }
```

```
      });
    }
  }
}).start();
```

The `Space` Subclass

For those who have worked on layouts and visual interfaces, the `Space` view is one that is both helpful and brings on somewhat lucid nightmares. This view is reserved to add "space" between other views and layout objects.

The benefit to using a `Space` is that it is a lightweight view that can be easily inserted and modified to fit your needs without you having to do an absolute layout or extra work trying to figure out how relative spacing would work on complex layouts.

Adding a `Space` is done by adding the following to your layout XML:

```
<Space
  android:layout_width="1dp"
  android:layout_height="40dp" />
```

The `SurfaceView` Subclass

The `SurfaceView` is used when rendering visuals to the screen. This may be as complex as providing a playback surface for a live camera feed, or it can be used for rendering images on a transparent surface.

The `SurfaceView` has two major callbacks that act as lifecycle mechanisms that you can use to your advantage: `SurfaceHolder.Callback.surfaceCreated()` and `SurfaceHolder.Callback.surfaceDestroyed()`. The time in between these methods is where any work with drawing on the surface should take place. Failing to do so may cause your application to crash and will get your animation threads out of sync.

Adding a `SurfaceView` requires adding the following to your layout XML:

```
<SurfaceView
  android:id="@+id/surfaceView"
  android:layout_width="match_parent"
  android:layout_height="match_parent"
  android:layout_weight="1" />
```

Depending on how you are going to use your `SurfaceView`, you may want to use the following callback methods:

- surfaceChanged()
- surfaceCreated()
- surfaceDestroyed()

Each of these callback methods gives you an opportunity to initialize values, change them, and more importantly free some system resources up when it is released. If you are using a `SurfaceView` for rendering video from the device camera, it is essential that you release control of the camera during the `surfaceDestroyed()` method. Failing to release the camera will throw errors when you attempt to resume usage of the camera in either another application or when your application is resumed. This is due to a new instance attempting to open on a resource that is finite and currently marked as in use.

The `TextView` Subclass

The `TextView` is likely the first view added to your project. If you create a new project in Android Studio that follows the default options, you will be given a project that contains a `TextView` with a string value of "Hello World" in it.

To add a `TextView`, you need to add the following code to your layout XML file:

```
<TextView
  android:text="@string/hello_world"
  android:layout_width="wrap_content"
  android:layout_height="wrap_content" />
```

Note that in the previous example, the value for the `TextView` is taken from `@string/hello_world`. This value is inside of the `strings.xml` file that is in your `res/values` folder for your project. The value is defined in `strings.xml` as follows:

```
<string name="hello_world">Hello world!</string>
```

The `TextView` also contains a large number of options that can be used to help format, adjust, and display text in your application. For a full list of properties, visit http://developer.android.com/reference/android/widget/TextView.html.

The `TextureView` Subclass

The `TextureView` is similar to the `SurfaceView` but carries the distinction of being tied directly to hardware acceleration. OpenGL and video can be rendered to the `TextureView`, but if hardware acceleration is not used for the rendering, nothing will be displayed. Another difference when compared to `SurfaceView` is that `TextureView` can be treated like a `View`. This allows you to set various properties including setting transparency.

In similarity to `SurfaceView`, some methods need to be used with `TextureView` in order for proper functionality. You should first create your `TextureView` and then use either `getSurfaceTexture()` or `TextureView.SurfaceTextureListener` before using `setContentView()`.

Callback methods should also be used for logic handling while working with the `TextureView`. Paramount among these callback methods is the `onSurfaceTextureAvailable()` method. Due to `TextureView` only allowing one content provider to manipulate it at a time, the onSurfaceTextureAvailable() method can allow you to handle IO exceptions and to make sure you actually have access to write to it.

The onSurfaceTextureDestroyed() method should also be used to release the content provider to prevent application and resource crashing.

The ViewGroup Subclass

The ViewGroup is a special view that is used for combining multiple views into a layout. This is useful for creating unique and custom layouts. These views are also called "compound views" and, although they are flexible, they may degrade performance and render poorly based on the number of children included, as well as the amount of processing that needs to be done for layout parameters.

CardView

The CardView is part of the ViewGroup that was introduced in Lollipop as part of the v7 support library. This view uses the Material design interface to display views on "cards." This is a nice view for displaying compact information in a native Material style. To use the CardView, you can load the support library and wrap your view elements in it. The following demonstrates an example:

```
<RelativeLayout
  xmlns:android="http://schemas.android.com/apk/res/android"
  xmlns:tools="http://schemas.android.com/tools"
  android:layout_width="match_parent"
  android:layout_height="match_parent"
  android:paddingLeft="@dimen/activity_horizontal_margin"
  android:paddingRight="@dimen/activity_horizontal_margin"
  android:paddingTop="@dimen/activity_vertical_margin"
  android:paddingBottom="@dimen/activity_vertical_margin"
  tools:context=".MainActivity">

  <android.support.v7.widget.CardView
    xmlns:card_view="http://schemas.android.com/apk/res-auto"
    android:id="@+id/card_view"
    android:layout_gravity="center"
    android:layout_width="200dp"
    android:layout_height="200dp"
    card_view:cardCornerRadius="4dp"
    android:layout_centerVertical="true"
    android:layout_centerHorizontal="true">

  <TextView android:text="@string/hello_world"
    android:layout_width="wrap_content"
    android:layout_height="wrap_content" />
  </android.support.v7.widget.CardView>
 </RelativeLayout>
```

This example shows a card in the center of the screen. The color and corner radius can be changed via attributes in the `<android.support.v7.widget.CardView>` element. Using `card_view:cardBackgroundColor` will allow you to change the background color, and using `card_view:cardCornerRadius` will allow you to change the corner radius value.

> **Note**
>
> Using the `CardView` support library requires you to edit your Gradle build files. You need to add the following line to the `dependencies` section in your `build.gradle` file:
>
> ```
> dependencies {
>   compile 'com.android.support:cardview-v7:21.+'
> }
> ```
>
> You should change the version number targeted on the end to match your project target.

RecyclerView

The `RecyclerView` was also added in Lollipop as part of the v7 support library. This view is a replacement for the aging `ListView`. It brings with it the ability to use a `LinearLayoutManager`, `StaggeredLayoutManager`, and `GridLayoutManager` as well as animation and decoration support. The following shows how you can add this view to your layout XML:

```
<android.support.v7.widget.RecyclerView
    android:id="@+id/my_recycler_view"
    android:scrollbars="vertical"
    android:layout_width="match_parent"
    android:layout_height="match_parent"/>
```

Similar to with a `ListView`, after you have added the `RecyclerView` to your layout, you then need to instantiate it, connect it to a layout manager, and then set up an adapter to display data.

You instantiate the `RecyclerView` by setting it up as follows:

```
myRecyclerView = (RecyclerView) findViewById(R.id.my_recycler_view);
```

The following shows connecting to a layout manager using the `LinearLayoutManager` that is part of the v7 support library:

```
myLayoutManager = new LinearLayoutManager(this);
myRecyclerView.setLayoutManager(myLayoutManager);
```

All that is left is to attach the data from an adapter to the `RecyclerView`. The following demonstrates how this is accomplished:

```
myAdapter = new MyAdapter(myDataset);
myRecyclerView.setAdapter(myAdapter);
```

The `ViewStub` Subclass

The `ViewStub` is a special view that is used to create views on demand in a reserved space. The `ViewStub` is placed in a layout where you want to place a view or other layout elements at a later time. When the `ViewStub` is displayed—either by setting its visibility with `setVisibility(View.VISIBLE)` or by using the `inflate()` method—it is removed and the layout it specifies is then injected into the page.

The following shows the XML needed to include a `ViewStub` in your layout XML file:

```
<ViewStub
    android:id="@+id/stub"
    android:inflatedId="@+id/panel_import"
    android:layout="@layout/progress_overlay"
    android:layout_width="match_parent"
    android:layout_height="wrap_content"
    android:layout_gravity="bottom" />
```

When the `ViewStub` is inflated, it will use the layout specified by the `android:layout` property. The newly inflated view will then be accessible via code by the ID specified by the `android:inflatedId` property.

Creating a Custom View

When developing your own application, you may need a view that doesn't come "out of the box." When this occurs you have two options: You can create a class for your own custom view or you may extend one of the existing views.

To create your own, you need to create a new class, have it extend `View`, and have it override at least one method. You will also be adding the variables and logic needed to handle the custom properties you will be adding to your view. The following shows a custom view along with the values used as custom properties:

```
public class MyView extends View {
  private int viewColor, viewBgColor;

  public MyView(Context context, AttributeSet attrs) {
    super(context, attrs);

    TypedArray a = context.getTheme().obtainStyledAttributes(attrs,
      R.styleable.MyView, 0, 0);

    try {
      viewColor = a.getInteger(R.styleable.MyView_viewColor);
      viewBgColor = a.getInteger(R.styleable.MyView_viewBgColor)
    } finally {
      a.recycle();
    }
```

```
    @Override
    protected void onDraw(Canvas canvas) {
      // draw your view
    }
  }
}
```

You want to be able to pass values through the XML when used with your application layout XML. To do this you can add an XML file to the `res/values` folder. This folder houses `<resources>` with child `<declare-styleable>` elements. The following shows an example of a custom view XML file:

```xml
<?xml version="1.0" encoding="utf-8"?>
<resources>
  <declare-styleable name="MyView">
    <attr name="viewColor" />
    <attr name="viewBgColor" />
  </declare-styleable>
</resources>
```

Now you can add your custom view to your application layout, but you need to add a property so that your custom view can be found. This is done by adding the following line to your layout element:

```
xmlns:custom="http://schemas.android.com/apk/res/com.dutsonpa.mycustomview"
```

Notice that you need to change the value to match your namespace by replacing `com.dutsonpa.myview` with your own package name. Once you add that to your layout element, you can add your custom view. This is done by referencing the package and then adjusting or setting the values you want to use. The following shows an example of a custom view being added with values being set:

```
<com.dutsonpa.mycustomview.myview
  android:id="@+id/"
  custom:viewColor="#33FF33"
  custom:viewBgColor="#333333" />
```

Notice that Android properties may be used and that your custom properties are used by employing `custom:valueName`. This provides some flexibility by allowing some built-in features to be mixed with your custom attributes.

The last thing you should do is add getter and setter methods for your attributes. These can be added to your class as follows:

```
public void getViewColor() {
  return viewColor;
}
```

```
public void getViewBgColor() {
  return viewBgColor;
}

public void setViewColor(int newViewColor) {
  viewColor=newViewColor;
  invalidate();
  requestLayout();
}

public void setViewBgColor(int newViewBgColor) {
  viewBgColor=newViewBgColor;
  invalidate();
  requestLayout();
}
```

By using `invalidate()` and `requestLayout()`, the layout is forced to redraw using the `onDraw()` method that is being employed by the custom view.

Summary

In this chapter, you learned what views are and how they are used in applications. You learned that views have multiple subclasses that can be used as is or extended by making a custom `View`.

You learned about the main subclasses and how to implement them into your application layout XML file, as well as some code that may be used to accompany them.

You also learned about two views that were introduced with Android Lollipop: `CardView` and `RecyclerView`. These views are complex `ViewGroups` that can help display data in the Material design style and update the aging `ListView`.

6

Layout

Android applications are made to be seen, touched, and interacted with. To achieve this, you need to create a layout that your application will use to display the interface to the user. There are several ways to create your layout, and this chapter introduces you to the various layouts available and how they can be used in your application.

Layout Basics

You have two ways to control the layout you use in your application. As you learned in Chapter 5, "Views," Views and ViewGroups can be created programmatically and edited. Some developers will be more comfortable creating and destroying layouts in this manner, but the application layout can also be created via XML.

When creating a new project in Android Studio, you will find a file in the res/layout folder that should be named after your Activity. If your Activity was named "main," then you will find a file named activity_main.xml. If you are not using Android Studio or would rather create your own layout file, this can be done by creating your XML file in the same folder, res/layout, and then referencing the layout file in your Activity class. The following shows referencing the file in the onCreate() method of the Activity class:

```
@Override
protected void onCreate(Bundle savedInstanceState) {
  super.onCreate(savedInstanceState);
  setContentView(R.layout.custom_main.xml);
}
```

The most important part of this sample code is the line setContentView(R.layout.custom_main.xml);. This is how the custom XML, custom_main.xml, is referenced and used. By changing the referenced file, you can use different layout files. This may not seem beneficial at first; however, if you happen to be experimenting with several different layouts, you can quickly swap them out without having to copy and paste or copy over your existing layout file.

Layout Measurements

The layout XML structure is a fairly simple XML syntax that contains properties you can use to help define how the layout and any child objects it contains are displayed. It is important to note that some properties affect how the layout is sized. In these instances, you should do your best to avoid pixel (px) values and instead use density-independent pixels (dp).

The reason why you should avoid using px units, whenever possible, is that when working with the myriad of devices available, you will find that not all pixels are the same. In the dark days before mobile devices gained popularity, most monitors that were used with computers all contained roughly the same pixel density as each other. This allowed a fairly standard unit of measurement to be used because pixels were a simple 1:1 ratio. Things started to get shaken up a bit when various hardware manufacturers found that they could create smaller screens with pixels that could fit in roughly half the same space as a standard pixel would take up. The ratio for pixel calculations suddenly switched to 2:1. This allowed incredibly detailed images and visuals onscreen that could be displayed with high clarity and sharpness. Whether it is fortunate or unfortunate is up for debate; however, increasing the pixel density didn't stop a 2:1, and now there are devices that have pixel ratios of 3:1, 4:1, and higher. Figure 6.1 demonstrates this problem on devices with different resolutions and pixel density ratios.

Figure 6.1   The image is set to 640px by 360px; however, it displays in a different size on a 9" 281ppi tablet (left), a 5" 565ppi phone (middle), and an 8" 283ppi tablet (right).

To alleviate this particular issue, the density-independent pixel was created. This measurement unit comes built in with a little extra math to figure out the pixel density of the screen and runs that against the entered number of dp units that a layout or object should take. This solves the pixel measurement problem by always returning the exact number of pixels to use.

You may find when you are developing that even though you are using dp units, your design or layout will not fit or starts to look a bit ridiculous on very large or small screens. Starting with Android 3.2, screens were grouped together based on the amount of dp units they contain. This makes it possible for you to use different layout files that fit the screen used to view your application.

The size groupings are as follows:

- **ldpi**: 120dpi
- **mdpi**: 160dpi
- **hdpi**: 240dpi
- **xhdpi**: 320dpi
- **xxhdpi**: 480dpi
- **xxxhdpi**: 640dpi

Using these groupings, you can provide not only layouts, but also other assets such as images. To provide these resources, you need to create folders and place the resources you want loaded for devices that match that screen size. For example, if you want to provide a special layout for extra-dense devices, you could create a folder called layout-xhdpi in your /res folder. You would then place your layout XML file there. Note that it must be the same name as the layout XML file in the /res/layout folder.

As you are defining the size of the elements in your layout, you should be aware of the wrap_content and match_parent settings. When you have an element that is going to be dynamic in size, you may want to use wrap_content because this will allow the view or widget to expand based on the content it contains. If you would like to force content to be constricted by the size of the parent container or view group, you should use match_parent.

When working with text, you should use scale-independent pixels (sp), which will scale displayed text based on user preferences as well as the screen density of the device. Because the sp unit will take into consideration user preferences, it is not a safe unit of measurement to use when setting the dimensions of layouts.

Layout Coordinates

Each layout type or container has a way of allowing you to place specific items; however, you can also get specific positioning information programmatically by using the getTop() and getLeft() methods. Similar to how web developers position elements, views are treated as rectangular objects that are placed on an X/Y axis, with 0 being the very top and left locations. Figure 6.2 shows a view positioned at 0,0 on an X/Y axis.

You can leverage two helper functions, getBottom() and getRight(), to figure out the bottom and right locations of a view. These are helper functions because they are shortcuts to combining two functions to determine view placement. Using getBottom() is a shortcut to using `getTop()` + `getHeight()`. Using `getRight()` is a shortcut to using `getLeft()` + `getWidth()`.

Figure 6.2   Using `getTop()` and `getLeft()` would return 0 for each function because the view is placed at the very top-left location.

Now that you are aware of the properties and values that are used when adding elements to your layout XML, it is time to learn about the various layout styles that you can use in your application.

Layout Containers

Each layout starts with a basic container that you use to fill with child views. Each layout style has a reason why it should be used, as well as reasons why it might not be the best choice for your application. In this section, you learn about linear, relative, table, and frame layouts, as well as `WebView`, which is a special container that is used to display web content.

Linear Layout

The linear layout is named after the way it uses direction to align child elements. You can align child elements in either a horizontal or vertical fashion. This orientation is adjusted by setting the value of the `android:orientation` property in the `<LinearLayout>` element.

The following shows the contents of a layout XML file using a linear layout with buttons and text:

```
<LinearLayout xmlns:android="http://schemas.android.com/apk/res/android"
  xmlns:tools="http://schemas.android.com/tools"
  android:layout_width="match_parent"
  android:layout_height="match_parent"
  android:paddingLeft="@dimen/activity_horizontal_margin"
  android:paddingRight="@dimen/activity_horizontal_margin"
  android:paddingTop="@dimen/activity_vertical_margin"
  android:paddingBottom="@dimen/activity_vertical_margin"
  tools:context=".MainActivity"
  android:orientation="vertical">

  <Button
    android:layout_width="match_parent"
    android:layout_height="wrap_content"
    android:text="Button 1"/>
  <Button
    android:layout_width="match_parent"
    android:layout_height="wrap_content"
    android:text="Button 2"/>
  <Button
    android:layout_width="match_parent"
    android:layout_height="wrap_content"
    android:text="Button 3"/>
  <TextView
    android:layout_width="match_parent"
    android:layout_height="wrap_content"
    android:text="This is vertical orientation"
    android:gravity="center"/>

</LinearLayout>
```

The android:orientation has been set to vertical, which allows all child elements to be stacked vertically. It is also important to note that elements have had the android:layout_width property set to match_parent. This allows the elements to be full width. Figure 6.3 shows this layout displayed on an Android device.

It is not possible to use android:layout_height="match_parent" when displaying elements vertically because every element would stretch to fill the screen and leave each element stacked on top of the other.

You can adjust how much room each child view takes by setting the android:layout_weight property. This takes a numeric value that is then used to decide how much space a particular child view should be allowed to take. If you decide that you want all child views to take the same amount of space, you can either set each view to android:layout_height with a value of 0dp for an equal vertical orientation or you can set each view to android:layout_width with a value of 0dp for an equal horizontal orientation.

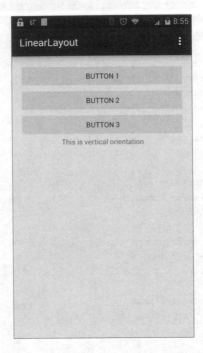

Figure 6.3   The buttons and text are positioned starting at the top of the layout and continuing down vertically.

To change the orientation to horizontal, you should change the value of the android:orientation property to horizontal, and then each child element will need to have the android:layout_height and android:layout_width properties adjusted.

Figure 6.4 demonstrates the same layout adjusted to be displayed horizontally.

Relative Layout

The relative layout is used when you have a complex user interface that requires specific sizing and relies on knowing where a view or layout element will be. It thus is named because elements are placed based on the relative proximity or position of other elements in the layout as well as to the containing layout.

The relative layout provides a somewhat flexible and adaptable interface. Elements can be told to position based off of the center, left, right, top, or bottom of the parent view. This can also be combined with placement values off of other child views that are already positioned.

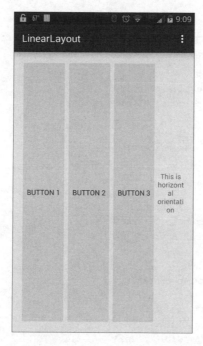

Figure 6.4   Text becomes almost impossible to read when there are too many elements being forced into a cramped area.

The following shows a layout XML file that uses a relative layout to position text and four buttons:

```
<RelativeLayout xmlns:android="http://schemas.android.com/apk/res/android"
  xmlns:tools="http://schemas.android.com/tools"
  android:layout_width="match_parent"
  android:layout_height="match_parent"
  android:paddingLeft="@dimen/activity_horizontal_margin"
  android:paddingRight="@dimen/activity_horizontal_margin"
  android:paddingTop-"@dimen/activity_vertical_margin"
  android:paddingBottom="@dimen/activity_vertical_margin"
  tools:context=".MainActivity">

  <TextView
    android:text="Relative layouts allow flexible positioning"
    android:layout_width="wrap_content"
    android:layout_height="wrap_content"
    android:layout_alignParentTop="true"
    android:layout_centerHorizontal="true" />
```

```
<Button
  android:layout_width="wrap_content"
  android:layout_height="wrap_content"
  android:text="Button 1"
  android:id="@+id/button"
  android:layout_centerVertical="true"
  android:layout_centerHorizontal="true" />

<Button
  android:layout_width="wrap_content"
  android:layout_height="wrap_content"
  android:text="Button 2"
  android:id="@+id/button2"
  android:layout_below="@id/button"
  android:layout_alignParentLeft="true"
  android:layout_alignParentStart="true" />

<Button
  android:layout_width="wrap_content"
  android:layout_height="wrap_content"
  android:text="Button 3"
  android:id="@+id/button3"
  android:layout_alignTop="@id/button2"
  android:layout_alignParentRight="true"
  android:layout_alignParentEnd="true" />

<Button
  android:layout_width="wrap_content"
  android:layout_height="wrap_content"
  android:text="Button 4"
  android:id="@+id/button4"
  android:layout_below="@id/button2"
  android:layout_centerHorizontal="true" />

</RelativeLayout>
```

Rather than use `gravity` to adjust how text is displayed, the `TextView` is placed at the top of the page in the center by using `android:layout_alignParentTop="true"` and `android:layout_centerHorizontal="true"`. Buttons 2, 3, and 4 are positioned based off of Button 1, which is placed directly in the center of the layout. Some extra properties are also used to align Buttons 2 and 3 to the left and right sides of the layout. Figure 6.5 demonstrates what the layout appears like when viewed on an Android device.

Another reason you should consider using a relative layout is that rather than create complex layouts by nesting multiple linear layouts, you can create the same type of interface without complicating the layout. By avoiding nesting layouts, you are able to keep the layout "flat." This decreases the amount of processing needed to display your layout and speeds up the screen rendering of your layout.

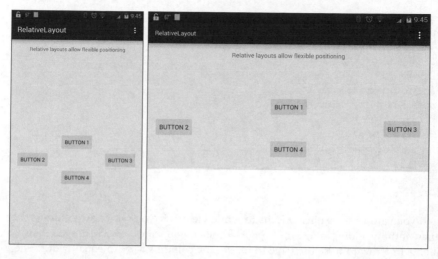

Figure 6.5   Regardless of device orientation, Button 1 is always at the center of the screen.

Table Layout

Table layouts are similar to how HTML table elements work. A table layout aligns child elements into rows and columns. Unlike tables in HTML, cell borders are never displayed and cells may be empty.

The table layout introduces some interesting formatting logic. By using `android:gravity`, you can adjust the text layout for elements. This may be needed as the size of columns is determined by the column that needs the most width or has the largest content.

You may think that you will just adjust the width of each element manually, but each child added to the table layout will default to a width of `match_parent`. The height is changeable, but has a default value of `wrap_content`. The following demonstrates a table layout with two rows containing `TextViews` and `Buttons`:

```
<TableLayout xmlns:android="http://schemas.android.com/apk/res/android"
  android:layout_width="match_parent"
  android:layout_height="match_parent"
  android:stretchColumns="1"
  android:padding="10dp">

  <TableRow>
    <TextView
      android:text="Name:"
      android:padding="5dp"/>
    <TextView
      android:text="Jonathan Generic"
      android:gravity="end"
```

```
      android:padding="5dp"/>
  </TableRow>

  <TableRow>
    <Button
      android:text="Button 1"
      android:id="@+id/button"/>
    <Button
      android:text="Button2"
      android:id="@+id/button2" />
  </TableRow>

</TableLayout>
```

Although you cannot set explicit widths for child elements, you can create columns that are the same width by adding `android:layout_width="0dp"` and `android:layout_weight="1"` to elements in a row to force the table to render the columns with an equal width. The following shows the properties applied to the `<Button>` elements:

```
<TableRow>
  <Button
    android:layout_width="0dp"
    android:layout_weight="1"
    android:text="Button 1"
    android:id="@+id/button"/>
  <Button
    android:layout_width="0dp"
    android:layout_weight="1"
    android:text="Button2"
    android:id="@+id/button2" />
</TableRow>
```

This also requires that the `<TableLayout>` element contains a property of `android:stretchColumns="1"`. Figure 6.6 shows how this fix was used to change the button alignment.

Table layouts are best for displaying tabular data. This is data or visuals that require a grid or specific spacing to allow the user to read and comprehend data quickly without trying to decipher a design to get the data they are looking for.

Frame Layout

The frame layout is used either when you would like to reserve screen space for a single view or when you are creating overlays that have a z-index effect. The spatial effect is achieved due to how the frame layout handles child elements. It positions them into a stack, with the first item added on the bottom and the last item added on the top.

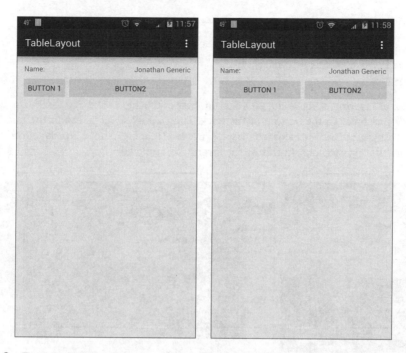

Figure 6.6   The buttons auto-align, leaving one small and the other large (left). With properties set, the buttons take an equal full column width (right).

The following demonstrates a frame layout that contains two TextViews and an ImageView:

```
<FrameLayout
  xmlns:android-"http://schemas.android.com/apk/res/android"
  android:layout_width="fill_parent"
  android:layout_height="fill_parent">

  <TextView
    android:layout_width="match_parent"
    android:layout_height="wrap_content"
    android:text="This text is under the image in the stack"/>

  <ImageView
    android:layout_width="match_parent"
    android:layout_height="wrap_content"
    android:src="@drawable/car"
    android:layout_gravity="center"/>

  <TextView
    android:layout_width="wrap_content"
    android:layout_height="wrap_content"
```

```
        android:text="This text is over the image"
        android:textColor="#ffffff"
        android:id="@+id/textView"
        android:layout_gravity="center" />
</FrameLayout>
```

The z-index or layering effect occurs in a first-in, first-out fashion. The first `TextView` is placed on the very first level, or the bottom of the stack. The `ImageView` is placed in the middle, above the first `TextView` but below the last `TextView`. Figure 6.7 shows this layout in two different orientations to help show how the layering is rendered.

Figure 6.7   When rotated to landscape, the first `TextView` appears cut off as the text goes behind the `ImageView`.

A frame layout can be used for overlay information or can be used with animation to add a little visual flair to your application. You should keep the child views contained in the layout to as few as possible in order to minimize managing the views in the stack. You can nest `<FrameLayout>` elements should you need to manipulate different sets or combine views together.

WebView

A `WebView` is not specifically a layout container; instead, it is a special view that allows you to display a web page inside of your application. This view is typically used to provide a help page or show the End-User License Agreement, or it is used inside of applications that allow you to open links in a browser without leaving the application. These applications are commonly social network or news applications. By allowing users to view web content without leaving your application, you are giving them a more powerful application that becomes an all-in-one solution for their needs. `WebViews` are also special because they get their own update through Google Play, which is similar to how Google Play Services are kept up to date.

A `WebView` also has the unique ability to pass some information between web page and device. This allows some features of the device to be triggered from the web page. This does not impede security because `WebViews` are still sandboxed to prevent full system access.

To add a `WebView` to your application, you need to add the following code to your layout XML file:

```
<WebView  xmlns:android="http://schemas.android.com/apk/res/android"
    android:id="@+id/webview"
    android:layout_width="match_parent"
    android:layout_height="match_parent" />
```

Note that if you are loading data from an Internet resource, you must also include the following permission in your application manifest:

```
<uses-permission android:name="android.permission.INTERNET" />
```

The URL that you want to load can then be passed to the view through your application logic by using the `.loadUrl()` method.

> **Tip**
>
> By default, `WebView` will not allow JavaScript to execute. If you require JavaScript processing, including triggering native functions such as a toast in your application, you must set the application to allow it. This can be done by adjusting the `WebView` settings like so:
>
> ```
> WebView myWebView = (WebView) findViewById(R.id.webview);
> WebSettings webSettings = myWebView.getSettings();
> webSettings.setJavaScriptEnabled(true);
> ```

Methods that you want to be accessible via JavaScript must be public and must use the `@JavascriptInterface` annotation. The annotation is required when working with Android API level 17 and above.

Summary

In this chapter, you learned about how layouts can be created and managed for your application. You learned about different size values and that pixels may be calculated differently depending on the device a user has. This means that using dp values is a safe way to adjust layout sizing.

You learned about how linear, relative, table, frame layout elements are added to your application layout XML and how they can be used. This included examples of when each type of layout is beneficial and should be considered.

Finally, you learned that a special view called a `WebView` can be used to display web content and why you may want to include a `WebView` in your application.

7

App Widgets

Part of the charm of using the Android platform is the ability to customize your experience. This can be done by moving and adjusting applications as well as adding widgets to your home and lock screens. Widgets were originally introduced in Android 1.5 (Cupcake) and have been a hit ever since. As newer versions of Android have been released, improvements have been made to how widgets (also known as app widgets) are placed, formatted, and displayed. In this chapter, you learn how app widgets are created.

A simple way to classify app widgets is as useful extensions of a full application. That is not to say that they must come bundled with a full application, but by doing so you can offer a fully functional detailed application along with streamlined widgets.

Widgets are not limited to only providing information; they can house several different views and can be used as controls for other applications by listening for and responding to different Intents. When working with Android 4.2+, app widgets are not limited to the home screen but can be added to the lock screen as well. This allows users the ability to see summaries, get quick information, and more, without having to unlock their device.

> ### Note
> Due to specific interaction that is already used by the main UI, widgets are limited to vertical scrolling and tapping only. Keeping this in mind will help you create a better widget and save you from trying to implement gestures and interactions that will not be possible.

When creating an app widget, you need to follow four steps:

1. Create a layout XML for the app widget.
2. Create an `AppWidgetProviderInfo` object via XML.
3. Create an `AppWidgetProvider` class file to contain widget logic.
4. Modify the application manifest to support the widget.

There is not a specific order in which the preceding steps must be implemented, but all four must be completed for an app widget to work.

> **Tip**
>
> Using Android Studio allows you to create all the necessary files for an app widget in just a few clicks:
>
> 1. Create a new base application.
> 2. Right-click the res folder and choose New, Widget, App Widget.
> 3. Name the widget and choose your placement, resizable option, width, and height.
> 4. A new `AppWidgetProvider` class file, an XML layout file, and `AppWidgetProvider` object XML will be generated and placed in your project; your application manifest will also be updated automatically.

App Widget Layouts

In the same way that a standard application has a layout XML file, app widgets also take advantage of a layout XML file. This file is generally stored in the same location as the application XML file. When you're working with Android Studio, this means that the file will be found in `/res/layout`. Naming the file is personal preference, but to keep things consistent, it should be named after the app widget, similarly to how the application layout is named after the Activity that it represents.

Just like the layout for an application or Activity, the app widget layout file is used to display various layout containers. Unlike standard Activities or views, app widgets are based on Remote Views and, as such, are limited to the following layout containers:

- `FrameLayout`
- `LinearLayout`
- `RelativeLayout`
- `GridLayout`

They also are limited to the following widgets and views:

- `AnalogClock`
- `Button`
- `Chronometer`
- `ImageButton`
- `ImageView`

- ProgressBar

- TextView

- ViewFlipper

- ListView

- GridView

- StackView

- AdapterViewFlipper

To put this together, Listing 7.1 demonstrates an app widget layout XML file.

Listing 7.1   **Sample Layout XML File for an App Widget**

```
<RelativeLayout xmlns:android="http://schemas.android.com/apk/res/android"
   android:layout_width="match_parent" android:layout_height="match_parent"
   android:padding="@dimen/widget_margin" android:background="#A4C639">

   <TextView android:id="@+id/appwidget_text"
      android:layout_width="wrap_content"
      android:layout_height="wrap_content" android:layout_centerHorizontal="true"
      android:layout_centerVertical="true" android:text="@string/appwidget_text"
      android:textColor="#ffffff" android:textSize="24sp"
      android:textStyle="bold|italic"
      android:layout_margin="8dp"
      android:contentDescription="@string/appwidget_text"
      android:background="#A4C639" />
</RelativeLayout>
```

On the first line of Listing 7.1, you can see that a `RelativeLayout` element is used with some basic settings to help shape the appearance of the widget. You should take special note of the `android:padding="@dimen/widget_margin"` property. By default, this is set to `8dp`; however, because the reference here, the value will change based on the screen size of the device. This is done by pulling the value from the `res/values/dimens.xml`, `res/values-v14/dimens.xml`, and `res/values-w820dp/dimens.xml` files.

Prior to API 14 (Android 4.0 Ice Cream Sandwich), app widget margins were not automatically configured and margins could extend from edge to edge, from widget to widget, and to the entire screen. Because this could potentially lead to a poor user experience, an 8dp margin is added to app widgets by the system for API 14+. To make your app widget work on as many devices as possible and still retain proper style standards, you can create two resources and invoke them based on the API that the device running your app widget is currently on. The first resource should be placed in the file `/res/values/dimens.xml`. This file should contain the following:

```
<resources>
  <dimen name="activity_horizontal_margin">16dp</dimen>
  <dimen name="activity_vertical_margin">16dp</dimen>

  <dimen name="widget_margin">8dp</dimen>
</resources>
```

The addition of the `dimen` element with a property of `name="widget_margin"` sets a global value of `8dp` that is used by all. Because this is a global setting, you need to add another file that is used by Android devices running API level 14+. This is done by adding another resource located at `/res/values-v14/dimens.xml`. This should contain the following:

```
<resources>
  <dimen name="widget_margin">0dp</dimen>
</resources>
```

This value overwrites the previous global and will allow the Android system to apply the correct margins to the app widget.

With the `RelativeLayout` element for the app widget taken care of, let's look at the `TextView` found in Listing 7.1. This `TextView` has several properties that should be read over carefully. Properties such as `android:layout_centerVertical="true"` and `android:layout_centerHorizontal="true"` have been added. These properties have been applied to help keep content where it should be. App widgets by nature should be forgiving due to being resized and needing to accommodate devices with varying pixel densities. By using a centering technique, you can be sure that your app widget will appear nearly the same on every device that it is shown on.

Figure 7.1 demonstrates how this app widget renders on an Android device.

The layout for the app widget is only one of half of how the widget is displayed. The `AppWidgetProviderInfo` object contains other options that change how your app widget is displayed.

The `AppWidgetProviderInfo` Object

The `AppWidgetProviderInfo` object is an XML metadata file located in the `/res/xml/` folder. It is used to contain the following settings and information for the app widget:

- Minimum width
- Minimum height
- Update frequency
- Preview image
- Widget category

- Initial layout for home screen
- Initial layout for lock screen
- Option to resize

Figure 7.1   The widget appears with a background and text styles applied.

App Widget Sizing

The recommended and default maximum width and height for a widget is 4×4 cells. It is possible to program your layout to be larger than this, but you will run into compatibility problems when running on the app widget on different devices. You can set the minimum width and height of your app widget by using the properties android:minWidth and android:minHeight. Because there are so many devices with different resolutions, screen sizes, and pixel densities, you should use dp units when setting the values for these properties.

You can use the following formula to figure out how many dp units should be placed in these properties to match a cell unit:

```
Number of cells = (i*70) - 30
```

In this formula, i is the number of cells you would like to use. Using this formula, you can determine the following sizing information:

- 1 cell = 40dp
- 2 cells = 110dp
- 3 cells = 180dp
- 4 cells = 250dp

With that information, you can create an app widget that fits the layout you want. For example, if your layout looks best at 2 cells wide by 1 cell tall, you would set the size by using `android:minWidth="110dp" android:minHeight="40dp"`.

Update Frequency

The `android:updatePeriodMillis` property is used to adjust how often your app widget will run through the `onUpdate()` method. This setting does not guarantee that the update method will be run at the exact moment you specify, but it will run near when specified. It should be noted that no matter how small of a number you place as the value for the property, the system will not run the update more than once every 30 minutes (180,000ms).

This setting should be handled with care because it will impact the user's battery. The recommendation is to set your update to at least 60 minutes. No matter what update timing you use, the update will schedule a job for the device to run around the specified time. This means that even if the device is sleeping, it will be forced to wake up, execute the update, and then wait to become idle before sleeping again.

If you would like to let the device sleep and only update when awake, it is possible to set this property to `0` and use an alarm Intent with the `AlarmManager` set as type `RTC` or `ELAPSED_ REALTIME` to control the updating frequency of the app widget.

Preview Image

The `previewImage` property was added in API 11 (Android 3.0 Honeycomb) and allows you to specify a drawable asset that will be used on the widget selection screen as a preview of what your widget will look like. Figure 7.2 shows the widget selection screen on a device.

There is a utility installed by default in the Android emulator called Widget Preview. When you open this application, you are given the option of selecting a widget that is installed on the device. After you have picked your widget, it is then displayed and you are given the option of taking a snapshot or emailing the preview image. Figure 7.3 shows the widget selection and preview screens of this application.

If you do not have an account set up on your emulator, the application may crash when you attempt to email the asset to yourself. If you save the preview, it will be saved to the `Download` folder on the emulated device. You can use the `adb` command from terminal to pull the file to your desktop.

Figure 7.2   Creating a preview that matches what your app widget looks like will help users decide which widget to use.

Figure 7.3   Your widget should appear on the list (left). Once selected, the widget is rendered and can be saved (right).

Once the asset has been saved, you can place it in the `/res/drawables` folder of your project. It can then be referenced by setting the value to it like so:

```
android:previewImage="@drawable/example_appwidget_preview"
```

You are not limited to providing a resource that looks exactly like your widget; however, for the best user experience, try to match the preview to what your widget will look like.

Widget Category

App widgets originated on the home screen, but starting with API 17 (Android 4.2 Jelly Bean) app widgets were allows to be added to the lock screen. To accommodate this addition, the `android:widgetCategory` property is used. This property can accept the following values:

- `home_screen`
- `keyguard`
- `home_screen|keyguard`

The `home_screen` value is the standard setting that allows the app widget to be placed on the main UI screen. Using a value of `keyguard` will place the widget only on the lock screen. When you specify this value, the app widget will not appear as an option to be placed on the home screen. Using a value of `home_screen|keyguard` allows your widget to be placed on both the home screen and the lock screen.

Warning

Be careful with what a widget is allowed to do and display when allowing access from the lock screen. If personal or private information is displayed through your app widget, it will show on the lock screen, potentially compromising user data should the device ever be misplaced or stolen.

Widget Category Layout

When providing the app widget access to the home screen and/or lock screen, it makes sense that you may want to offer a different layout. This can help with displaying sensitive information or by providing a layout that is more streamlined for a quick glance without extra interaction.

To specify a specific layout for the home screen and lock screen, you use the `android:initialLayout` and `android:initialKeyguardLayout` properties. If you want both to use the same layout, you would set the properties to the same value, like so:

```
android:initialLayout="@layout/my_app_widget"
android:initialKeyguardLayout="@layout/my_app_widget"
```

By using `@layout/my_app_widget`, the layout stored in `/res/layout/my_app_widget.xml` will be used for displaying and positioning elements on the widget. To change layout based on screen, you just need to reference another file for the value.

Note that the property contains the word "initial," because you have the ability to programmatically change the layout file that is used, but when the app widget is first rendered, it will use the file listed as the value of this property.

Resizable Mode

The ability to resize widgets was added in API 11 (Android 3.0 Honeycomb). This was when the ability to tap and hold an app widget to resize it was introduced. Not all widgets will resize, and the option of allowing the resize is based on the value placed in the `android:resizeMode` property.

The `android:resizeMode` property can accept `none`, `horizontal`, and `vertical`. Beginning with API 12 (Android 3.1 Honeycomb), another option was introduced allowing resizing to occur on both axes by supplying the value of `horizontal|vertical`.

Sample `AppWidgetProviderInfo` Object

Now that you have seen what goes into an `AppProviderWidgetInfo` object, you should be familiar with the following sample file:

```xml
<?xml version="1.0" encoding="utf-8"?>
<appwidget-provider xmlns:android="http://schemas.android.com/apk/res/android"
    android:minWidth="110dp" android:minHeight="40dp"
    android:updatePeriodMillis="86400000"
    android:previewImage="@drawable/example_appwidget_preview"
    android:initialLayout="@layout/my_app_widget"
    android:resizeMode="horizontal|vertical"
    android:widgetCategory="home_screen"
    android:initialKeyguardLayout="@layout/my_app_widget"></appwidget-provider>
```

Note that in the previous widget layout, the `android:initialKeyguardLayout` attribute is set. This does not need to be defined when working with a home screen–only widget, but is included here because Android Studio currently includes the value when creating a widget. If you do not plan on creating a lock screen widget, this attribute can be safely removed.

This file can be named anything you want, but should reside in the `/res/xml` folder. As per XML guidelines, the file should begin with an XML declaration and then any document elements. The `<appwidget-provider>` is then declared with a namespace of `http://schemas.android.com/apk/res/android`. Inside, you will find all the previously mentioned properties that help define how your app widget is displayed.

The `AppWidgetProvider` Class

The `AppWidgetProvider` class should reside in your source package and can be named anything that makes sense to you. For ease of maintenance and development, I recommend naming it after the app widget you are creating.

As an example, I have created an application named "MyAppWidget" with an Activity named `MainActivity`. This means that both `MainActivity.java` and `MyAppWidget.java` will be found at `src/main/java/com/dutsonpa/appwidget/`. Note that your package name should replace mine in the path.

The class file should extend `AppWidgetProvider` and contain at least the `onUpdate()` method. The following methods may be used:

- `onUpdate()`: Runs during the update lifecycle of the app widget

- `onAppWidgetOptionsChanged()`: Runs on widget creation and every time the widget is resized

- `onDeleted(Context, int[])`: Runs whenever an app widget is removed

- `onEnabled(Context)`: Runs when the first instance of a widget is added

- `onDisabled(Context)`: Runs when the last instance of a widget is removed

- `onReceive(Context, Intent)`: Not generally needed, but will run for every broadcast and before any other callback methods

Among the listed callback methods, the `onUpdate()` method is paramount because it is where Intents are parsed and executed. This is also where you attach click events by using `setOnClickPendingIntent(int, PendingIntent)`. You should also consider setting up services within this method to handle any long polling or web requests. Because `AppWidgetProvider` is an extension of `BroadcastReceiver`, it may be shut down at any time. By using the services within the `onUpdate()` method, you can avoid application crashes caused by Application Not Responding (ANR) errors.

Listing 7.2 shows a sample `AppWidgetProvider` class that could be used as a starting point for working with an app widget.

Listing 7.2   **Sample `AppWidgetProvider` Class**

```
package com.dutsonpa.myappwidget;

import android.appwidget.AppWidgetManager;
import android.appwidget.AppWidgetProvider;
import android.content.Context;
import android.widget.RemoteViews;

public class MyAppWidget extends AppWidgetProvider {
```

```
@Override
public void onUpdate(Context context,
                        AppWidgetManager appWidgetManager, int[] appWidgetIds) {
  // Loop to make sure all widgets are updated
  final int N = appWidgetIds.length;
  for (int i = 0; i < N; i++) {
    // add widget logic here
    updateAppWidget(context, appWidgetManager, appWidgetIds[i]);
  }
}


@Override
public void onEnabled(Context context) {
  // Code here will run on launch of app widget
}

@Override
public void onDisabled(Context context) {
  // Code here will run when the last widget is disabled
}

static void updateAppWidget(Context context,
                            AppWidgetManager appWidgetManager,
                            int appWidgetId) {

  // Set widget text
  CharSequence widgetText = context.getString(R.string.appwidget_text);
  // App widgets use RemoteViews to manipulate widget view data
  RemoteViews views = new RemoteViews(context.getPackageName(),
    R.layout.my_app_widget);
  views.setTextViewText(R.id.appwidget_text, widgetText);

  // Pass updates to the widget
  appWidgetManager.updateAppWidget(appWidgetId, views);
}
}
```

The class file should feel familiar; it starts with the required imports, moves to the class declaration, and extends AppWidgetProvider. You can then see that several methods have been set up with comments to help guide you through each section.

The onUpdate() method contains a for loop that identifies if more than one of your widgets has been added to the user's screen. By using the for loop, you can be sure that logic changes and updates that should be executed will be, instead of only happening on one app widget. Other logic, such as click events, services, and Intent handling, should happen here.

The onEnabled() method is added so that if you need to set anything up for initialization, you may do so here. Note that this is a run-once method, and after being called and executed, it will not run again until all instances of the app widget are removed and one is added again.

The onDisabled() method is added so that logic from either onUpdate() or onCreate() can be executed to clean up any local variables, temp files, or databases.

A method named updateAppWidget() is also created to pass updates to the widget. This method will generally be called from onUpdate(). Remember that app widgets do not use standard views, but use RemoveViews instead. This is why the updateAppWidget() method uses them to change the text that is displayed in the widget.

> **Tip**
>
> The onAppWidgetOptionsChanged() method is used to change settings and options whenever the app widget is resized. You can get current information from the app widget by using getAppWidgetOptions().

Application Manifest Entries

The final piece that takes an app widget from idea to implementation is to modify your application manifest XML file. The modification consists of adding a <receiver> with an <intent-filter> element and a <meta-data> element.

The <receiver> should contain an android:name property with a value of your AppWidgetProvider class. A child <intent-filter> should then contain an <action> with a property and value of android:name="android.appwidget.action.APPWIDGET_UPDATE".

A <meta-data> element should be added as a sibling to the <intent-filter> element. This is a self-closing element, but it should contain the android:name="android.appwidget.provider" and android:resource properties. The value of android:resource should be set to the AppWidgetProviderInfo object XML file. As an example, if I had created an XML file named my_app_widget_info.xml in the res/xml folder, the property would read as follows:

android:resource="@xml/my_app_widget_info"

The following shows an example of what would be added to your Application Manifest XML:

```
<receiver android:name=".MyAppWidget" >
  <intent-filter>
    <action android:name="android.appwidget.action.APPWIDGET_UPDATE" />
  </intent-filter>

  <meta-data
    android:name="android.appwidget.provider"
    android:resource="@xml/my_app_widget_info" />
</receiver>
```

Summary

In this chapter, you learned about what app widgets are and the four basic steps involved in creating one. You learned about how layouts work with app widgets and how you can create two layouts that are used for the lock screen and home screen.

You learned about creating an XML file that houses information that the app widget uses to control interaction and meta information as an `AppWidgetProviderInfo` object. You also learned about creating a class to control widget logic and where it is placed in your application.

Finally, you learned how to modify your Application Manifest XML to contain the elements needed for the app widget to receive Intents and how to tie together the class and object file to relay resources between the app widget on the screen and the underlying logic that makes it function how you want.

## 8

Application Design: Using MVC

Creating your first Android application exposes you to how an application is put together, but it does not give you an understanding of how the application is wired together. Each piece of the application works together to create an experience that transfers data between the user and the device.

This chapter introduces you to Model-View-Controller (MVC) architecture. This architecture style meshes well with Android development, and you are shown how various Android components fit this style of development. This includes working with asynchronous methods, threads, tasks, content providers, and services.

The MVC pattern has been used in software development for many years and is a clean architecture style that allows developers to separate business or application logic from display logic.

The Model manages data and really only cares about the data's integrity. The View is what is shown to the user and serves as the interaction point at which a user can manipulate data. The Controller is the glue that holds the system together; it allows for transport and accessibility between the Model and the View. Figure 8.1 shows how this process works.

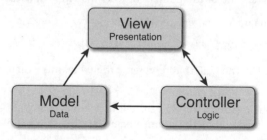

Figure 8.1   A diagram of the Model-View-Controller architecture demonstrates how the logic, data, and presentation layers work together.

Model

The primary role of a Model is to contain and manage data. In Android development, a component that acts like a Model is a content provider. A content provider not only allows you to collect and create connections to data in your application, but it allows you to create a resource that multiple applications can access.

Access to content providers from other applications requires them to have permission to access the data that will be returned. This allows users to be informed of what an application will have access to, including content providers that you have created to share data.

Some system content providers are available for use and will require you to specify permissions for access in your application. If you do not plan on sharing your content provider with any other applications, you do not need to worry about setting up extra permissions because content providers will always have read and write access from the application in which they originate.

The data that is stored in a content provider is placed in a table (similar to a rational database such as SQLite). This allows you to update, insert, and delete data in the content provider.

Running an update, insert, or delete will require you to use one of the matching methods in `ContentResolver`.

Here's how to update data in a content provider:

```
getContentResolver().update(Uri uri, ContentValues values, String where,
  String[] selectionArgs);
```

Note that `uri` is the Uniform Resource Identifier (URI), which is used to define the location of the content provider. The `values` are the new field values, with the key being the column name. Be aware that passing a null will erase the data in the specified column. The `where` value is a filter that mimics the functionality of an SQL `WHERE` statement. This allows you to be specific with the data that should be updated. The `selectionArgs` are used as the binding parameters for the selection or `values`. Depending on the update you are making, the value passed for `selectionArgs` may be `null`.

This method will return an `int` of the number of rows that were updated.

Here's how to insert data into a content provider:

```
getContentResolver.insert(Uri url, ContentValues values);
```

The value of `url` should be the URL that represents the table into which you are going to insert data.

The values passed through `values` should be the initial values that will be used when the new row is created. The key used will be the column name, and passing a null value will create an empty row.

This method will return the URL of the newly created row.

Here's how to delete data from a content provider:

```
getContentResolver.delete(Uri url, String where, String[] selectionArgs)
```

Similar to the other methods, the `url` should be the URI of the table or content provider that contains the row to be removed.

The `where` should contain the values that help you make a specific selection. This is used the same as a `WHERE` statement would work in SQL. After the method is run, it will return an `int` of the number of rows that were deleted.

> **Note**
>
> When working with content providers, you may notice that the built-in content providers contain a column name constant of `_ID` due to it being a requirement of Android SQLite. This is not necessarily a required column; however, if you create your own content provider and want to display the contents of it in a `ListView`, then you must have this column.

View

In MVC architecture, the View is exactly what it sounds like: the portion of the application that the viewer views. The View is responsible for dealing with visual display and translating user input into data that can be handled by the rest of the application.

In Android development, this boils down to Views and Activities. These were covered in detail in Chapter 5, "Views," so refer to that chapter for a refresher. To summarize, Activities are used to manage a single set of events. This means that when an application is launched, the Activity begins a lifecycle. This lifecycle is as follows:

1. The Activity is launched.
2. The `onCreate()` method is run.
3. The `onStart()` method is run.
4. The `onResume()` method is run.
5. The `onPause()` method runs when the user leaves the Activity, and `onResume()` is run when the user returns to the Activity. This may include system dialogs.
6. The `onStop()` method is called when the Activity is no longer viewable to the user. If the user returns, the `onRestart()` method will run before the application is reinstituted into the lifecycle by calling `onStart()` again.
7. The `onDestroy()` method is called when the Activity has been determined by the system to be closed down and has any resources reallocated back to the system.

An Android view will contain the visible and intractable pieces that are shown to the user by displaying widgets and custom views.

Through the addition of event listeners, such as onClick(), onLongClick(), and onKey(), information is allowed to pass between the presentation (the View of MVC) to the controller, which ties the Model and View together.

Controller

As previously mentioned, the Controller is responsible for holding the system together by facilitating the exchange of data between the View and the Model.

In Android development, the Controller can be thought of as the logic that is placed inside of event handlers as well as services.

A service is a component that can perform operations that are on going or that need to run for extended periods of time. A service can continue to run even when the user switches to another application; however, unless strictly specified, it is part of the application. This means that when the application is destroyed, the service will also be terminated.

An example of service behavior is starting media, such as an audio stream, and then changing to the home screen or another application while the audio is still playing. You may also use a service to fetch news, RSS feeds, or even stock listings.

Services require registration in the application manifest XML file. This can be set as a `<service>` element with a name:

```
<manifest>
<!-- other manifest elements -->
  <application>
    <service android:name=".myService" />
    <!-- other manifest elements -->
  </application>
<!-- other manifest elements -->
</manifest>
```

For security reasons, note that the `<service>` element does not contain an Intent filter. This means that you will need to call this service explicitly.

Services have two states: started and bound. Both states are similar in starting a service, but different in how they handle data returns.

In the started state, you call the `startService()` method to inform the system that you need to have the service scheduled to start. The service will then be started and run to completion. When finished, the service will self-terminate. In rare circumstances, it will return information back to the application.

To start a service through the `startService()` method, you can implement the following:

```
Intent intent = newIntent(this, MyService.class);
startService(intent);
```

In the bound state, the service is connected to an application via the `bindService()` method. This allows information to be passed from service to application and back. When you set a service in this state, it will only be active as long as a component is actively connected to the service. Should the connections to it stop, so will the bound service.

To start a bound service, you can implement the following:

```
Intent intent = new Intent(this, MyService.class);
bindService(intent, myConnection, 0)
```

The three arguments passed here are the Intent service, a `ServiceConnection`, and flags. Depending on what you need your service to do, you may wish to pass different flag values. Here are the possible values you can use:

- **BIND_AUTO_CREATE**: Creates the service as long as the binding exists.
- **BIND_DEBUG_UNBIND**: Saves the callstack from `unbindService` for viewing or printing. This does cause a memory leak, however.
- **BIND_NOT_FOREGROUND**: Stops the service from gaining a higher priority than the application.
- **BIND_ABOVE_CLIENT**: Used to inform the system that the service is more important than the application.
- **BIND_ALLOW_OOM_MANAGEMENT**: Allows the process used to manage the service to be treated as a normal application, allowing restarts and candidacy for termination based on the time it has been running.
- **BIND_WAIVE_PRIORITY**: Allows the system to perform schedule and memory management.
- **0**: Used when you do not want to specify a value.

Should you find that you need a service that can run indefinitely and be allowed to enable application components to bind, you can use the `onBind()` callback method. When implementing logic that uses the `onBind()` method, remember that you may want or need to use the `onUnbind()` method.

Services also have an `onCreate()` method that runs when the service first starts as well as an `onDestroy()` method that runs upon service termination.

> **Note**
>
> Application performance can be severely compromised if you are performing CPU-intensive operations on the main application thread. When using a service, make sure to start a new process for the service. Failure to do so may end in an Application Not Responding (ANR) error.

Starting a service from an `IntentService` allows long-running services to be managed on a separate thread from the main UI thread and should be strongly considered when creating services to use with your application.

Working Asynchronously

When creating an application, there are times when you may want to perform an action without interrupting application processing. This process is known as asynchronous processing and is not limited to application development.

Web developers have struggled against loading scripts and processes for years. In HTML5, the addition of the `async` property to a `<script>` element allows scripts to be queued up and requested without stopping the rendering of the web page.

Android applications are visually run on one UI thread that is not thread-safe. This means that you must do all visual updates on the UI thread, but it also means that you cannot use operations that slow down or interrupt the UI thread, such as network or Web API operations. If you do manage to interrupt the thread, your application will stall and you may experience an ANR error due to exceptions being thrown by the system.

To get around the limitations of the UI thread, you can create worker threads. This still requires a bit of finesse because you have to be careful not to create a process that is not thread-safe. You can leverage three methods to help maintain thread-safe operations:

- **`runOnUiThread(Runnable action)`**: Will queue the task to run on the UI thread. If the task is already on the UI thread, it will run immediately.

- **`post(Runnable action)`**: Adds the action to the message queue to be run on the UI thread. Returns `true` if the action is successfully placed into the queue.

- **`postDelayed(Runnable action, long delayMillis)`**: Adds the action to the message queue, with the condition of waiting to run until the specified time has been reached. Returns `true` if the action is successfully placed into queue.

The following is an example of using the `post()` method to perform thread-safe work:

```
new Thread(new Runnable() {
  public void run() {
    // create bitmap and retrieve from network
    final Bitmap bitmap =
        loadNetworkImage("http://example.com/my-image.png");
    // Use .post() method on ImageView to place image
    myImageView.post(new Runnable() {
      public void run() {
        // When queue is reached, place image
        myImageView.setImageBitmap(bitmap);
      }
```

```
    });
  }
}).start();
```

Depending on the work you are doing, you may also consider using AsyncTask. The AsyncTask will move processes from the main UI thread to a background process and return results without interrupting the rendering process of the application.

AsyncTask

The AsyncTask should be used with regard to the name it bears. This means you have a somewhat simple or short task that needs to be done.

Using AsyncTask requires you to set up a subclass with at least one method. Three parameterized types are used with AsyncTask: Params, Progress, and Result. Should you not want to use a particular argument, you may use Void.

The following demonstrates a skeleton AsyncTask subclass with a method to run the AsyncTask:

```
private class MyAsyncTask extends AsyncTask<String, Integer, String> {
  @Override
  protected String doInBackground(String... parameter) {
    // code to run in background as an AsyncTask
  }
  @Override
  protected void onProgressUpdate(Integer... progress){
    // code to run for update of AsyncTask
  }
  @Override
  protected void onPostExecute(String result) {
    // return data from AsyncTask as well as clean up
  }
}

// run the AsyncTask
public void executeAsync(View view) {
  MyAsyncTask task = new MyAsyncTask();
  task.execute("String value passed to AsyncTask");
}
```

If the AsyncTask is set to update a progress indicator, the onProgressUpdate() method could be used to pass information to update the indicator. The onPostExecute() method is used to return data to a view, widget, or other component.

Performing service-level operations with an AsyncTask opens up potential application and memory problems. One such potential problem is that an AsyncTask does not recognize configuration changes that cause Activities to be destroyed and re-created. That includes device orientation changes. If the `AsyncTask` happens to be in the middle of processing when the screen is rotated, your progress is lost and an exception will be thrown.

Getting past this issue requires keeping track of the `AsyncTask` instance by either implementing `setRetainInstance(true)` or creating a fragment with logic to check whether the `AsyncTask` is running when the orientation is changed.

Summary

In this chapter, you learned about Model-View-Controller architecture and how it can be applied to Android application development.

You learned that content providers are similar to Models and that information can be accessed between applications by using a content provider, but applications that do not wish to share data may still use a content provider.

You learned that Views and Activities make up the View component of MVC architecture and that activities follow a lifecycle that helps developers understand when callback methods are executed.

You learned that services can make up the Controller component of MVC architecture. Services are long-running components that do not strictly follow application lifecycles and are perfect for keeping things running even when the application is paused.

Finally, you learned about running processes asynchronously to avoid ANR errors and to speed up your application. You learned methods to pass data to the UI thread in a thread-safe manner, and you learned when you should use `AsyncTask`.

9

Drawing and Animation

Creating rich experiences in Android applications cannot be done with amazing code alone. There must be visual allure—something that draws users in and gives their minds something to play with for those moments between view changes, swipes, and loading events.

This can be done with shapes, drawables, bitmaps, 3D graphics, and animation. This chapter explains the classes, frameworks, and best practices to add visuals to your application.

Graphics

Whether you are displaying a bitmap or using OpenGL ES to create textures and shapes, there are multiple ways to display visuals with Android. In this section, you learn about bitmaps, drawables, and rendering with OpenGL ES.

Bitmaps

Bitmaps are collections of pixel information that contain data that can be used to construct an image. Bitmaps are commonly used as icons and image assets in applications.

The supported file types when working with Android include PNG, JPEG, and GIF. If at all possible, you should avoid GIF files and use PNG files because the format will give you the best features of GIF along with a rich color palette and alpha channels.

To display an image in your application, you may want to start with an `ImageView`. An `ImageView` is a widget that is used specifically for displaying image content.

> **Warning**
>
> You may want to use large bitmaps to increase the detail and presentation of image assets used in your application. This may seem like a great idea, but you need to remember that mobile devices are limited on the amount of memory available. An image snapped with a device camera may come out to 5248×3936 (20 megapixels). To put this image into memory with a bitmap configuration of ARGB_8888 will take almost 79MB of system memory. This will immediately take up all available system memory and your application will crash, displaying an OutOfMemoryError.

To avoid potential application crashes due to a lack of memory, you can scale your images before you load them. This can be done with an ImageView by setting the scaling type.

Each scaling type will do something different with your image, and you will need to do as much testing as possible to avoid aspect ratio and zooming issues.

The available scale types are as follows:

- **CENTER (android:scaleType="center")**: Even though this is a scale type, the image will be centered with no scaling applied.

- **CENTER_CROP (android:scaleType="centerCrop")**: This will scale while matching the aspect ratio of the image to the maximum size of the parent container, but will cut off any part of the image that does not fit.

- **CENTER_INSIDE (android:scaleType="centerInside")**: This will scale while matching the aspect ratio of the image to the maximum size of the parent container while showing all of the image.

- **FIT_CENTER (android:scaleType="fitCenter")**: Uses a matrix to resize the image to fit while maintaining the aspect ratio and places the image in the center of the container.

- **FIT_END (android:scaleType="fitEnd")**: Uses a matrix to resize the image to fit while maintaining aspect ratio and aligning the image to the bottom-right corner of the container.

- **FIT_START (android:scaleType="fitStart")**: Uses a matrix to resize the image to fit while maintaining the aspect ratio and aligning the image to the top-left corner of the container.

- **FIT_XY (android:scaleType="fitXY")**: Uses a matrix to scale the width and height of the image independently to fit a container. Does not maintain the aspect ratio of the image.

- **MATRIX (android:scaleType="matrix")**: Uses a matrix to scale the image. Does not maintain the aspect ratio when scaling to fit the container.

The following shows an example of an `ImageView` added to a layout XML file:

```
<ImageView
    android:layout_width="wrap_content"
    android:layout_height="wrap_content"
    android:src="@drawable/skyline" />
```

Figure 9.1 shows how these settings change the way a picture is displayed.

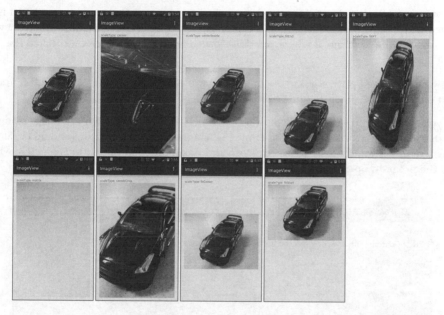

Figure 9.1   The `scaleType` settings used in the top row, moving from left to right: `none`, `center`, `centerInside`, `fitEnd`, and `fitX`. The settings used in the bottom row, moving from left to right: `matrix`, `centerCrop`, `fitCenter`, and `fitStart`.

NinePatch

A NinePatch is an image made from a bitmap that is capable of being stretched when displayed. The stretched areas of the image are made from repeating pixels and saved in PNG format with a .9.png extension. Figure 9.2 shows what a NinePatch looks like.

Figure 9.2   This NinePatch is used for the background and coloring of a button.

If you examine the NinePatch closely, you can see that there is 1 pixel of padding around the main image and that there are black lines around the top, left, right, and bottom. These lines define which areas of the NinePatch are repeatable that will be used as the stretchable area.

NinePatch files do not have to be perfectly square; you can use rectangles, circles, and even have some areas that contain an image or logo and will not be stretched. This allows you to create custom buttons and backgrounds that match the theme of your application that are the smallest size possible while working on as many different screens as possible.

To create your own NinePatch file, you can use the Draw 9-patch tool (draw9patch) that is included with the Android SDK. This tool can be launched from the sdk/tools directory via the command-line or terminal where you downloaded and uncompressed or installed the Android SDK.

When you open the utility, it asks you for a file to work with. If you do not have a file, you should either acquire or create one before proceeding.

Once you select the image file that you want to work with, you are shown the image along with information that will help you determine where the repeatable sections should be, along with where they should not be repeated. This window should look similar to Figure 9.3, which shows the program open with an image that contains a slight gradient.

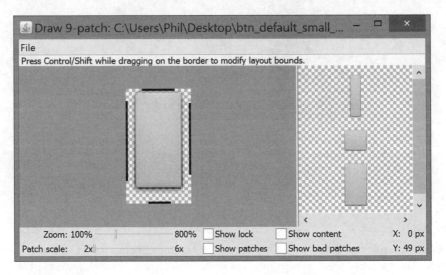

Figure 9.3   The Draw 9-patch tool allows you to edit, preview what your NinePatch will look like, and export .9.png files

After you have adjusted the image to your liking, you can then save the image out by using the File menu and selecting "Save 9-patch." This will bring up a prompt of where you would like to save your newly created NinePatch file.

You can now use your custom NinePatch in your application by placing it in the `/res/drawable/` folder of your project and referencing it in your layout XML file. The following demonstrates using the custom NinePatch (named `customninepatch.9.png`) as the background for a button:

```
<Button
  android:layout_height="wrap_content"
  android:layout_width="wrap_content"
  android:background="@drawable/customninepatch" />
```

Drawables

The term drawable is a generic description of resources that can be drawn. Android has support for many built-in drawable objects, as well as the ability to allow you to create your own.

When something visual is rendered on the screen, this counts as a drawable. This explains why graphical resources, such as PNG files, count as a drawable. It also gives reason to why image assets are stored in the `res/drawables` directory of your project.

Note

Images placed in the `res/drawable` directory may be automatically optimized and replaced by more memory-efficient versions. If you prefer to keep the exact file you put in, you should place the drawable resource in the `res/raw` folder.

Some drawables do not require a resource to be placed in the `res/drawable` directory. Instead, you may be interested in using primitive shapes.

Using a primitive shape will help with memory and also allow you to create visuals purely from code. The following is an example of drawing a square shape in a custom view:

```
// Create variable for ImageView
ImageView myDrawnImageView;

// populate the variable
myDrawnImageView = (ImageView) this.findViewById(R.id.myDrawnImageView);

// Need to get dimensions of the screen
Display display = getWindowManager().getDefaultDisplay();
Point size = new Point();
display.getSize(size);
int screen_width = size.x;
int screen_height = size.y;

// Create a bitmap
Bitmap bitmap = Bitmap.createBitmap((int) screen_width, (int) screen_height,
Bitmap.Config.ARGB_8888);
```

```
// Create a canvas and attach the bitmap
Canvas canvas = new Canvas(bitmap);
myDrawnImageView.setImageBitmap(bitmap);

// use Paint() and drawRect() to draw a rectangle
Paint p = new Paint();
p.setColor(Color.BLUE);
p.setStyle(Paint.Style.FILL_AND_STROKE);
p.setStrokeWidth(40);
float rectLeft = 80;
float rectTop = 80;
float rectRight = 200;
float rectBottom = 200;
canvas.drawRect(rectLeft, rectTop, rectRight, rectBottom, p);
```

Note that in the previous snippet, both a stroke and fill are set. You do not have to set a stroke if it will be the same color as the fill, but you will have to adjust the size of your drawable to make up for the lost space that the stroke covered. Figure 9.4 shows the square that was created.

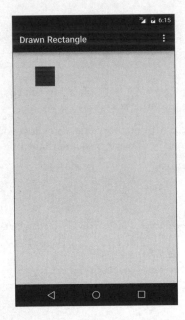

Figure 9.4   A blue square has been drawn using a bitmap, a canvas, and the `drawRect()` method.

Shapes can also be defined in XML by using the `<shape>` element. This is done by creating an XML file and placing it in the `res/drawable` directory.

In the same manner as working with bitmaps, the asset will be identified by the name of the XML file. If the file was named `my_circle.xml`, it would be referenced by `my_circle`.

The following is an example of a custom shape defined in XML:

```xml
<?xml version="1.0" encoding="utf-8"?>
<shape xmlns:android="http://schemas.android.com/apk/res/android"
    android:shape="oval">
    <solid android:color="#FF00FF00"/>
</shape>
```

This shape will draw either a green oval or a circle. By defining the basic elements of the shape, a `View` can reference this shape as the background and apply various constraints to show it as either a circle or an oval.

Figure 9.5 shows what the shape looks like when rendered as a background for a view with a height and width of `50dp`.

Figure 9.5   With a rendering container that shares the same width and height, a small green circle is rendered on the screen, even though the shape is defined as an oval.

You can also use system drawables in your projects. These resources can, however, be a double-edged sword. They enable you to match the system theme, allowing a user to quickly understand what the icon or image means, but if used improperly, they confuse and destroy the trust a user may have for your application.

Another issue you may run into is that because they are part of the system, they may change from version to version. This means that you have no control over the past, present, or future visual styles.

Should you find that you still want to use these resources, visit http://androiddrawables.com/. Here, you will find a list of available resources and what they look like in various versions of Android.

OpenGL ES

OpenGL for Embedded Systems (OpenGL ES) has been supported by Android from version 1.0 of the Android system. This, however, does not mean that every version of OpenGL ES is compatible with every version of Android.

As a quick reference, the following lists the version of OpenGL that can be used with various Android versions:

- OpenGL ES 1.0–1.1 supports Android 1.0+.

- OpenGL ES 2.0 supports Android 2.2+.

- OpenGL ES 3.0 supports Android 4.3+, provided the manufacturer has built in support for the graphics pipeline.

- OpenGL ES 3.1 supports Android 5.0+.

> **Tip**
>
> Due to breaking changes with OpenGL ES 1.4 and 2.0, you cannot mix and match the API calls and usage. OpenGL ES 3.X is backward compatible with 2.0. This allows you to code for 3.0 and set your feature level to 2.0 and then use a runtime check to see if the device will support 3.0, allowing the use of the advanced 3.X features.

To use OpenGL ES in your application without the APK, you first need to modify your application manifest to add OpenGL ES as a feature. Depending on the version you plan on using, this can be done as follows:

```
<!-- to use version OpenGL ES 2.0 - Android 2.2+ -->
<uses-feature android:glEsVersion="0x00020000" android:required="true" />

<!-- to use version OpenGL ES 3.0 - Android 4.3+ -->
<uses-feature android:glEsVersion="0x00030000" android:required="true" />

<!-- to use version OpenGL ES 3.1 - Android 5.0+ -->
<uses-feature android:glEsVersion="0x00030001" android:required="true" />
```

While you are modifying your application manifest, if you plan on using texture compression, you need to declare it in the manifest as well. Remember that not all texture compression types are compatible with all Android devices. By placing the type of compression used in the manifest, you allow the Play store to filter out your application from devices that cannot support the compression type.

Now that you have your application manifest properly set up, you are ready to start using OpenGL ES in your application. To do this you will want to work with the GLSurfaceView and GLSurfaceView.Renderer.

In your Activity, you will want to start by creating the GLSurfaceView object and then setting it as the primary view in the onCreate() callback method. After setting the GLSurfaceView as the main view, you will also need to implement callback methods for the GLSurfaceView. The following shows a minimal framework that could be used to set up a GLSurfaceView in an application:

```
// Create GLSurfaceView object
private GLSurfaceView myGLSView;

@Override
public void onCreate(Bundle savedInstanceState) {
  super.onCreate(savedInstanceState);

  // Set myGLSView to the MyGLSurfaceView class
  myGLSView = new MyGLSurfaceView(this);
  // Set the myGLSView as the main view for the activity
  setContentView(mGLSurfaceView);
}

@Override
protected void onResume()
{
  super.onResume();
  // set the onResume callback of the GLSurfaceView
  myGLSView.onResume();
}

@Override
protected void onPause()
{
  super.onPause();
  // set the onPause callback of the GLSurfaceView
  myGLSView.onPause();
}
```

In the previous example, the myGLSView object is set to an inner class. This allows you to set the version of OpenGL ES that you want to use as well as to set up the renderer. The following shows another minimal setup of that class:

```
class MyGLSurfaceView extends GLSurfaceView {

  private final MyGLRenderer myRenderer;

  public MyGLSurfaceView(Context context){
    super(context);

    // Set context to OpenGL ES 2.0
    setEGLContextClientVersion(2);

    // Set the renderer
    myRenderer = new MyGLRenderer();

    // Set the Renderer for drawing on the GLSurfaceView
    setRenderer(myRenderer);
  }

}
```

The renderer also points to another class to handle the initial setup and implementation of the
onDrawFrame() and onSurfaceChanged() methods. This is shown as follows:

```
public class MyGLRenderer implements GLSurfaceView.Renderer {

  public void onSurfaceCreated(GL10 unused, EGLConfig config) {
    // Set the background frame color
    GLES20.glClearColor(0.0f, 0.0f, 0.0f, 1.0f);
  }

  public void onDrawFrame(GL10 unused) {
    // Redraw background color
    GLES20.glClear(GLES20.GL_COLOR_BUFFER_BIT);
  }

  public void onSurfaceChanged(GL10 unused, int width, int height) {
    GLES20.glViewport(0, 0, width, height);
  }
}
```

To then begin drawing shapes, you need to create a class for your shape, create the coordinates
of your shape, pass the coordinates by using a ByteBuffer, and then draw it out. An example
of creating a triangle follows:

```
public void myTriangle() {

  private FloatBuffer vertexBuffer;

    // Set number of coordinates
    static final int COORDS_PER_VERTEX = 3;
```

```
static float triangleCoords[] = {
  10.0f, 200f, 0.0f,
  10.0f, 100f, 0.0f,
  100f, 100f, 0.0f
};

// Set color with red, green, blue and alpha (opacity) values
float color[] = { 0.5f, 1.0f, 0.5f, 1.0f };

public Triangle() {
    // Set ByteBuffer for shape coordinates
    ByteBuffer bb = ByteBuffer.allocateDirect(triangleCoords.length * 4);
    // Set native byte order per device setting
    bb.order(ByteOrder.nativeOrder());

    // Set a floating point buffer from the ByteBuffer
    vertexBuffer = bb.asFloatBuffer();
    // add the coordinates to the vertexBuffer
    vertexBuffer.put(triangleCoords);
    // set the buffer to read the first coordinate
    vertexBuffer.position(0);
}
}
```

Beyond drawing shapes, you will want to study the official docs for working with OpenGL ES at https://www.khronos.org/opengles/. This will give you the specifications for the available versions of OpenGL ES as well as online reference manuals and cards.

For those looking for a "bare-metal" approach to using OpenGL ES, you can use the Native Development Kit (NDK), which you may also want to use for calculation-intensive operations, including writing RenderScript.

Animation

If you are not using a 2D- or 3D-rendering engine for your application, you can still add some eye candy and visual splendor to it by using view and property animations.

View Animation

A view animation is used when you have two views and would like to animate between them. Those with animation experience know that when a transition is built between one view and another, there are many in-between (or tween) frames that must be drawn to smoothly show the change between one view and another.

Note that even if you are not building a transition, the tween frames are still needed to animate a single view with changes such as scale, rotation, and translation. The view animation does all the math, calculation, and drawing for you to handle smoothly animating changes to views.

To create a view animation, either you can use an XML file that contains the details of the animation and is stored in the /res/anim directory of your project or you can use the AnimationSet and Animator classes to define an animation with Java.

To define an animation in XML, you need to define a <set> element that will contain sub-elements to start defining an animation.

There are four basic animation effects you can use:

- **alpha**: Controls the opacity or visibility
- **rotate**: Controls the degree of rotation
- **scale**: Controls size
- **translate**: Controls the placement in both the X and Y planes

Each of these animation basics can be used in the animation XML. The following demonstrates a sample animation XML:

```
<scale
  android:interpolator="@android:anim/accelerate_decelerate_interpolator"
  android:fromXScale="1.0"
  android:toXScale="1.5"
  android:fromYScale="1.0"
  android:toYScale="0.5"
  android:pivotX="50%"
  android:pivotY="50%"
  android:fillAfter="false"
  android:duration="800" />
```

The <scale> element designates that this animation will scale what it is used with. The properties listed are how the scale is controlled. It is worth noting that the easing of the effect is controlled by an interpolator. This is set with android:interpolator with many different values that can be used. A list of subclasses that can be used can be found at http://developer.android.com/reference/android/view/animation/BaseInterpolator.html.

If you want to perform more than one animation, you may use a <set> element and even nest more <set> elements to run animations in sequence or at the same time.

For a complete list of the properties that can be used with view animation, visit http://developer.android.com/guide/topics/resources/animation-resource.html.

Property Animation

View animation is great for working with specific animations and views, but not everything that you may want to animate is a view or is one of the four basic animations.

Property animation allows you to animate properties of any object, including views. This opens up new options because you may not have thought about animating properties such as text and background color.

Similar to using a view animation, you can use XML to define a property animation. Property animation XML files can contain <set> elements as well as <objectAnimator> and <valueAnimator> elements to control the animations. Unlike a view animation XML, property animation XML files should be placed in the res/animator directory of your project.

The following shows an example of a property animation XML file:

```
<set android:ordering="sequentially">
  <set>
    <objectAnimator
      android:propertyName="x"
      android:duration="600"
      android:valueTo="500"
      android:valueType="intType"/>
    <objectAnimator
      android:propertyName="y"
      android:duration="600"
      android:valueTo="350"
      android:valueType="intType"/>
  </set>
  <objectAnimator
    android:propertyName="alpha"
    android:duration="800"
    android:valueTo="1f"/>
</set>
```

In similarity to view animation XML files, the <set> element can be used to control when and if animations will run together or separately. In this example, there is a containing <set> element with a property of android:ordering="sequentially" that informs the system to start at the top and run through any child <set> elements before running the next animation.

To call the animation that was defined in XML, you need to inflate the XML into an AnimatorSet object as well as use the setTarget() method to attach the animation to a target. This can be done as follows:

```
AnimatorSet aniSet = (AnimatorSet) AnimatorInflater.loadAnimator(myContext,
    R.anim.property_animator);
aniSet.setTarget(myObject);
aniSet.start();
```

Note that R.anim.property_animator is used to load the XML file even though it is stored in the res/animator directory. This is normal behavior and has more to do with the layout editor for the legacy Eclipse ADT plugin, which only checks the res/animator folder for resources.

Due to the extra control and complexity of using a property animation, more set up is required to create animations than using a view animation. Three subclasses extend the `Animator` class that you will be using to adjust and create property animations:

- **ValueAnimator**: This subclass handles the calculation for values used in the animation.

- **ObjectAnimator**: This is actually a subclass of `ValueAnimator` that is used to target an object with an animation value.

- **AnimatorSet**: This is used to create sets of animations that relate to each other.

ValueAnimator

The `ValueAnimator` allows you to change the values of an object. This is done by setting a beginning and ending value, a duration (in milliseconds), and then starting the animation.

Note that because `ValueAnimator` cannot change an object or property directly, you must implement `ValueAnimator.AnimatorUpdateListener`.

The following demonstrates setting up a `ValueAnimator`:

```
// set up a beginning and ending value
ValueAnimator animation = ValueAnimator.ofInt(1,20);

// set duration of animation to 1.5 seconds
animation.setDuration(1500);

// begin animation
animation.start();
```

Instead of calling `animation.start()`, you may instead want to perform an animated value change based on the current event of an animation.

To do this, use one of the animation event listeners:

- **onAnimationStart()**: Runs on animation start.

- **onAnimationRepeat()**: Runs when an animation is repeated.

- **onAnimationCancel()**: Runs when an animation is stopped or cancelled.

- **onAnimationEnd()**: Runs at the end of an animation regardless of how it was ended. This is also called when `onAnimationCancel()` is called.

ObjectAnimator

Whereas the `ValueAnimator` could not be directly called on an object, the `ObjectAnimator` allows you to target an object property. The following shows how to use an `ObjectAnimator`:

```
// Target myObject for an alpha animation
ObjectAnimator oAnimation = ObjectAnimator.ofFloat(myObject, "alpha", 0f);

// Set the duration to 1.5 seconds
oAnimation.setDuration(1500);

// Start the animation
oAnimation.start();
```

As commented, the object myObject has been targeted to have the alpha property adjusted to 0 (not visible) over a duration of 1.5 seconds when the animation starts.

AnimatorSet

Animations can be combined to have multiple properties changed at the same time, start running at the same time, or run in a specific sequence by using an AnimatorSet.

The following shows several animations created with ObjectAnimator that will be added to a set and executed in order:

```
// Change alpha and set to 1.5 second duration
ObjectAnimator fadeOut = ObjectAnimator.ofFloat(myObj, "alpha", 0f);
fadeOut.setDuration(1500);

// Change the position of the object with 1.5 second duration
ObjectAnimator transX = ObjectAnimator.ofFloat(myObj, "translationX", -300f,
0f);
transX.setDuration(1500);

// Change alpha from 0 to 1 with a 1.5 second duration
ObjectAnimator fadeIn = ObjectAnimator.ofFloat(myObj, "alpha", 0f, 1f);
fadeIn.setDuration(1500);

// create AnimatorSet
AnimatorSet animatorSet = new AnimatorSet();

// fadeOut first, then run fadeIn and transX
animatorSet.play(fadeIn).with(transX).after(fadeOut);

// start the animation sequence
animatorSet.start();
```

By using the play(), with(), and after() methods, you can control when animations in an AnimatorSet will run. The animation used in the after() method will run first and the other methods will run when it completes.

Drawable Animation

The last type of animation you may wish to use is a drawable animation. The best way to think of this is like creating a flipbook, or even an animated GIF.

A drawable animation is composed of a list of drawables that will be played frame by frame. These resources are grouped in an `<animation-list>` element in an XML file that is stored in the `/res/drawable` directory of your project. The following shows an example of an XML file:

```xml
<animation-list xmlns:android="http://schemas.android.com/apk/res/android"
  android:oneshot="false">
  <item android:drawable="@drawable/andy_run1" android:duration="200" />
  <item android:drawable="@drawable/andy_run2" android:duration="200" />
  <item android:drawable="@drawable/andy_run3" android:duration="200" />
  <item android:drawable="@drawable/andy_run4" android:duration="200" />
  <item android:drawable="@drawable/andy_run5" android:duration="200" />
</animation-list>
```

Note the use of `android:oneshot="false"`. This means that the animation will continually run from start to end. Should you decide that you would only like to run the animation one time, you can change the value from `false` to `true`.

The XML file is then referenced from your code during the `onCreate()` method. You can then invoke the animation in a variety of ways, including using an `onTouchEvent`:

```java
// set up the animation for use
ImageView andyImage = (ImageView) findViewById(R.id.andy_image);
andyImage.setBackgroundResource(R.drawable.andy_running);
andyAnimation = (AnimationDrawable) andyImage.getBackground();

// ...

public boolean onTouchEvent(MotionEvent event) {
  if (event.getAction() == MotionEvent.ACTION_DOWN) {
    andyAnimation.start();
    return true;
  }
  return super.onTouchEvent(event);
}
```

> **Tip**
>
> Some animations may need to use many bitmaps in order to appear smooth and buttery. This means that you need to take care in choosing the animation you would like to perform and strike a balance between file size and how smooth the animation appears. This is especially important when working with animations on wearable devices.

Transition Framework

The transition framework was added in Android 4.4 and allows developers to create scenes that can then be transitioned. This is useful when you have two different view hierarchies that you want to change between.

This will be accomplished by using the starting and ending layouts as scenes and then applying a transition to them that is controlled with a `TransitionManager`.

> **Warning**
>
> Views that contain `AdapterView` or `ListView` are not compatible with the transition framework. Attempting to use one anyway may result in an unresponsive UI.

Because there are going to be two scenes, I define these in XML. First, the contents of `/res/layout/scene_a.xml`:

```xml
<?xml version="1.0" encoding="utf-8"?>
<RelativeLayout xmlns:android="http://schemas.android.com/apk/res/android"
  android:id="@+id/scene_container"
  android:layout_width="match_parent"
  android:layout_height="match_parent" >

  <TextView
    android:layout_width="wrap_content"
    android:layout_height="wrap_content"
    android:text="TextView 1"
    android:id="@+id/textView"
    android:layout_alignParentTop="true"
    android:layout_alignParentStart="true" />

  <TextView
    android:layout_width="wrap_content"
    android:layout_height="wrap_content"
    android:text="TextView 2"
    android:id="@+id/textView2"
    android:layout_alignParentTop="true"
    android:layout_alignParentEnd="true" />

  <Button
    android:layout_width="wrap_content"
    android:layout_height="wrap_content"
    android:text="Go!"
    android:id="@+id/button"
    android:layout_centerVertical="true"
    android:layout_centerHorizontal="true" />

</RelativeLayout>
```

The contents of /res/layout/scene_b.xml:

```xml
<?xml version="1.0" encoding="utf-8"?>
<RelativeLayout xmlns:android="http://schemas.android.com/apk/res/android"
  android:id="@+id/scene_container"
  android:layout_width="match_parent"
  android:layout_height="match_parent" >

  <TextView
    android:layout_width="wrap_content"
    android:layout_height="wrap_content"
    android:text="TextView 2"
    android:id="@+id/textView2"
    android:layout_alignParentTop="true"
    android:layout_alignParentStart="true" />

  <TextView
    android:layout_width="wrap_content"
    android:layout_height="wrap_content"
    android:text="TextView 1"
    android:id="@+id/textView"
    android:layout_alignParentTop="true"
    android:layout_alignParentEnd="true" />

</RelativeLayout>
```

Rather than using three different layout XML files, I instead give the RelativeLayout an ID of scene_container to signify that this is the containing element that will contain the transitioned scenes. It is important that the ID is set because it is used to initially set the scene.

The following demonstrates the code needed to set the scenes and transition to them:

```java
Scene mySceneA;
Scene mySceneB;

@Override
protected void onCreate(Bundle savedInstanceState) {
  super.onCreate(savedInstanceState);
  setContentView(R.layout.scene_a);

  RelativeLayout mySceneRoot = (RelativeLayout)findViewById(R.id.scene_container);
  mySceneA = Scene.getSceneForLayout(mySceneRoot, R.layout.scene_a, this);
  mySceneB = Scene.getSceneForLayout(mySceneRoot, R.layout.scene_b, this);

  Button button = (Button)findViewById(R.id.button);
  button.setOnClickListener(new View.OnClickListener() {
    @Override
    public void onClick(View v) {
```

```
        TransitionManager.go(mySceneB);
    }
  });
}
```

When this code is run, the default transition will execute. This may vary per the version of Android used, but generally this equates to a fade-out, then fade-in transition.

If you want to specify a transition yourself, you can either create a transition in XML or it can be invoked by using a particular subclass such as Fade().

By using a transitionSet in a transition XML file, you can apply multiple transitions. The following is an example of a transition XML file that resides at res/transitions/ transition_fader.xml in your project:

```
<transitionSet xmlns:android="http://schemas.android.com/apk/res/android"
    android:transitionOrdering="sequential">
  <fade android:fadingMode="fade_out" />
  <changeBounds />
  <fade android:fadingMode="fade_in" />
</transitionSet>
```

This transition will run sequentially (thanks to the android:transitionOrdering= "sequential" setting) and fade elements out, apply property changes, and then fade the elements back in.

If you decide to use an XML file for your transition, you will need to inflate it into your code. This can be done as follows:

```
Transition myTransitionFader = TransitionInflater.from(this)
    .inflateTransition(R.transition.transition_fader)
```

Now that the scenes and transition have been defined, you can kick the transition off by running the following:

```
TransitionManager.go(mySceneB, myTransitionFader);
```

Summary

In this chapter, you learned about the tools, utilities, and frameworks that can be leveraged to add visuals to your application that will deliver the interface magic that unites the data and presentation of your application.

Starting out with bitmaps, you learned that you can use PNG, JPEG, and GIF images in your application. You also learned how these can be displayed in an ImageView.

You learned about NinePatches and how they can be small image resource files that can be used for backgrounds and contain repeatable sections that will stretch. Using the `draw9patch` tool in the `sdk/tools` directory brings up an application that can be used to import and adjust NinePatches.

You also learned about drawables, including using ones that come bundled in each version of Android. You learned that images that are placed into the `res/drawables` folder may be optimized and come out at a different quality level. You also learned that by using drawables and a canvas, you can create 2D objects with primitive shapes.

You then learned a little about using OpenGL ES and the versions that are compatible with each version of Android. You were given an example of creating a `GLSurfaceView` to render the visuals on and how to set some properties.

Finally, you were shown how animations work, including how to animate views, properties, and drawables. You were also shown how the transition framework could be used to do the calculations and display the changing from one scene to another.

10

Networking

Networking in Android has been an area that has steadily improved with each release of Android. Whereas network connections were once created and executed no matter what, through the use of the Volley library, they can now be queued to send, process, and even be canceled. In this chapter, you will learn about connecting to the Internet through an HTTP client, how to work with XML, and why using `AsyncTask` for network communication is necessary for your application, and how you can start using Volley.

Accessing the Internet

Unless your application is completely standalone, you will probably need to connect to the Internet. Saving information, accessing data feeds, or even getting updated files will require you to access the Internet.

To connect to the Internet, your application manifest will require the following permissions:

```
<uses-permission android:name="android.permission.INTERNET" />
<uses-permission android:name="android.permission.ACCESS_NETWORK_STATE" />
```

The `INTERNET` permission is used to allow your application to make outbound requests to the Internet. The `ACCESS_NETWORK_STATE` permission is used to allow access to either the radio or the Wi-Fi adapter on your device.

It is also important to remember that network activity must occur in a separate thread than the main or UI thread. Any attempt to perform network operations on the main thread causes a runtime exception or an Application Not Responding error.

Network Detection

An important aspect of using the networking features of Android is making sure that you actually have a connection before attempting to use it. Being able to detect when you have a connection is also useful for queuing data until a connection becomes available.

Checking for a connection involves getting a `ConnectivityManager` and then using the `getActiveNetworkInfo()` method and subsequently the `isConnected()` method on the active network. Listing 10.1 shows sample code from an Activity that demonstrates how this is done.

Listing 10.1   **Checking Network Status**

```
public void onClick(View view) {

  ConnectivityManager connMgr = (ConnectivityManager)
    getSystemService(Context.CONNECTIVITY_SERVICE);
  NetworkInfo networkInfo = connMgr.getActiveNetworkInfo();
  if(networkInfo != null && networkInfo.isConnected()) {
    Toast connectedToast = Toast.makeText(getApplicationContext(),
      "Network connected!", Toast.LENGTH_SHORT);
    connectedToast.show();
  } else {
    Toast disconnectedToast = Toast.makeText(getApplicationContext(),
      "No network connection!", Toast.LENGTH_SHORT);
    disconnectedToast.show();
  }

}
```

In the previous sample, an `onClick()` method is used to trigger a check for the connection state. The `connMgr` is created and used in conjunction with `networkInfo` to retrieve the current status of the network. If `networkInfo` is not empty and the network is connected, a toast will appear onscreen informing the user that the network is connected. Consequently, if `networkInfo` is empty or does not return `true` for `isConnected()`, then a toast will appear on the device with a message of "No network connection."

Note that either a Wi-Fi or mobile data connection will trigger `isConnected()` to return `true`. For testing purposes, you should be able to use airplane mode to disable any network connections, allowing you to test your application without a network connection. If you would like to specifically check for either Wi-Fi or mobile data, you will need to specify the type when getting `networkInfo`.

To check for Wi-Fi, use the following snippet:

```
NetworkInfo networkInfo = connMgr.getNetworkInfo(ConnectivityManager.TYPE_WIFI);
```

Checking for a mobile data connection would change the snippet to be as follows:

```
NetworkInfo networkInfo = connMgr.getNetworkInfo(ConnectivityManager.TYPE_MOBILE);
```

Figure 10.1 shows an application running this code and the toast messages that appear when a button is pressed.

Figure 10.1   The network is connected for the phone on the left. The phone on the right, however, does not have a network connection.

Using an HTTP Client

Developers who have been with Android since the beginning are probably familiar with using both the HttpURLConnection and Apache HttpConnection HTTP clients. As it stands now, Google recommends the use of the HttpURLConnection client for any new applications that are targeted at Gingerbread (Android 2.3, API level 10) and up.

When using an HTTP client, you will start by creating the client, preparing the request, handling the return, and making sure to close the connection. Closing the request is important so that device resources can be released and used again.

Listing 10.2 demonstrates the code needed to create and release an HTTP connection using HttpURLConnection.

Listing 10.2   **Creating and Closing an HTTP Connection**

```
URL url = new URL("http://www.google.com/");
HttpURLConnection urlConnection = (HttpURLConnection) url.openConnection();
try {
  // save the response to an InputStream
  InputStream in = new BufferedInputStream(urlConnection.getInputStream());
  // parse the response
  parseStream(in);
} finally {
  // release the connection
  urlConnection.disconnect();
}
```

Note that this example shows the basic method for creating and closing a connection but will require you to create your own method for parsing the response.

Working with a secure or HTTPS connection is the same. When this is the case, an `HttpsURLConnection` will be returned.

With each release of Android, new trusted Certificate Authorities are added; this means that if you are attempting to connect to a site that has a certificate signed by a trusted CA, your connection will be fine. Should you run into a handshake error, you will need to add the connection to your application as a trusted resource. See https://developer.android.com/training/articles/security-ssl.html for more information.

When using an HTTP client, information not only can be read from a connection, but information can also be posted through the connection. The process of posting information is similar to getting information. A connection is created, the connection is set to send data, data is sent, and then the connection is closed. Listing 10.3 demonstrates how this is achieved.

Listing 10.3   **Creating a Connection that Will Post Data**

```
// create the connection
HttpURLConnection urlConnection = (HttpURLConnection) url.openConnection();
try {
  // I am going to push, so setDoOutput should be true
  urlConnection.setDoOutput(true);
  // I do not know the exact size of the response body
  urlConnection.setChunkedStreamingMode(0);

  // create the response body
  OutputStream out = new BufferedOutputStream(urlConnection.getOutputStream());
  // use a function to send information through the connection
  writeStream(out);

  // save the response to an InputStream
  InputStream in = new BufferedInputStream(urlConnection.getInputStream());
  // parse the response
  parseStream(in);
} finally {
  // close the connection
  urlConnection.disconnect();
}
```

Now that you have seen how to get and send data with an HTTP client, it is time to learn about using XML.

Parsing XML

XML remains a popular choice for data delivery. Whether the data is for creating pins on a map or a data feed for updated content on a website, there is a fairly good chance that you will end up dealing with XML.

To get started parsing XML, you need to do the following:

1. Decide what elements that you will be using.

2. Instantiate your parser.

1. Read the XML feed.

4. Parse the results.

5. Consume the XML.

Deciding what elements to use should be part of your application architecture. You should have a good idea of what the XML structure is, and which elements you are interested in dealing with. If you have a feed with elements that you are not interested in using, you can skip these elements during your parsing procedure.

Google currently recommends using `XmlPullParser` when working with XML. The following snippets show the instantiation of the parser:

```
XmlPullParser parser = Xml.newPullParser();
```

Note that you can decide to ignore parsing namespaces by setting FEATURE_PROCESS_ NAMESPACE to `false`. The following shows how this is done through the use of the `setFeature()` method:

```
parser.setFeature(XmlPullParser.FEATURE_PROCESS_NAMESPACES, false);
```

As you parse the XML data, you will want to create functions to read each element that you need. This is helpful because each tag may contain different types of data, and it allows you to handle the data in the manner of your choosing. Listing 10.4 demonstrates using two functions to find the element you want and then read the text value from the element.

Listing 10.4   **Getting a Text Value from an XML Element**

```
private String readFirstName(XmlPullParser parser) throws IOException,
XmlPullParserException {
  parser.require(XmlPullParser.START_TAG, ns, "firstname");
  String firstName = readText(parser);
  parser.require(XmlPullParser.END_TAG, ns, "firstname");
  return firstName;
}
```

```
private String readText(XmlPullParser parser) throws IOException,
XmlPullParserException {
  String textValue = "";
  if (parser.next() == XmlPullParser.TEXT) {
    textValue = parser.getText();
    parser.nextTag();
  }
  return textValue;
}
```

Looking at Listing 10.4, you can see the `require()` method is initially used to define the start tag that is searched for in the parsed XML file; in this case, it will look for `<firstname>`. When that tag is found, a string named `firstName` is set to the returned value of the `readText()` function.

To retrieve the text from inside of the `<firstname>` element, the `readText()` function creates an empty string and then parses the element for text. If text is found, the string will be populated; otherwise, the function will return the empty string.

If you wanted to parse the value of a specific property, this can be done by using the `getAttributeValue(String namespace, String name)` method of `XmlPullParser`, like so:

```
String altPropertyValue = parser.getAttributeValue(null, "alt");
```

When you need to parse tags that are nested, use a method that allows you to skip tags. This is important to make sure that you get the data you want. Listing 10.5 shows a skip function that you may find useful.

Listing 10.5 A Skip Function for Parsing Nested XML Elements

```
private void skip(XmlPullParser parser) throws XmlPullParserException,
IOException {
  // if the current event does not match the start tag, throw exception
  if (parser.getEventType() != XmlPullParser.START_TAG) {
    throw new IllegalStateException();
  }
  // create a counter to keep track of depth
  int depth = 1;
  // use while loop to find the end of the element
  while (depth != 0) {
    // use switch to move through nested elements
    switch (parser.next()) {
      case XmlPullParser.END_TAG:
      depth--;
      break;
      case XmlPullParser.START_TAG:
      depth++;
```

```
        break;
      }
    }
}
```

Because the counter, or depth, is set to 1, the switch will be triggered based on the type of event or element encountered. The while loop is used to keep the processing going until the value of depth is set to 0, which is the closing element.

Consuming XML will vary based on your application and needs; however, this will generally consist of the previous steps combined with an AsyncTask to make the data request, save the output to a stream, and then process the stream to pull the values you need.

Using an AsyncTask is paramount to application success and to avoid working on the main UI thread. In the next section, you learn why this is needed and how to create and work with AsyncTask.

Handling Network Operations Asynchronously

Users expect applications to run on their devices as fast as possible. This includes any lag, jank, or stuttering that your application may perform on the user interface (UI) level. It should not come as a surprise that, by default, the Android system prohibits certain activities and processing from happening on the main UI thread. This is solved, however, by using AsyncTask for various logic handling.

In the case of network handling, you should be using AsyncTask to offload your communication and processing logic. Remember that you should also inform the user that a network event has started; otherwise, you may end up with a user creating multiple connections or operations while waiting for the first request to return.

For your application, you may find it useful to determine if the URL you are requesting is available or if it is currently experiencing an error. By using the getResponseCode() method, you can determine the status of the server you are connecting to. Listing 10.6 demonstrates this in action.

Listing 10.6   **Using `getResponseCode()` to Determine Server Status**

```
private class CheckUrlTask extends AsyncTask<String, Void, String> {
@Override
  protected String doInBackground(String... urls) {
    try {
      return urlResponse(urls[0]);
    } catch (IOException e) {
      return "Unable to retrieve web page. URL may be invalid.";
    }
  }
```

```
    // onPostExecute displays the results of the AsyncTask.
    @Override
    protected void onPostExecute(String result) {
      Toast responseToast = Toast.makeText(getApplicationContext(),
        "URL responded with "+result, Toast.LENGTH_SHORT);
      responseToast.show();
    }
  }

  private String urlResponse(String checkUrl) throws IOException {
    InputStream is = null;

    try {
      URL url = new URL(checkUrl);
      HttpURLConnection conn = (HttpURLConnection) url.openConnection();
      conn.setReadTimeout(10000 /* milliseconds */);
      conn.setConnectTimeout(15000 /* milliseconds */);
      conn.setRequestMethod("GET");
      conn.setDoInput(true);
      // Attempt connection
      conn.connect();
      int response = conn.getResponseCode();

      Log.d(DEBUG_TAG, "The response is: " + response);
      is = conn.getInputStream();

      return String.valueOf(response);

      // Close the InputStream
    } finally {
      if (is != null) {
        is.close();
      }
    }
  }
```

The CheckUrlTask class extends AsyncTask, allowing it to run separately from the UI thread. This helps keep applications responsive and protects the application from crashing in case of any network lag or delay. In fact, without specifically ordering your application to run network tasks on the UI thread, you will receive a NetworkOnMainThread error when your application runs. When CheckUrlTask() runs, it attempts to load the URL passed to it, and by using onPostExecute(), it displays a toast with the results returned from the urlResponse() method.

The urlResponse() method creates an InputStream that is used to contain the value of an HTTP request made to a remote server.

Another way to deal with network connections, including queuing and canceling, is to use Volley.

Volley

Volley is an HTTP library that is useful to developers who want to build scheduling and management into their network connections. Volley is particularly useful for fetching items to update widgets, return search results, or even as a network resource cache. The Volley library is available for download from the Android Open Source Project at https://android.googlesource. com/platform/frameworks/volley. To get started using Volley, you will need to find a compiled `volley.jar` file, clone the repository, and import the clone as a library project, or you will need to run the build scripts to make your own `volley.jar` file.

To clone the repository with Git, run the following command:

```
git clone https://android.googlesource.com/platform/frameworks/volley
```

After you have cloned the repository, open a terminal window and move into the folder and run the following build script (note that you must have Apache Ant installed in order for the build to work):

```
android update project -p .
ant jar
```

If running `ant` in your terminal does not work, make sure you have added the bin folder of Ant to your system path or environment variables.

When the build script is complete, you should have a `volley.jar` file that you can use in your Android project. Depending on the IDE you are using, this may be as simple as copying the file into your libs folder, or you may have to copy it as well as right-click the .jar file and choose Add as Library, and then perform a clean/build of your application.

Once the jar or library project has been added to your application, make sure you have added the `android.permission.INTERNET` to your application manifest.

Because Volley was created to make things easier for developers, several convenience methods have been built to help you perform otherwise manual tasks. To demonstrate this, instead of having to manually create a queue to handle network requests, you can use the following:

```
RequestQueue queue = Volley.newRequestQueue(this);
```

This creates a queue that can then be used to process requests that have been added. To add a request, you need to create one and then use the `.add()` method on your queue object. The following demonstrates how this is done:

```
String url = "http://developer.android.com/";
StringRequest stringRequest = new StringRequest(Request.Method.GET, url,
    new Response.Listener() {
      @Override
```

```
        public void onResponse(String response) {
            // the server responded, handle response here
        }
    }, new Response.ErrorListener() {
      @Override
      public void onErrorResponse(VolleyError error) {
          // add error message here
      }
    });
queue.add(stringRequest);
```

Multiple requests can be built and will then be handled by worker threads in the background.
Results are delivered to the main UI thread, allowing you to update controls and widgets.
Requests that require data may be updated by data that is in the cache, thus speeding up
processes and saving on network trips.

Another benefit of using Volley is that you can stop requests in the queue should you no
longer need them. To stop requests, tag them to the Activity that calls them. This can be done
as follows:

```
public static final String TAG = "DataRequestTag";
StringRequest stringRequest;
RequestQueue queue;

// Tag the request
stringRequest.setTag(TAG);

// Queue the request
queue.add(stringRequest);
```

Now that the requests have been tagged, you can cancel them from processing from the
onStop() method of your Activity:

```
@Override
protected void onStop () {
    super.onStop();
    if (queue != null) {
        queue.cancelAll(TAG);
    }
}
```

So far, we have covered using a `stringRequest`, but a few other requests are built into Volley.
You can also make an `ImageRequest`, `JsonObjectRequest`, and `JsonArrayRequest`.

When making an `ImageRequest`, you need to have an `ImageView` to place your image as
well as the URL where the image lives. Once you have these, you can make the request. An
`ImageRequest` may look like the following:

```
ImageRequest request = new ImageRequest(url,
    new Response.Listener() {
        @Override
        public void onResponse(Bitmap bitmap) {
            // set the image
            mImageView.setImageBitmap(bitmap);
        }
    }, 0, 0, null,
    new Response.ErrorListener() {
        public void onErrorResponse(VolleyError error) {
            // handle the error with error resource
            mImageView.setImageResource(R.drawable.image_load_error);
        }
    });
```

You may have noticed that this example is missing the `add()` method. This is because you may want to work with a singleton class when using images. If you need an example of setting up a singleton, you can find one at https://developer.android.com/training/volley/requestqueue.html#singleton.

After adding the class, you can then queue the `imageRequest`, as follows:

```
MySingleton.getInstance(this).addToRequestQueue(request);
```

To work with a JSON array or object, you should either use `JsonArrayRequest` or `JsonObjectRequest`, respectively. The following demonstrates working with a JSON object:

```
JsonObjectRequest jsonObjRequest = new JsonObjectRequest
        (Request.Method.GET, url, null, new Response.Listener() {

    @Override
    public void onResponse(JSONObject response) {
        // handle the response
    }
}, new Response.ErrorListener() {

    @Override
    public void onErrorResponse(VolleyError error) {
        // handle the error
    }
});
```

Working with JSON data may also require the use of the singleton class, making use of the queue, similar to how the `imageRequest` was performed:

```
MySingleton.getInstance(this).addToRequestQueue(jsonObjRequest);
```

Summary

In this chapter, you learned about using an HTTP client and how to connect and send data. You also learned how to parse through XML files for data, and that using a skip method can help you return the data you want. You also learned why `AsyncTasks` are used when working with network functions. Lastly, you learned that, by using the Volley library, you can gain finer control over your network connections and requests.

## 11

Working with Location Data

Many applications may benefit from adding support or processing location data. There are many examples of how location can be used and why it is important. In this chapter, you learn ways to access and use user location data.

At first glance, it may seem simple to work with location data. Most Android devices contain a GPS or similar sensor, so it may be easy to believe that by simply turning this sensor on you should have access to the data you want.

This, however, is not the case. A user may not wish to turn on their device sensors because it diminishes battery life and may not return a perceivable benefit. Some users may also not want their exact movements and locations recorded and will turn off all location services and providers.

This is not the end of the road, though, because Android offers several options to work with location data. Depending on the data you will be working with, you need permissions for your application to access sensor data.

Permissions

Due to the sensitivity of working with location data, a permission request needs to be added to your application. You can request the use of either a coarse or fine location.

The ACCESS_COARSE_LOCATION permission does not use the GPS sensor data and returns a location that is accurate to within about one city block. This information is distilled through cell-tower and Wi-Fi data from the device.

For many applications, this is an acceptable amount of location data because enough information will be returned to be used to display information relevant to the user's city or area.

Adding this permission is the same as adding other permissions into your application manifest:

```
<uses-permission android:name="android.permission.ACCESS_COARSE_LOCATION"/>
```

Applications that serve current weather conditions or city- or area-specific advertisements would benefit from this type of location data. In each of these application types, the precise location of a user is not necessarily needed.

> **Note**
>
> If you are using an advertisement service in your application, you should review their require-ments because some advertisers require the precise or fine location of a user in order to com-ply with their terms of service. If you want to extend battery life and not require the use of GPS information, you may want to find another advertising service.

To turn things up a notch and acquire the precise location of a user by use of GPS or similar sensor data as well as the passive location provider, you can use the ACCESS_FINE_LOCATION:

```
<uses-permission android:name="android.permission.ACCESS_FINE_LOCATION"/>
```

To demonstrate the difference in how these locations are reported, a simple application can be built that gets the device location and displays it when the buttons are pressed. This can be built using an Activity, a service, and a layout, as well as by adding permissions to the applica-tion manifest. Listing 11.1 shows the contents of the Activity for the application.

Listing 11.1 **Contents of `MainActivity.java`**

```
package com.dutsonpa.mylocation;

import android.app.AlertDialog;
import android.content.DialogInterface;
import android.content.Intent;
import android.location.Location;
import android.location.LocationManager;
import android.os.Bundle;
import android.provider.Settings;
import android.support.v7.app.AppCompatActivity;
import android.view.Menu;
import android.view.MenuItem;
import android.view.View;
import android.widget.Button;
import android.widget.TextView;
import android.widget.Toast;



public class MainActivity extends AppCompatActivity {

    Button buttonFineLocation;
    Button buttonCoarseLocation;
```

```java
MyLocationService myLocationService;
TextView textViewResults;

@Override
protected void onCreate(Bundle savedInstanceState) {
  super.onCreate(savedInstanceState);
  setContentView(R.layout.activity_main);
  textViewResults = (TextView)findViewById(R.id.textViewResults);
  // use a service for location to avoid blocking the UI thread
  myLocationService = new MyLocationService(MainActivity.this);

  // set up GPS button click
  buttonFineLocation = (Button) findViewById(R.id.buttonFineLocation);
  buttonFineLocation.setOnClickListener(new View.OnClickListener() {
    @Override
    public void onClick(View v) {

      Location fineLocation =
          myLocationService.getLocation(LocationManager.GPS_PROVIDER);

      if (fineLocation != null) {
        double latitude = fineLocation.getLatitude();
        double longitude = fineLocation.getLongitude();
        textViewResults.setText("GPS: \nLatitude: " + latitude
            + "\nLongitude: " + longitude);
      } else {
        // The GPS is not currently enabled, the user needs to enable it
        showProviderDialog("GPS");
        textViewResults.setText("Please enable the GPS to receive location");
      }
    }
  });

  // set up Network Provider button click
  buttonCoarseLocation = (Button) findViewById(R.id.buttonCoarseLocation);
  buttonCoarseLocation.setOnClickListener(new View.OnClickListener() {
    @Override
    public void onClick(View v) {
      // get the location from the service
      Location coarseLocation = myLocationService
      .getLocation(LocationManager.NETWORK_PROVIDER);
      if (coarseLocation != null) {
        double latitude = coarseLocation.getLatitude();
        double longitude = coarseLocation.getLongitude();
```

```
            textViewResults.setText("Network Provided: \nLatitude: " + latitude
                + "\nLongitude: " + longitude);
        } else {
            // There is not network provider, the user needs to enable it
            showProviderDialog("NETWORK");
            textViewResults.setText("Please enable WiFi to receive location");
        }
    }
  });
}

public void showProviderDialog(String provider) {

  // Build an AlertDialog
  AlertDialog.Builder alertDialogBuilder = new AlertDialog.Builder(this)
  .setTitle(provider + " SETTINGS")
  .setMessage(provider
    + " is not enabled. Would you like to enable it in the settings menu?")
  .setPositiveButton("Settings",
    new DialogInterface.OnClickListener() {
      public void onClick(DialogInterface dialog, int which) {
        Intent intent = new Intent(
          Settings.ACTION_LOCATION_SOURCE_SETTINGS);
        MainActivity.this.startActivity(intent);
      }
    })
  .setNegativeButton("Cancel",
    new DialogInterface.OnClickListener() {
      public void onClick(DialogInterface dialog, int which) {
        dialog.cancel();
      }
    });

      // Show the AlertDialog
  AlertDialog alertDialog = alertDialogBuilder.show();
}

@Override
public boolean onCreateOptionsMenu(Menu menu) {
  // Inflate the menu; this adds items to the action bar if it is present.
  getMenuInflater().inflate(R.menu.menu_main, menu);
  return true;
}

@Override
```

```
public boolean onOptionsItemSelected(MenuItem item) {
  // Handle action bar item clicks here. The action bar will
  // automatically handle clicks on the Home/Up button, so long
  // as you specify a parent activity in AndroidManifest.xml.
  int id = item.getItemId();

  //noinspection SimplifiableIfStatement
  if (id == R.id.action_settings) {
    return true;
  }

  return super.onOptionsItemSelected(item);
 }
}
```

Stepping through the Activity, you will find that it contains the definition for two buttons: the service that will be used to get the location, and a `TextView` definition. The `onCreate()` method sets the layout to be used and then sets the value for the `TextView`. The service is also defined, and the Activity is passed as the context that is needed by the service. This service is used to prevent blocking on the UI thread and needs to be used in order to avoid Application Not Responding errors and exceptions.

The click events for the buttons are then defined. Each one contains a check to see if a location is available from either the GPS or the network provider. When a location exists, the latitude and longitude are set as `double` values and then inserted into the `TextView` on the page.

If the location is not available, the `showProviderDialog()` method is called and it passes a `String` of either `GPS` or `NETWORK`. This method uses a builder pattern to assemble an `AlertDialog`. This pattern is used to set all the elements of the `AlertDialog` before it is then displayed via an `AlertDialog` variable that's set equal to `alertDialogBuild.show()`.

Using an `AlertDialog` allows you to inform the user of sensor status and allows them an opportunity to get to the device settings to enable data to be collected. Because the alert dialog contains a "positive" button and a "negative" button, users can choose to cancel the operation if they do not want to enable the location sensors.

Figure 11.1 shows an alert dialog displayed onscreen when the device does not have any network data available.

> **Note**
>
> You cannot directly turn on the GPS with your application. This would violate the trust and security your application has with the user. You can detect if the GPS is disabled and allow the user to turn it on through the system settings. This gives the end user the comfort of controlling when applications are reporting location data.

Figure 11.1   By clicking the Settings button, the user is taken to the location-sharing settings of the device.

Listing 11.2 shows the contents of the service that is referenced from the main activity.

Listing 11.2   **Contents of `MyLocationService.java`**

```java
package com.dutsonpa.mylocation;

import android.app.Service;
import android.content.Context;
import android.content.Intent;
import android.location.Location;
import android.location.LocationListener;
import android.location.LocationManager;
import android.os.Bundle;
import android.os.IBinder;

public class MyLocationService extends Service implements LocationListener {

    protected LocationManager locationManager;
    Location location;

    // create a distance value in meters to use for update frequency
    private static final long UPDATE_DISTANCE_FILTER = 10;
```

```java
// create a 2 minute time value for use as update frequency
private static final long UPDATE_MIN_FREQUENCY = 1000 * 60 * 2;

/*
 * Note that using a value of "0" for the variables above will request
 * updates as often as the device can provide, however this will require
 * much more battery usage, avoid using "0" if possible
 */

public MyLocationService(Context context) {
  locationManager = (LocationManager)
    context.getSystemService(LOCATION_SERVICE);
}

// create a getter for location
public Location getLocation(String provider) {
  // Is a location provider enabled?
  if (locationManager.isProviderEnabled(provider)){
    locationManager.requestLocationUpdates(provider, UPDATE_MIN_FREQUENCY,
      UPDATE_DISTANCE_FILTER, this);
    // Has it been 2 minutes or moved 10 meters?
    if (locationManager != null){
      // There is a provider and it is time to send a location update
      location = locationManager.getLastKnownLocation(provider);
      return location;
    }
  }
  // Location provider is not enabled, return null
  return null;
}

@Override
public IBinder onBind(Intent intent) {
  return null;
}

@Override
public void onLocationChanged(Location location) {
  // specific logic for location change
}

@Override
public void onStatusChanged(String provider, int status, Bundle extras) {
  // specific logic for a status change
}
```

```
@Override
public void onProviderEnabled(String provider) {
  // specific logic for a provider being enabled
}

@Override
public void onProviderDisabled(String provider) {
  // specific logic for a provider being disabled
}
}
```

Starting with the class declaration, you can see that LocationListener is implemented. This is an interface that allows the location information to be updated. It contains four public methods that you can use for performing specific logic during the lifecycle of location management. In this example, these public classes are not used but are shown with an @Override notation and a comment within that explains what each does.

The LocationManager is defined that is used to manage what location provider is available as well as to manage the frequency of the updates. Location is also defined as an object, so that location data can be set and passed through the service.

A method named MyLocationService is defined that requires a context passed to it. In turn, it sets the value for the LocationManager object so that it has a properly defined context.

The getLocation() method is the "getter" method that does most of the lifting in this service. It starts out by checking for an enabled location provider. If a location is not found, the method will return a null value. When a location provider exists, you can use the requestLocationUpdates() method by providing the provider being used, the update time frequency, the updated distance frequency, and this, which refers to the LocationListener implemented in this class.

When an update is found, the locationManager is populated and then set to use the getLastKnownLocation() method. This method will populate the location with longitude and latitude data for the last known location from the device.

Now that the service has been created, you will need to make sure you have set up proper permissions in your application manifest. Due to this application using the GPS for location data, you will need to use ACCESS_FINE_LOCATION.

Note

By using ACCESS_FINE_LOCATION, you are using a greater permission request than ACCESS_COARSE_LOCATION. Because of this, you do not need to include both permissions because the coarse location permission is implied.

The layout for the application contains a RelativeLayout with two TextViews and two Buttons. Listing 11.3 shows the contents of the layout used in the application.

Listing 11.3 **Contents of `activity_main.xml`**

```xml
<RelativeLayout xmlns:android="http://schemas.android.com/apk/res/android"

  xmlns:tools="http://schemas.android.com/tools"
  android:layout_width="match_parent"
  android:layout_height="match_parent"
  android:paddingLeft="@dimen/activity_horizontal_margin"
  android:paddingRight="@dimen/activity_horizontal_margin"
  android:paddingTop="@dimen/activity_vertical_margin"
  android:paddingBottom="@dimen/activity_vertical_margin" tools:context=".
MainActivity">

  <TextView android:text="@string/hello_world"
    android:layout_width="wrap_content"
    android:layout_height="wrap_content"
    android:id="@+id/textView" />

  <Button
    android:layout_width="wrap_content"
    android:layout_height="wrap_content"
    android:text="GPS (FINE) Location"
    android:id="@+id/buttonFineLocation"
    android:layout_marginTop="50dp"
    android:layout_below="@+id/textView"
    android:layout_centerHorizontal="true" />

  <Button
    android:layout_width="wrap_content"
    android:layout_height="wrap_content"
    android:text="Network Provided (COARSE) Location"
    android:id="@+id/buttonCoarseLocation"
    android:layout_below="@+id/buttonFineLocation"
    android:layout_centerHorizontal="true" />

  <TextView
    android:layout_width="wrap_content"
    android:layout_height="wrap_content"
    android:text="Location Data will appear here"
    android:id="@+id/textViewResults"
    android:layout_alignParentBottom="true"
    android:layout_centerHorizontal="true" />
</RelativeLayout>
```

In the layout XML, you can see that the IDs have been set that are referenced and used in the main activity. You should also notice that some values have been hard-coded rather than using the traditional `strings.xml` file. There is an example in the first `TextView` of using the `strings.xml` file, and this should be followed in all your applications. The hard-coded values in the other `TextView` as well as both `Buttons` are displayed for ease of reading and understanding this example.

Google Play Services Locations API

In the previous example, the `android.location` package was used to demonstrate working with fine and coarse location data. This package is still a viable option; however, Google strongly recommends converting all existing applications and writing all new applications using the Locations API.

One of the major benefits of using the Locations API is that you give Google the responsibility of managing compatibility and thus allow it to push updates that will not require you to rewrite your code in order to take advantage of new optimizations.

A practical benefit of using the Locations API is the Fused Location Provider. This provider uses some clever algorithms to determine an accurate guess of where a user is with minimal impact to battery life, allowing you a much finer control of location awareness while also extending the amount of time the device can remain powered and functional. It also allows you to set some parameters manually to increase or decrease precision and frequency of location data when you need it.

> **Note**
>
> Using Google Play Services requires the device running your app to be running at least Android 2.3 and have access to the Google Play Store. Some builds of Android may not be compatible, including popular third-party custom ROMs and some devices that are based on Android but choose not to include Google Play Services and applications.

Working with Google Play Services is covered in depth in Chapter 15, "Google Play Services." However, Listing 11.4 shows an activity that uses the Locations API to retrieve the current location.

Listing 11.4   **Activity Using the Locations API**

```
package com.dutsonpa.locationsapi;

import android.app.Activity;
import android.content.DialogInterface;
import android.content.DialogInterface.OnCancelListener;
import android.content.Intent;
import android.content.IntentSender.SendIntentException;
import android.location.Location;
import android.os.Bundle;
import android.util.Log;
```

```java
import android.widget.TextView;
import android.widget.Toast;

import com.google.android.gms.common.ConnectionResult;
import com.google.android.gms.common.GooglePlayServicesUtil;
import com.google.android.gms.common.api.GoogleApiClient;
import com.google.android.gms.location.LocationServices;


public class GooglePlayServicesActivity extends Activity implements
GoogleApiClient.ConnectionCallbacks,
GoogleApiClient.OnConnectionFailedListener {

  private static final String TAG = "GooglePlayServicesActiv";
  private static final String KEY_IN_RESOLUTION = "is_in_resolution";
  protected static final int REQUEST_CODE_RESOLUTION = 1;
  private GoogleApiClient mGoogleApiClient;
  private boolean mIsInResolution;
  /** Set variables other variables **/
  protected Location myLastLocation;
  protected TextView myTextView;

  @Override
  protected void onCreate(Bundle savedInstanceState) {
    super.onCreate(savedInstanceState);
    if (savedInstanceState != null) {
      mIsInResolution = savedInstanceState.getBoolean(KEY_IN_RESOLUTION, false);
    }
    setContentView(R.layout.activity_google_play_services);

    myTextView = (TextView) findViewById(R.id.textView);
  }

  @Override
  protected void onStart() {
    super.onStart();
    if (mGoogleApiClient == null) {
      mGoogleApiClient = new GoogleApiClient.Builder(this)
      // Notice the addApi(LocationServices.API) added below
      .addConnectionCallbacks(this)
      .addOnConnectionFailedListener(this)
      .addApi(LocationServices.API)
      .build();
    }
    mGoogleApiClient.connect();
  }
```

```java
@Override
protected void onStop() {
  if (mGoogleApiClient != null) {
    mGoogleApiClient.disconnect();
  }
  super.onStop();
}

@Override
protected void onSaveInstanceState(Bundle outState) {
  super.onSaveInstanceState(outState);
  outState.putBoolean(KEY_IN_RESOLUTION, mIsInResolution);
}

@Override
protected void onActivityResult(int requestCode, int resultCode, Intent data) {
  super.onActivityResult(requestCode, resultCode, data);
  switch (requestCode) {
    case REQUEST_CODE_RESOLUTION:
    retryConnecting();
    break;
  }
}

private void retryConnecting() {
  mIsInResolution = false;
  if (!mGoogleApiClient.isConnecting()) {
    mGoogleApiClient.connect();
  }
}

@Override
public void onConnected(Bundle connectionHint) {
  Log.i(TAG, "GoogleApiClient connected");
    // create a location object by using the Location API
  myLastLocation =
    LocationServices.FusedLocationApi.getLastLocation(mGoogleApiClient);
  if (myLastLocation != null) {
    myTextView.setText("Latitude: "+ myLastLocation.getLatitude()
      + "\nLongitude: " + myLastLocation.getLongitude());
  } else {
    Toast.makeText(this, "Location data not available",
      Toast.LENGTH_LONG).show();
  }
}
```

```
@Override
public void onConnectionSuspended(int cause) {
  Log.i(TAG, "GoogleApiClient connection suspended");
  retryConnecting();
}

@Override
public void onConnectionFailed(ConnectionResult result) {
  Log.i(TAG, "GoogleApiClient connection failed: " + result.toString());
  if (!result.hasResolution()) {
    GooglePlayServicesUtil.getErrorDialog(
      result.getErrorCode(), this, 0, new OnCancelListener() {
        @Override
        public void onCancel(DialogInterface dialog) {
          retryConnecting();
        }
      }).show();
    return;
  }
  if (mIsInResolution) {
    return;
  }
  mIsInResolution = true;
  try {
    result.startResolutionForResult(this, REQUEST_CODE_RESOLUTION);
  } catch (SendIntentException e) {
    Log.e(TAG, "Exception while starting resolution activity", e);
    retryConnecting();
  }
}
}
}
```

When using the Google Play Services, you must build an API client that will manage your connection to the Google Play Services. This also means that some of the Activity lifecycle must be managed to help keep state between the API client and the device.

For example, the onStop() method is used to disconnect the API client as soon as the activity becomes invisible. When the activity is started, the client is reconnected if it still exists, or re-created if it had been destroyed.

During the creation in the onStart() method, the methods that you want to use are initialized. This is noted in the code example as the addApi(LocationServices.API) portion of code used to build the mGoogleApiClient object.

Because most of the code is related to working with Google Services, the other point I draw your attention to is the onConnected() method. In this method, you can see that when the client has been connected, the myLastLocation object is set to contain the location of the device. This is done by using getLastLocation(), which is part of the FusedLocationApi method within the Location API.

The FusedLocationApi is the Fused Location Provider, and it uses any location data that it currently has to make a best guess on the current location of the device. Depending on the resolution or accuracy level being used by the app, or other apps using the Location API, this may be accurate to within a few feet for a fine level or accuracy, or a city block (roughly 100 meters) if coarse location data is being used.

Using the Location API to get location updates can be done by creating a LocationRequest object and then setting the update frequency and accuracy that you want to use. The following snippet shows a method that is used to create a location request update:

```
protected void createLocationRequest() {
  myLocationRequest = new LocationRequest();
  // set the length of update requests
  myLocationRequest.setInterval(UPDATE_INTERVAL_IN_MILLISECONDS);
  // set a maximum of how often an update can be requested
  myLocationRequest.setFastestInterval(FASTEST_UPDATE_INTERVAL_IN_MILLISECONDS);
  // set the accuracy of the requested location
  myLocationRequest.setPriority(LocationRequest.PRIORITY_HIGH_ACCURACY);
}
```

In this example, you can see that a LocationRequest is created and then has properties set that will influence how often it is updated and how accurate it should be. Even with some of these values set, you should be aware that they may not run at the time you want them. The setInterval() will set a request up; however, if another app is also running and using the Location API with a faster interval, your application will receive faster updates than you may set here.

To get around this timing issue, the setFastestInterval method is used to specify a maximum amount of updates your application can handle. This can be helpful to you because you may be using some processor time to draw updates to a map or to update various aspects of your UI. If you are constantly having to run logic to handle an update, you could experience screen flicker or application jank.

The setPriority() method allows you to control the accuracy of the location that is returned. If you only need a rough guesstimate for a location (such as a weather application), you could use PRIORITY_LOW_POWER. This uses minimal power and provides a location with city-level accuracy. Should you want a little more precision, you can step up to PRIORITY_BALANCED_POWER_ACCURACY, which is nearly the same resolution as using coarse accuracy. If you are working on an application that needs to access the GPS or fine-level accuracy, you can use PRIORITY_HIGH_ACCURACY.

Should you find that you need a location, but are not interested in using any battery to use the location, you can use a setting of PRIORITY_NO_POWER. This allows the location data to be piggy-backed from another application that is requesting data. This is not ideal for situations where you need relatively accurate information, but it can be helpful if you need the location for a region and want to save as much battery power as possible.

Summary

This chapter discussed how to access location data through the location providers included in the Android platform.

You started out by learning how the `android.location` package can be used to locate a device based on either coarse or fine accuracy. You learned that using location data requires adding a permission to your application manifest and that using the fine level of accuracy will use more battery life than using a network-provided location.

You were shown a sample application that updates based on a time period or distance to request a location update. This was shown as an example of how to minimize battery impact while providing an acceptable level of location accuracy.

Lastly, you learned that you can leverage the Google Play Services Location API to set up a client that uses the Fused Location Provider to return location data. This provider allows you to minimize location requests and even use minimal power in your application by using another application that is requesting location data to share it with your application.

12

Multimedia

Creating an application that can display data and take user input is fine; however, applications that contain video and audio can do much more than simply provide something to look at or listen to. By adding multimedia to your application, you can draw a user in and provide another dimension for user feedback and manipulation. In this chapter, you learn how to work with audio and video within your application.

Working with Audio

Audio is an almost ever-present obligatory addition to many of the applications and system functionalities of your Android device. Most notifications have an audio cue attached to them, as do messaging and contact applications.

Within the Android system, sound playback has been implemented with a variety of support codecs. These codecs allow for container files to be played back on the device. Table 12.1 lists the supported audio codecs that you can use in your application.

Table 12.1 **Supported Audio Codecs and Containers**

Codec	File Format	Information
AAC LC, HE-AACv1, HE-AACv2, AAC ELD	.3gp, .mp4, .mp4a, .aac, .ts	Note that decoding .aac files was added in 3.1, and encoding support was added in 4.0. ADIF is not supported, and MPEG-TS files can only be played back and not scrubbed. AAC LC, HE-AACv1, and HE-AACv2 support mono/stereo/5.0/5.1 sources with sampling rates from 8KHz to 48KHz. AAC ELD supports mono/stereo with sampling rates from 16KHz to 48KHz.
AMR-NB	.3gp	Encoding and decoding are fully supported with files sampled at 8KHz.

Codec	File Format	Information
AMR-WB	.3gp	Encoding and decoding are fully supported with files sampled at 16KHz.
FLAC	.flac	Decoding support was added in 3.1. Supports mono/stereo sources up to 48KHz at 24 bit. Note that if the device does not have adequate hardware to play back at maximum quality, it will be down-sampled to 44KHz at 16 bit; however, a dither and low-pass filter will not be applied and may distort playback.
MP3	.mp3	Decoding is supported. Supports mono/stereo sources with rates of 8–320Kbps with either constant or variable bitrate.
MIDI	.mid, .xmf, .mxmf, .rtttl, .rtx, .ota, .imy	Decoding is supported for Type 0 and Type 1 MIDI, DLS Version 1 and 2, XMF, Mobile XMF, Ringtone, and iMelody files.
Vorbis	.ogg, .mkv	Decoding support for .ogg files works for all versions of Android. Support for .mkv was added in Android 4.0.
PCM/WAVE	.wav	Offers decoding for 8-bit and 16-bit PCM files with sampling rates of 8000Hz, 16,000Hz, and 44,100Hz. Encoding support was added in 4.1.
Opus	.mkv	Decoding support was added in 5.0.

Audio Playback

Android has a few different ways for leveraging audio playback. One of the most common ways is to use a SoundPool. Depending on the structure and functionality of your application, MediaPlayer can also be directly used.

Starting with the first version of the Android API, the SoundPool class has been used to manage sound playback. This is done by leveraging the internal MediaPlay service and decoding audio into raw 16-bit PCM streams that can then be used in your application. SoundPool is ideal for loading short, quick sounds that are used in games, events such as taps and clicks, and sounds that provide system feedback. SoundPool is not ideal for loading large audio files such as music and soundtracks because all sounds are loaded into a small shared memory pool. Larger audio files should instead be played back using MediaPlayer. Audio that you customize with filters and effects should be processed through AudioTrack.

The upside is that this allows you to ship compressed audio files with your application, which saves you from forcing users to download an application that is mostly large audio files.

The downside to this is that the files must be decoded before they are ready for use. Depending on the size and duration of the audio source, this has the potential of adding a significant delay to the playback of the file. To best alleviate this, you should consider loading the required audio sources before they will be needed for playback. This can be done during a "loading" sequence, or in the background of the application when it is starting.

As per current application design patterns, a splash screen should be shown to reinforce branding and also to load resources that will be needed by the application. If your application has only one "loading" screen, this is a suitable place for preparing audio streams.

You may also be worried about resource management because loading a soundtrack, sound effects, and other audio cues may quickly overtake the available system resources. This is a valid concern and one that you do have some control over. When using SoundPool, you can designate the maximum number of samples that can be active at a given time. This limit can be further tweaked with a priority setting so that the essential audio streams will not be discarded when too many samples are requested.

To use SoundPool, you need to declare the variable as well the samples you want to use. This is done as follows:

```
private SoundPool mSoundPool;
int sound1 = 0;
int sound2 = 0;
int sound3 = 0;
```

> **Note**
>
> To help eliminate bottlenecks in processing audio, starting with API 21 rigid design patterns are enforced. Because of this, you must either create two blocks of code to execute the proper block based on the version of Android running on the device, or create restricted applications that will only work for targeted versions of Android.

Due to the difference in the internals of media players starting with Lollipop (API 21), you need to do the following if you plan on supporting multiple versions of Android:

```
// For KitKat 4.4.4 and below,
// the warning is suppressed so you can support current versions of Android
@SuppressWarnings("deprecation")
protected void legacySoundPool() {
  // change values as needed
  mSoundPool = new SoundPool(6, AudioManager.STREAM_MUSIC, 0);
}


// Starting with API 21, you must use the builder pattern to achieve
// proper performance of SoundPool
@TargetApi(Build.VERSION_CODES.LOLLIPOP)
protected void builderSoundPool() {
  // change values as needed
```

```
AudioAttributes attributes = new AudioAttributes.Builder()
    .setUsage(AudioAttributes.USAGE_GAME)
    .setContentType(AudioAttributes.CONTENT_TYPE_MUSIC)
    .build();

mSoundPool = new
    SoundPool.Builder().setAudioAttributes(attributes).setMaxStreams(6).build();
}

// Now that methods have been created to handle both pre and post API 21
// The proper method can be called when you need to use SoundPool
if (Build.VERSION.SDK_INT >= Build.VERSION_CODES.LOLLIPOP) {
    builderSoundPool();
} else{
    legacySoundPool();
}
```

In this code block, two methods were created to help get around various player issues as well as to initialize the SoundPool. In the legacySoundPool() method, SoundPool is used as a constructor. The SoundPool constructor takes several arguments.

The first argument is the maximum number of audio streams that will play simultaneously. The second argument is the type of audio that will be streamed. This value is used to make some internal optimizations for how the audio is handled within the AudioManager. A value of STREAM_MUSIC is the most common and is suitable for gaming applications. The third argument is more of a placeholder that is used to adjust the quality of the audio sample.

When using a builder to invoke SoundPool, you need to use AudioAttributes and helper methods to set the values you want to use with the SoundPool by chaining them together. This is seen in the preceding code block as the .setUsage() and .setContentType() methods for the AudioAttributes, and using setAudioAttributes() and setMaxStreams() to set the attributes and values needed for the SoundPool.

After a SoundPool object is ready for use, you need to use a try-catch block to set up your audio assets and load them into the sound pool. The following shows a sample block for loading an audio asset:

```
builderSoundPool();
try {
  AssetManager assetManager = getAssets();
  AssetFileDescriptor descriptor;

  // open the sound asset, then load it into the SoundPool
  descriptor = assetManager.openFd("pewpew.mp3");
  sound1 = soundPool.load(descriptor, 0);
} catch(IOException e) {
  // You need to put your error handling logic here
}
```

After an asset is successfully loaded into the `SoundPool` using the `load()` method, you can call that asset to play with the `play()` method. This method takes several arguments:

- The first argument is the `soundID`, which is returned from the `load()` method.

- The second argument is `leftVolume`, which changes how loud the playback will be on the left channel (the range is from `0.0` to `1.0`).

- The third argument is `rightVolume`, which changes how loud the playback will be on the right channel (the range is from `0.0` to `1.0`).

- The fourth argument is the priority, which is used to determine if the sound should be stopped based on the maximum number of simultaneous audio streams that can be played back (note that `0` is the lowest priority).

- The fifth argument is used to determine if the audio stream is a one-shot or loop; using any number greater than or equal to `0` will end playback at the end of the file, whereas a value of `-1` will play the sound as a loop.

- The sixth argument is used to determine the playback rate of the audio file; a value of `0.5` will play back at half-rate, whereas a value of `2` will play back at twice the default rate.

The following is an example of playing audio back with the `play()` method:

```
mSoundPool.play(sound1, 1, 1, 0, 0, 1);
```

If you need to stop a sound that is playing, do so by using the `stop()` method and passing the `soundID` of the item you want to stop playing. The following shows an example of stopping `sound1` from playing:

```
mSoundPool.stop(sound1);
```

> **Tip**
>
> To effectively use a `SoundPool`, consider creating "sound packs" that can be loaded for a specific Activity and then released when the Activity is closed or destroyed. This can be done by calling `mSoundPlayer.release()`. When the `release` method is called, all loaded audio samples as well as any used memory are released. This allows you to create an application that minimizes load time and will have the right sounds ready when the user needs them.

Now that you know how to play audio files, it is time to learn about how to capture or record them.

Audio Recording

Audio can be recorded or captured through the use of the `MediaRecorder` class. This API is used to perform the necessary steps to record audio to your device.

> **Note**
>
> The Android emulator is a useful tool; however, it does not contain the ability to allow you to test the recording behavior of an actual device. When adding an audio-capture feature to your application, you need to test with a real device.

To record audio, do the following:

1. Initialize the recorder.

2. Set the audio source via `setAudioSource()`.

3. Set the output format via `setOutputFormat()`.

4. Set the encoder to use via `setAudioEncoder()`.

5. Set the file output via `setOutputFile()`.

6. Ready the device to record via `prepare()`.

7. Start the recording via `start()`.

8. End the recording via `stop()`.

9. Either reuse the object with `reset()` or release the object with `release()`.

In practice, this would appear as follows in your application logic:

```
MediaRecorder mRecorder = new MediaRecorder();
// use the device microphone
mRecorder.setAudioSource(MediaRecorder.AudioSource.MIC);
mRecorder.setOutputFormat(MediaRecorder.OutputFormat.THREE_GPP);
mRecorder.setAudioEncoder(MediaRecorder.AudioEncoder.AMR_NB);
// replace OUTPUT_LOCATION with the proper filesystem path or variable
mRecoder.setOutputFile(OUTPUT_LOCATION);
try {
  mRecoder.prepare();
} catch (IllegalStateException e) {
  // handle the error here
} catch (IOException e) {
  // handle the error here
}

try {
  mRecorder.start();
} catch (IllegalStateException e) {
  // handle the error here
}
```

```
try {
  // use a button, timer, or other method to call the following:
  mRecoder.stop();
} catch (IllegalStateException e) {
  // handle the error here
}
// If you want to use the same MediaRecoder object use this
mRecorder.reset();
// If you want to discard the MediaRecoder object use this
mRecorder.release();
mRecoder = null;
```

Playing the recording back can be done via the `MediaPlayer` class. `MediaPlayer` can be used to play back not only audio files but also video files. `MediaPlayer` needs to be initialized and then pointed to the file to play; it then uses the `prepare()` and `start()` methods to begin playback.

The following two methods demonstrate how you can start and stop playback of audio files:

```
private void startPlayback() {
  mPlayer = new MediaPlayer();
  try {
    // change FILETOPLAY to the path and file that you want to playback
    mPlayer.setDataSource(FILETOPLAY);
    // already in a try/catch block, no need to wrap prepare() in another
    mPlayer.prepare();
    mPlayer.start();
  } catch (IllegalStateException e) {
    // handle the error here
  } catch (IOException e) {
    // handle the error here
  }
}

private void stopPlayback() {
  mPlayer.release();
  mPlayer = null;
}
```

Now that you understand how audio works with Android, let's look at how video works.

Working with Video

Similar to how Android supports a wide variety of audio formats and codecs, it also supports a variety of video containers and codecs. Table 12.2 lists the supported video formats.

Table 12.2 **Supported Video Codecs and Containers**

Codec	File Format	Information
H.263	.3gp, .mp4	Provides encoder and decoder support in all versions of Android.
H.264 AVC	.3gp, .mp4, .ts	Provides encoding support in Android 3.0+ and decoder support for all versions in the Baseline Profile. Also note that the .ts format only works with AAC audio and with Android 3.0+.
H.265 HEVC	.mp4	The decoder supports Main Profile Level 3 on mobile devices and Main Profile Level 4.1 with Android TV. HEVC support was added in Android 5.0+.
MPEG-4 SP	.3gp	Provides decoder support in all versions of Android.
VP8	.webm, .mkv	Provides decoder support for Android 2.3.3+ and encoder support for Android 4.3+. Note that this format can be a streamed format for Android 4.0+, and .mkv files are supported in Android 4.0+.
VP9	.webm, .mkv	The decoder is supported in Android 4.4+, and .mkv files are supported in Android 4.0+.

Video Playback

Video files can be played back in a variety of different ways, including using the `MediaPlayer` class. However, there is a View that specifically exists for playing back video files.

Unlike audio files, video needs access to the screen. This means that you either need to use a `VideoView` or `SurfaceView`. Note that, depending on what your application does, you may find it easier to work with a `VideoView`.

When using a `VideoView`, note that if the Activity is moved into the background, the View will not retain state automatically. This means that you need to pause and save the playback state on pause and restore the video on resume of the Activity.

Adding a `VideoView` can be as simple as dragging and dropping it from the Design view of Android Studio into your layout. Alternatively, you can add the following XML to your layout XML file:

```
<VideoView
  android:id="@+id/myVideoView"
  android:layout_width="match_parent"
  android:layout_height="match_parent"
  android:layout_centerInParent="true" />
```

Now that you have the `VideoView` added to your layout, you will want to play a video in it. To work with a remote or streaming video, you need to create a URI for it. This can be done as follows:

```
// change the value to an actual video, this is only an example
String videoAddress = "https://video.website.com/video.mp4";
Uri videoURI = Uri.parse(videoAddress);
```

For applications that will be streaming video files, you need to add the `INTERNET` permission to your application manifest. As a reminder, this is done by adding the following permission to your application manifest XML:

```
<uses-permission android:name="android.permission.INTERNET" />
```

The video can then be programmatically attached to the `VideoView` by referencing the `ViewView` and using the `setVideoURI()` method. This is shown as follows:

```
VideoView myVideoView = (VideoView)findViewById(R.id.myVideoView);
myVideoView.setVideoURI(videoURI);
```

If you only wanted to play a video without user interaction, you could finish here by using the `start()` method on the `VideoView` object. However, if you want to add scrubbing and other controls, you can use the `MediaController` class with your `VideoView`. This is done by creating a `MediaController` object, anchoring it to the `VideoView`, and then setting the `MediaController` object to the `VideoView`, as follows:

```
MediaController myMediaController = new MediaController(this);
myMediaController.setAnchorView(myVideoView);
MyViewView.setMediaController(myMediaController);
```

If you want to use the `MediaPlayer` class rather than the `VideoView`, you will need to use a `SurfaceView`. The `SurfaceView` is a special view that is used as a canvas to be drawn on. Because video playback involves multiple frames being drawn, the `SurfaceView` is used as the screen to draw the frames on.

Adding a `SurfaceView` to your application is done in one of two ways: You can use the Design mode in Android Studio and then drag and drop the `SurfaceView` into your layout, or you can add the following code to your layout XML file:

```
<SurfaceView
  android:id="@+id/mySurfaceView"
  android:layout_width="match_parent"
  android:layout_height="match_parent" />
```

In your `Activity` class, you need to implement `SurfaceHolder.Callback` and `MediaPlayer.OnPreparedListener`. The following shows a sample of how your main Activity might look:

```
public class MainActivity extends Activity
    implements SurfaceHolder.Callback, OnPreparedListener {
  // your activity code
}
```

When you add the required implementations, Android Studio should automatically generate some method stubs for you. If it doesn't, add the following to your Activity:

```
@Override
public void surfaceChanged(SurfaceHolder arg0, int arg1, int arg2, int arg3) {
  // TODO Auto-generated method stub
}


@Override
public void surfaceCreated(SurfaceHolder arg0) {
  // MediaPlayer code will go in this method
}


@Override
public void surfaceDestroyed(SurfaceHolder arg0) {
  // TODO Auto-generated method stub
}


@Override
public void onPrepared(MediaPlayer mp) {
  // MediaPlayer start method should be called here
}
```

The next step is to create a few variables, set them, set up the MediaPlayer, and then start the player. The following shows an example of this:

```
// create variables
private MediaPlayer mPlayer;
private SufaceHolder mSurfaceHolder;
private SurfaceView mSurfaceView;
String videoAddress = "https://video.website.com/video.mp4";

// other code in your activity...

@Override
protected void onCreate(Bundle savedInstanceState) {
  // onCreate code...
  mSurfaceView = (SurfaceView) findViewById(R.id.mySurfaceView);
  mSurfaceHolder = mSurfaceView.getHolder();
  mSurfaceHolder.addCallback(this);
}

// other code in your activity...

@Override
public void surfaceCreated(SurfaceHolder arg0) {
  // Remember to handle the setup of the MediaPlayer for the version
  // of Android that you are targeting, make changes as needed
```

```
    try {
      mPlayer = new MediaPlayer();
      mPlayer.setDisplay(mSurfaceHolder);
      mPlayer.setDataSource(videoAddress);
      mPlayer.prepare();
      mPlayer.setOnPreparedListener(this);
      mPlayer.setAudioStreamType(AudioManager.STREAM_MUSIC);
    } catch (Exception e) {
      // handle the exception
    }
}

// other code in your activity...

@Override
public void onPrepared(MediaPlayer mp) {
  mPlayer.start();
}
```

In the preceding example, note the comments to help you place the code in the proper location in your application. When working with `MediaPlayer`, remember to use the builder pattern when working with API 21+.

You should also consider using a service to prepare playback for video and audio files to keep any potential sluggishness and ANR errors from wrecking your application.

Summary

In this chapter, you learned that Android has wide support for many types of media files. You learned that audio files can be bundled in your application as sound effects. You learned that these files can be included in a compressed format to save device space and then be processed into memory for playback.

You learned that there is a limit to how many files can be played simultaneously and that files loaded into memory can be bundled into sound packs that can be loaded when needed and released when finished to clear out used system resources.

You also learned that Android has broad support for video containers and codecs. Some video files, such as VP9 and WebM, offer better compression and quality than other files but are only supported in newer versions of Android.

Lastly, you learned that video files can be played back with a `VideoView`. You were shown how to include a `VideoView` and then use it in conjunction with a `MediaController` to add controls such as a play/pause button as well as a scrubbing bar. You also learned that videos can leverage the `MediaPlayer` class and be played back on a `SurfaceView`, and you were shown the basic setup of doing this in an Activity.

13

Optional Hardware APIs

Android devices come in many different shapes and sizes. Some also come with extra features or hardware. Not every device comes with every supported feature, but as a developer, you should be looking to provide experiences that will work with the myriad of available devices. Working with Bluetooth, NFC, USB, and other device sensors gives your application greater functionality and usefulness. In this chapter, you learn about how this hardware is implemented into Android and some of the ways that you can leverage device features.

Bluetooth

Bluetooth support in Android has come a considerable way since it was first introduced in API level 5. This form of Bluetooth is known as Bluetooth Classic. Starting with API 18, developers can take advantage of Bluetooth low energy (BLE), or Bluetooth Smart. BLE offers a version of the popular protocol that uses several enhancements to allow it to use less power, enabling both the receiver and the transmitter to save on power. It also brings with it the ability to work with new protocols, such as Eddystone, that allow the use of "beacons" to detect when a device is near and interact with it without pairing.

To take things even further when using Bluetooth with Android devices, the Generic Access Profile portion of the Bluetooth stack has been added in API level 21+.

Bluetooth communication can be broken down into three basic steps:

1. Discovery
2. Exploration
3. Interaction

During the discovery stage, two devices broadcast their availability to one another. When they find each other, the smart devices enter into pairing or information-exchange mode and begin broadcasting a unique address that can be received by other Bluetooth devices that are within the proximity of the Bluetooth radio.

Once the two devices discover one another, they move into the exploration stage. During exploration, a device sends a request to pair with the other one. Depending on the device and current Bluetooth support, a pairing may not be needed to exchange data because data can be passed via an exchanged encryption key.

This now moves the process into the interaction stage. Although this is not strictly required as a security measure, before the devices will move into a fully interactive mode, a device may request a passcode to be entered or a passcode exchanged to confirm that it is connecting to the intended device. Note that with BLE, this is not a standard "pairing mode" because the connections made are casual.

Whether you are working with Bluetooth Classic or BLE, the APIs you will work with are found in the `android.bluetooth` package. Also, accessing the Bluetooth radio requires user permissions, so you need to add the following to your application manifest XML:

```
<uses-permission android:name="android.permission.BLUETOOTH"/>
<uses-permission android:name="android.permission.BLUETOOTH_ADMIN"/>
```

The first permission allows access to the Bluetooth hardware, whereas the second permission allows access to enabling the Bluetooth radio as well as for using it for device discovery.

If you are working with BLE devices and want to filter your app so that only devices that support BLE can download your application from the Google Play store, you can use the following `<uses-feature>` element in conjunction with the previously mentioned permissions:

```
<uses-feature android:name="android.hardware.bluetooth_le" android:required="true"/>
```

Enabling Bluetooth

When working with Bluetooth Classic, you need to use the `BluetoothAdapter` class and the `getDefaultAdapter()` method to see if Bluetooth is available on the device. If there is an adapter available but not currently enabled, you can start an Intent to turn on Bluetooth. The following snippet demonstrates how this is done:

```
BluetoothAdapter myBluetooth = BluetoothAdapter.getDefaultAdapter();
if(!myBluetooth.isEnabled()) {
  Intent enableIntent = new Intent(BluetoothAdapter.ACTION_REQUEST_ENABLE);
  startActivityForResult(enableIntent, REQUEST_ENABLE_BT);
}
```

Enabling the BLE adapter is a similar process, but has the notable difference of using the `BluetoothManager` to get the adapter instead of just using the `BluetoothAdapter` class. After you create an adapter, you can check to see if the adapter exists and if it is enabled. The following code snippet shows how this is done:

```
private BluetoothAdapter myBluetoothAdapter;

final BluetoothManager bluetoothManager =
    (BluetoothManager) getSystemService(Context.BLUETOOTH_SERVICE);
myBluetoothAdapter = bluetoothManager.getAdapter();
```

```
if (myBluetoothAdapter == null || !myBluetoothAdapter.isEnabled()) {
  Intent enableIntent = new Intent(BluetoothAdapter.ACTION_REQUEST_ENABLE);
  startActivityForResult(enableIntent, REQUEST_ENABLE_BT);
}
```

Now that Bluetooth is enabled and ready for use, it is time to find nearby devices.

Discovering Devices with Bluetooth

If you have not paired with a device before and you are using Bluetooth Classic, you will want to scan for available devices that you can connect with. This can be done by using the startDiscovery() method, which begins a short scan of nearby devices that are currently available for connection. The following code snippet shows the use of a BroadcastReceiver to fire an Intent for Bluetooth devices that are found during the scan:

```
// Scanning for Bluetooth Classic
private final BroadcastReceiver myReceiver = new BroadcastReceiver() {
  public void onReceive(Context context, Intent intent) {
    String action = intent.getAction();
    if (BluetoothDevice.ACTION_FOUND.equals(action)) {
      // a bluetooth device has been found, create an object from the Intent
      BluetoothDevice device =
        intent.getParcelableExtra(BluetoothDevice.EXTRA_DEVICE);
      // Display the name and address of the found device
      mArrayAdapter.add(device.getName() + "\n" + device.getAddress());
    }
  }
};


// Register BroadcastReceiver
IntentFilter filter = new IntentFilter(BluetoothDevice.ACTION_FOUND);
registerReceiver(myReceiver, filter);
```

When you are finished scanning, you should use the cancelDiscovery() method. This allows resources and processor-intensive activities to stop and improve performance. You should also remember to unregister myReciver in the onDestroy() method of your application lifecycle.

If you have already paired with a device, you can save some device resources by getting a list of the previously paired devices and scanning to see if they are available. The following code snippet demonstrates how to retrieve the list of devices:

```
Set<BluetoothDevice> pairedDevices = myBluetoothAdapter.getBondedDevices();
if(pairedDevices.size() > 0) {
  for(BluetoothDevice device : pariedDevices) {
    // add found devices to a view
    myArrayAdapter.add(device.getName() + "\n" + device.getAddress());
  }
}
```

Because BLE devices can behave differently, there is a different method to use when you are scanning for them. The startLeScan() method scans for devices and then uses a callback to display scan results. The following code snippet shows both how to scan and a sample callback method to display the results:

```java
private BluetoothAdapter myBluetoothAdapter;
private boolean myScanning;
private Handler myHandler;

// Stop scanning after 20 seconds
private static final long SCAN_PERIOD = 20000;

private void scanLeDevice(final boolean enable) {
  if (enable) {
    // Stops scanning after a pre-defined scan period.
    myHandler.postDelayed(new Runnable() {
      @Override
      public void run() {
        myScanning = false;
        myBluetoothAdapter.stopLeScan(myLeScanCallback);
      }
    }, SCAN_PERIOD);

    myScanning = true;
    myBluetoothAdapter.startLeScan(myLeScanCallback);
  } else {
    myScanning = false;
    myBluetoothAdapter.stopLeScan(myLeScanCallback);
  }
}


private LeDeviceListAdapter myLeDeviceListAdapter;

// BLE  scan callback
private BluetoothAdapter.LeScanCallback myLeScanCallback =
    new BluetoothAdapter.LeScanCallback() {
  @Override
  public void onLeScan(final BluetoothDevice device, int rssi,
      byte[] scanRecord) {
    runOnUiThread(new Runnable() {
      @Override
      public void run() {
        myLeDeviceListAdapter.addDevice(device);
        myLeDeviceListAdapter.notifyDataSetChanged();
      }
    });
  }
};
```

Connecting via Bluetooth Classic

With Bluetooth Classic communications, one device needs to be the server. Note that a server can have multiple clients and acts as the go-between for any other connected devices. Clients cannot directly communicate with each other, so the server must forward and manage any data that would be shared between multiple clients.

To establish communication, a socket is opened and data is passed. To make sure that data is being passed to the correct client, you must pass the Universally Unique Identifier (UUID) when creating the socket. After the socket is created, the accept() method is used to listen, and, when it's finished, the close() method should be called to close the socket. You should be especially careful with the accept() method as it is blocking and therefore must not run on the main thread. The following code demonstrates how to set up the socket and accept communications as a server:

```
private class AcceptThread extends Thread {
  private final BluetoothServerSocket myServerSocket;

  public AcceptThread() {
    // Create a temp object for use with myServerSocket, because
    // myServerSocket is final
    BluetoothServerSocket tmp = null;
    try {
      // MY_UUID is the app UUID string
      tmp = mBluetoothAdapter.listenUsingRfcommWithServiceRecord(NAME, MY_UUID);
    } catch (IOException e) { }
    myServerSocket = tmp;
  }

  public void run() {
    BluetoothSocket socket = null;
    // make sure myServerSocket is not null
    if (myServerSocket != null) {
      // Use loop to keep the socket open for either error or data returned
      while (true) {
        try {
          socket = myServerSocket.accept();
        } catch (IOException e) {
          break;
        }
        if (socket != null) {
          // use a method to handle returned data in a different thread
          manageConnectedSocket(socket);
          myServerSocket.close();
          break;
        }
      }
```

```
    }
  }

  // This method will close the socket and the thread
  public void cancel() {
    try {
      myServerSocket.close();
    } catch (IOException e) { }
  }
}
```

To connect as a client, you need to create an object containing the BluetoothDevice of the server. You then need to pass a matching UUID that will be used to ensure you are communicating with the correct device. Just like communicating as a server, the connect() method is used to establish a connection and either get data or an error. The following sample code snippet shows the code required to connect as a client:

```
private class ConnectThread extends Thread {
  private final BluetoothSocket mySocket;
  private final BluetoothDevice myDevice;

  public ConnectThread(BluetoothDevice device) {
    // Create a temp object for mySocket, because mySocket is final
    BluetoothSocket tmp = null;
    myDevice = device;

    // Get a BluetoothSocket to connect with the BluetoothDevice
    try {
      // MY_UUID is the app UUID string
      tmp = device.createRfcomySocketToServiceRecord(MY_UUID);
    } catch (IOException e) { }
    mySocket = tmp;
  }

  public void run() {
    // Cancel discovery because it will slow down the connection
    mBluetoothAdapter.cancelDiscovery();

    try {
      // Use the socket to connect or throw an exception
      // This method is blocking
      mySocket.connect();
    } catch (IOException connectException) {
      // Unable to connect, close the socket
      try {
        mySocket.close();
      } catch (IOException closeException) { }
```

```
      return;
    }

    // use a method to handle returned data in a different thread
    manageConnectedSocket(mySocket);
  }

  // This method will close the socket and the thread
  public void cancel() {
    try {
      mySocket.close();
    } catch (IOException e) { }
  }
}
```

Communicating with BLE

As mentioned earlier, BLE makes a slight modification to the exploration and interaction phase of connectivity. Instead of devices being required to be paired or even provide a passcode, devices can be detected and perform a key exchange without interaction. These keys provide an encryption method that can be used to encrypt and decrypt data between the devices without the need of a successful pair between them.

Rather than determine a server and client relationship, you need to connect to the Generic Attribute Profile (GATT) server of the device. This can be done with the connectGatt() method. This method takes a context, a Boolean to determine autoConnect, and a reference to a callback method. This is done as follows:

```
myBluetoothGatt = device.connectGatt(this, false, myGattCallback);
```

The callback method may be invoked in a service or other form of logic. An example of the method being used inside of a service follows:

```
private final BluetoothGattCallback mGattCallback =
new BluetoothGattCallback() {
  @Override
  public void onConnectionStateChange(BluetoothGatt gatt, int status,
    int newState) {
    String intentAction;
    if (newState == BluetoothProfile.STATE_CONNECTED) {
      intentAction = ACTION_GATT_CONNECTED;
      myConnectionState = STATE_CONNECTED;
      broadcastUpdate(intentAction);
      Log.i(TAG, "Connected to GATT server.");
      Log.i(TAG, "Attempting to start service discovery:" +
        gatt.discoverServices());
```

```
    } else if (newState == BluetoothProfile.STATE_DISCONNECTED) {
      intentAction = ACTION_GATT_DISCONNECTED;
      myConnectionState = STATE_DISCONNECTED;
      Log.i(TAG, "Disconnected from GATT server.");
      broadcastUpdate(intentAction);
    }
  }

  @Override
  // New services discovered
  public void onServicesDiscovered(BluetoothGatt gatt, int status) {
    if (status == BluetoothGatt.GATT_SUCCESS) {
      // call an update method to announce service
      broadcastUpdate(ACTION_GATT_SERVICES_DISCOVERED);
    } else {
      Log.w(TAG, "onServicesDiscovered received: " + status);
    }
  }

  @Override
  // Result of a characteristic read operation
  public void onCharacteristicRead(BluetoothGatt gatt,
    BluetoothGattCharacteristic characteristic,
    int status) {
    if (status == BluetoothGatt.GATT_SUCCESS) {
      // call an update method to pass data
      broadcastUpdate(ACTION_DATA_AVAILABLE, characteristic);
    }
  }
};
```

In the instances where the GATT server is connected, or when data is passed, a method named
broadcastUpdate() is called. This method handles the custom logic that you will be processing. The following demonstrates using a StringBuilder to handle the data being passed:

```
private void broadcastUpdate(final String action) {
  final Intent intent = new Intent(action);
  sendBroadcast(intent);
}

private void broadcastUpdate(final String action,
  final BluetoothGattCharacteristic characteristic) {
  final Intent intent = new Intent(action);

  // Format data for HEX as this is not a Heart Rate Measurement Profile
  final byte[] data = characteristic.getValue();
  if (data != null && data.length > 0) {
```

```
    final StringBuilder stringBuilder = new StringBuilder(data.length);
    for(byte byteChar : data)
      stringBuilder.append(String.format("%02X ", byteChar));
    intent.putExtra(EXTRA_DATA, new String(data) + "\n" +
      stringBuilder.toString());
  }
  sendBroadcast(intent);
}
```

To handle the data sent through the Intent, you need to have a BroadcastReceiver set up. This receiver picks up more than just device data; it also listens for the state of the GATT server. By listening for events, you can handle for disconnection, connection, working with data, and handling services. The following is sample code for working with these events:

```
private final BroadcastReceiver mGattUpdateReceiver = new BroadcastReceiver() {
  @Override
  public void onReceive(Context context, Intent intent) {
    final String action = intent.getAction();
    if (BluetoothLeService.ACTION_GATT_CONNECTED.equals(action)) {
      myConnected = true;
      updateConnectionState(R.string.connected);
      invalidateOptionsMenu();
    } else if (BluetoothLeService.ACTION_GATT_DISCONNECTED.equals(action)) {
      myConnected = false;
      updateConnectionState(R.string.disconnected);
      invalidateOptionsMenu();
      clearUI();
    } else if (BluetoothLeService.
      ACTION_GATT_SERVICES_DISCOVERED.equals(action)) {
      // Update the UI for supported services and characteristics
      displayGattServices(mBluetoothLeService.getSupportedGattServices());
    } else if (BluetoothLeService.ACTION_DATA_AVAILABLE.equals(action)) {
      displayData(intent.getStringExtra(BluetoothLeService.EXTRA_DATA));
    }
  }
};
```

With the GATT server connected, you can then loop through BluetoothGattService to find available services and read and write data to and from them. You can also set up a listener for GATT notifications by using your myBluetoothGatt object and using the setCharacteristicNotification() method to inform the local system that a characteristic value has changed. To inform the remote system, you need to get the BluetoothGattDescriptor for the characteristic and use setValue(BluetoothGatt Descriptor.ENABLE_NOTIFICATION_VALUE) to set the value. You then use gatt. writeDescriptor to send the value to the remote system. When onDescriptorWrite in BluetoothGattCallback runs, you are then ready to receive updates. After you complete your setup, you can override the `onCharacteristicChanged()` method to broadcast an update when a GATT notification is available.

When you are finished communicating with a BLE device, use the `close()` method to release the connection. The following is an example of the `close()` method in use:

```
public void close() {
  if (myBluetoothGatt == null) {
    return;
  }
  myBluetoothGatt.close();
  myBluetoothGatt = null;
}
```

Near Field Communication

Near Field Communication (NFC) is a passive technology created by NXP Semiconductors that allows "tags" to be used with NFC-capable devices. It is a radio technology that has a very small operational field. This field is generally about 4cm, but can be as much as 10cm, depending on the radio of the device and the size of the tag.

Unlike Bluetooth beacons, NFC tags do not require a power source. This makes them ideal for use in semi-permanent locations and as a medium to automate tasks or distribute relevant information for a set location.

Information is stored in bits of data in NFC Data Exchange Format (NDEF) messages. Each NDEF message will contain at least one NDEF record. A record will contain the following fields:

- Three-bit type name format (TNF)
- Variable-length type
- Variable-length ID (optional)
- Variable-length payload

The TNF field can contain values that the Android system uses to determine how to handle the information presented in the rest of the NDEF message. The rest of the data is generally contained inside of a physical "tag." However, using technology similar to Android Beam, a device itself may take the role of a physical tag.

Note that not all NFC tags work with all Android devices. This is due to the format and type of NFC tag used compared to the NFC reader hardware inside of the Android device. As defined by the NFC Forum, there are several types of NFC tags:

- **Type 1**: Based on ISO/IEC 14443A, is readable and writeable, can be set to read-only, and has 96 bytes of space but is expandable to 2KB.
- **Type 2**: Based on ISO/IEC 14443A, is readable and writeable, can be set to read-only, and has 48 bytes of space but is expandable to 2KB.

- **Type 3**: Based on (JIS) X 6319-4, comes preconfigured either as readable and writeable or as read-only, and memory can be up to 1MB.

- **Type 4**: Compatible with ISO/IEC 14443, comes preconfigured either as readable and writeable or as read-only, and memory can be up to 32KB.

- **MIFARE Classic**: Compatible with ISO/IEC 14443, is readable and writeable, can be set to read-only, and has either 1KB or 4KB of space available.

These are the most common types of tags available; however, there are NFC tags in circulation that do not conform to the standards of the NFC Forum. These tags are not guaranteed to work with all NFC hardware. Depending on the device manufacturer, you may find that some Android devices can read tags that other devices cannot. The MIFARE classic is an example of a tag that may not be read or written to by some Android devices. This may be important to know because it may confuse some users who change devices and find that a set of tags no longer works with their new device.

Working with NFC in your application requires the use of the NFC permission. To add this permission to your application, you need to open your application manifest XML file and add the following to it:

```
<uses-permission android:name="android.permission.NFC"/>
```

As an extra step, you can also add a `<users-feature />` element to the manifest to have your application filtered by the Google Play store so that devices without NFC cannot download it. This is optional, but may save you from having to deal with upset users. Add the following to your application manifest XML to enable the Google Play filtering:

```
<uses-feature android:name="android.hardware.nfc"  android:required="true" />
```

When a tag is scanned by your device, it reads the data stored in the TNF and determines the MIME type or URI of the tag. The internal tag dispatch system is used to determine whether the tag is compatible, empty, or if it should be opened in a specific app. Determining which app to open relies on an Intent being created and then matched against any matching Activities.

If your app should respond to the Intent, you need to filter for one or more of the following Intents:

- `ACTION_NDEF_DISCOVERED`
- `ACTION_TECH_DISCOVERED`
- `ACTION_TAG_DISCOVERED`

`ACTION_NDEF_DISCOVERED`

To filter for this intent, you can either filter on the MIME type, or on the URI. The following shows a sample of filtering for a MIME type of `text/plain`:

```
<intent-filter>
  <action android:name="android.nfc.action.NDEF_DISCOVERED"/>
  <category android:name="android.intent.category.DEFAULT"/>
  <data android:mimeType="text/plain" />
</intent-filter>
```

Filtering on the URI is similar, but changes out the property of `<data>` element from `android:mimetype` to `android:scheme` with some added properties. The following shows how to filter for a URI of `http://www.android.com/index.html`:

```
<intent-filter>
  <action android:name="android.nfc.action.NDEF_DISCOVERED"/>
  <category android:name="android.intent.category.DEFAULT"/>
 <data android:scheme="http"
       android:host="www.android.com"
       android:pathPrefix="/index.html" />
</intent-filter>
```

ACTION_TECH_DISCOVERED

When filtering on this Intent, you need to create a resource XML file that contains all the technology types you want to monitor. This ensures that when a tag is scanned, your app only opens when the tag contains the technology your app is expecting to work with. This file should reside in the `/res/xml` folder of your project. An example of the XML file follows:

```
<resources xmlns:xliff="urn:oasis:names:tc:xliff:document:1.2">
  <tech-list>
    <tech>android.nfc.tech.IsoDep</tech>
    <tech>android.nfc.tech.NfcA</tech>
    <tech>android.nfc.tech.NfcB</tech>
    <tech>android.nfc.tech.NfcF</tech>
    <tech>android.nfc.tech.NfcV</tech>
    <tech>android.nfc.tech.Ndef</tech>
    <tech>android.nfc.tech.NdefFormatable</tech>
    <tech>android.nfc.tech.MifareClassic</tech>
    <tech>android.nfc.tech.MifareUltralight</tech>
  </tech-list>
</resources>
```

To reference your XML technology list, you need to add a `<meta-data>` tag to your application manifest XML. This will contain the path to your resource list. The following shows an example of the `<intent-filter>` and `<meta-data>` elements needed for working with `ACTION_TECH_DISCOVERED`:

```
<intent-filter>
  <action android:name="android.nfc.action.TECH_DISCOVERED"/>
</intent-filter>
```

```
<meta-data android:name="android.nfc.action.TECH_DISCOVERED"
          android:resource="@xml/nfc_tech_filter" />
```

Note that the resource path used in the `<meta-data>` element uses a property with a value of `@xml/nfc_tech_filter`. This value refers to the file `/res/xml/nfc_tech_filter.xml` in your project.

ACTION_TAG_DISCOVERED

The final Intent, and perhaps the easiest to implement a filter for, is `ACTION_TAG_DISCOVERED`. Because you are not filtering for what type of technology or information the tag contains, you can use the following `<intent-filter>`:

```
<intent-filter>
  <action android:name="android.nfc.action.TAG_DISCOVERED"/>
</intent-filter>
```

Reading and writing information to NFC tags requires you to define your own protocol stack. The following code demonstrates how to work with the fairly common MIFARE Ultralight tag:

```
package com.example.android.nfc;

import android.nfc.Tag;
import android.nfc.tech.MifareUltralight;
import android.util.Log;
import java.io.IOException;
import java.nio.charset.Charset;

public class MifareUltralightTagTester {

  private static final String TAG =
    MifareUltralightTagTester.class.getSimpleName();

  // Write to the tag:
  public void writeTag(Tag tag, String tagText) {
    MifareUltralight ultralight = MifareUltralight.get(tag);
    try {
      ultralight.connect();
      ultralight.writePage(4, "abcd".getBytes(Charset.forName("US-ASCII")));
      ultralight.writePage(5, "efgh".getBytes(Charset.forName("US-ASCII")));
      ultralight.writePage(6, "ijkl".getBytes(Charset.forName("US-ASCII")));
      ultralight.writePage(7, "mnop".getBytes(Charset.forName("US-ASCII")));
    } catch (IOException e) {
      Log.e(TAG, "IOException while closing MifareUltralight", e);
    } finally {
      if (ultralight != null) {
        try {
          ultralight.close();
```

```
      } catch (IOException e) {
        Log.e(TAG, "IOException while closing MifareUltralight", e);
      }
    }
  }
}

// Read the tag:
public String readTag(Tag tag) {
  MifareUltralight mifare = MifareUltralight.get(tag);
  try {
    mifare.connect();
    byte[] payload = mifare.readPages(4);
    return new String(payload, Charset.forName("US-ASCII"));
  } catch (IOException e) {
    Log.e(TAG, "IOException while writing MifareUltralight message", e);
  } finally {
    if (mifare != null) {
      try {
        mifare.close();
      }
      catch (IOException e) {
        Log.e(TAG, "Error closing tag", e);
      }
    }
  }
  return null;
}
}
```

You may be wondering how this code is expected to function in the instance when you have already defined an Intent to trigger when a tag is near the device. Without a solution to this problem, every time you place a tag near your phone, rather than writing it would constantly read the tag. This is where the Foreground Dispatch System comes into play.

The Foreground Dispatch System allows you to hijack an Intent and stop it from going to where it normally would. It requires you to add a PendingIntent in your application's onCreate() method as well as to use disableForegroundDispatch() in the onPause() method and enableForegroundDispatch() in the onResume() method. Finally, you must also create a method that will handle the data from the scanned NFC tag.

The following code snippet shows an example of the code needed to work with the Foreground Dispatch System:

```
@Override
protected void onCreate(Bundle savedInstanceState) {
  // your code for the method here
```

```
PendingIntent pendingIntent = PendingIntent.getActivity(
    this, 0, new Intent(this, getClass())
    .addFlags(Intent.FLAG_ACTIVITY_SINGLE_TOP), 0);

// add an IntentFilter to know what to intercept
IntentFilter ndef = new IntentFilter(NfcAdapter.ACTION_NDEF_DISCOVERED);
try {
  //  This will catch ALL MIME data types
  ndef.addDataType("*/*");
} catch (MalformedMimeTypeException e) {
  throw new RuntimeException("fail", e);
}
intentFiltersArray = new IntentFilter[] {ndef };

// the techListsArray is used to create a list of tech you will support
// this is used when enabling Foreground Dispatch
techListsArray = new String[][] { new String[] { NfcF.class.getName() } };
}


@Override
public void onPause() {
    super.onPause();
    // release to resume default scanning behavior
    myAdapter.disableForegroundDispatch(this);
}

@Override
public void onResume() {
    super.onResume();
    // enable to hijack default scanning behavior
    myAdapter.enableForegroundDispatch(this, pendingIntent, intentFiltersArray,
      techListsArray);
}

public void onNewIntent(Intent intent) {
    Tag tagFromIntent = intent.getParcelableExtra(NfcAdapter.EXTRA_TAG);
    // Logic here to handle tagFromIntent
}
```

Device Sensors

Android provides an API for sensors that device manufacturers may have added to their device.
The following is a list of sensors that are supported by Android 5.0:

- **Accelerometer**: Hardware
- **Ambient temperature**: Hardware
- **Gravity**: Software or hardware
- **Gyroscope**: Hardware
- **Light**: Hardware
- **Linear acceleration**: Software or hardware
- **Magnetic field**: Hardware
- **Pressure**: Hardware
- **Proximity**: Hardware
- **Relative humidity**: Hardware
- **Rotation vector**: Software or hardware

Sensors can be built into the device as sensor hardware, or they may be computed through software calculation. In these instances the values are calculated data taken from other sensors.

Many of these sensors should seem familiar to you, and some have even been leveraged as part of great experiments that have turned into defined standards. For example, the first generation of Cardboard used the magnetic field sensor to determine when an action should be performed. Other sensors are used by the Android system itself without you even realizing it; the proximity sensor is used to turn the screen off when you are taking a phone call.

Note that previous versions of Android do not support all the listed sensors. Note that in some previous versions of Android, an orientation sensor and a temperature sensor were available but have since become deprecated.

Detecting the Available Sensors

Not every sensor that has an API will be included in every device, so you should do your best to offer a fallback solution or to remove options that require the sensor to work.

To see what sensors are available, you should create a SensorManager object. This object will contain all the sensors that are either available or that match a particular set of sensors. The following code snippet shows how to populate the SensorManager object:

```
// create object
private SensorManager mySensorManager;

// in your onCreate or similar method:
mySensorManager = (SensorManager) getSystemService(Context.SENSOR_SERVICE);

// get all device sensors:
List<Sensor> allSensors = mySensorManager.getSensorList(Sensor.TYPE_ALL);
```

```
// get just the proximity sensor(s):
List<Sensor> proxSensors = mySensorManager.getSensorList(Sensor.TYPE_PROXIMITY);
```

In the previous snippet, it may seem confusing that a list is used for what appears to be a single sensor. A list is used because there may be multiple sensors on the device, and some by specific manufacturers that you may want to use. In this case, you could create a logic check that looks for a specific sensor and vendor before allowing the sensor to be used. The following snippet shows this in action:

```
// see if the device has a proximity sensor
if (mySensorManager.getDefaultSensor(Sensor.TYPE_PROXIMITY) != null) {
  List<Sensor> proxSensors =
     mySensorManager.getSensorList(Sensor.TYPE_PROXIMITY);
  // loop through the sensors to find a Samsung version 1 sensor
  for(int i=0; i<proxSensors.size(); i++) {
    if ((proxSensors.get(i).getVendor().contains("Samsung")) &&
       (proxSensors.get(i).getVersion() == 1)) {
      // Success! set a variable to the sensor
      mySensor = proxSensors.get(i);
      break;
    }
  }
}
```

If you can get away with using another sensor, you can modify the previous snippet by adding an else clause that then does another loop through a secondary sensor to determine availability.

> **Note**
>
> If your app must have a specific sensor available in order to function, you can use
> <uses-feature> with the sensor information added in your manifest to add filtering to
> your app via the Google Play store. This helps you avoid bad ratings from users who do
> not meet the system requirements of your app.

After determining that you have sensors available, you need to work with the data they provide.

Reading Sensor Data

To get started reading data, you want to set up an event listener. This can be done by using the SensorEventListener interface and working with the onAccuracyChanged() and onSensorChanged() methods.

Of these two methods, onAccuracyChanged() provides you with the current accuracy setting of the sensor you are working with. This provides a Sensor object with one of the following constants:

- SENSOR_STATUS_UNRELIABLE

- SENSOR_STATUS_ACCURACY_LOW

- SENSOR_STATUS_ACCURACY_MEDIUM

- SENSOR_STATUS_ACCURACY_HIGH

To perform your custom logic, you need to override the method and place your specific logic handling inside. The following is a sample snippet:

```
@Override
public final void onAccuracyChanged(Sensor sensor, int accuracy) {
  // Custom logic goes here for sensor accuracy changes
}
```

The other method, onSensorChanged(), provides you with a SensorEvent object that contains sensor accuracy, a timestamp of data provided, which sensor provided data, and the sensor data. Just like the onAccuracyChanged() method, you will need to override the method to perform your custom logic. The following is a snippet demonstrating the method override:

```
@Override
public final void onSensorChanged(SensorEvent event) {
  // The "event" may return multiple values
  // Create variables to contain event values
  // Perform custom logic based on sensor values
}
```

With custom logic set up, you can now use the SensorManager to register and unregister the event listeners in the onResume() and onPause() methods. When you register the event listener, you need to specify which sensor to listen to as well as the speed or sampling rate of the sensor. To register the event listener, use the following snippet of code:

```
// define the Sensor Manager and Sensor
private SensorManager mySensorManager;
private Sensor mySensor

//... other methods and activity lifecycle methods ...

@Override
protected void onResume() {
  super.onResume();
  mySensorManager.registerListener(this, mySensor,
    SensorManager.SENSOR_DELAY_NORMAL);
}
```

Notice the use of SENSOR_DELAY_NORMAL for the sensor sampling speed; this has a default value of 200,000 microseconds. You can set your own value in microseconds, or you can use the following values:

- **SENSOR_DELAY_GAME**: 20,000-microsecond delay

- **SENSOR_DELAY_UI**: 60,000-microsecond delay

- **SENSOR_DELAY_FASTEST**: 0-microsecond delay

Some sensors happily take a 0-microsecond delay but will not actually return information at that rate. They offer information back at the fastest available speed, however. You should also keep in mind that using a lower delay value creates an increase on power usage, thus resulting in reduced battery life for the user.

You should unregister sensor listeners when you are finished with them, including when pausing your application. Failure to unregister the sensors in use causes them to continue to collect data and use power. It should also be noted that unless a partial wake lock has been invoked, sensor collection will stop when the screen is turned off. An example of how to unregister the listener in the `onPause()` event lifecycle is shown next:

```
// define the SensorManager
private SensorManager mySensorManager;

// ... other methods and activity lifecycle methods ...

@Override
protected void onPause() {
  super.onPause();
  mySensorManager.unregisterListener(this);
}
```

Summary

In this chapter, you learned about using Bluetooth with your application. You learned that two standards of Bluetooth are available. Older devices use Bluetooth Classic, and newer devices can leverage the new features of BLE.

You also learned about NFC and the types of tags that can be used. You learned about working with NDEF and TNF records on NFC tags. You also learned how to detect support for NFC in the device and that filtering can be applied to have your application only work with devices that have NFC support. You then learned how to read and write information using the Foreground Dispatch System and how it is leveraged to allow you to intercept triggered Intents. This enables you to read and write data without worrying about other applications taking the focus away from the work you are doing with an NFC tag.

Finally, you learned about working with various device sensors that may be in a device. You learned how to detect sensors that are available as well as how to set up event listeners. You learned how to read data from the sensors by overriding the `onAccuracyChanged()` and `onSensorChanged()` methods. Just as you learned that registering the events is important, you also learned about the importance of unregistering sensor event listeners to not only stop collecting data, but to save on wasting device power.

## 14

Managing Account Data

Android has at one time or another been labeled as a difficult system to work with due to the fragmentation of the system. While detractors to the platform are quick to point out the potential flaws of working with a myriad of devices and hardware platforms, part of the strength of Android is the abundance of APIs and libraries available to back up, restore, and synchronize data. This allows users to move from one device to another without missing their information and applications. In this chapter, you learn about many of the Google-provided services as well as how to integrate with other services to handle the transportation and synchronization of user data.

Getting Accounts

Many Android devices require users to create or use an existing Google account to sign in and start using them. Some devices run customized versions of Android and do not require a Google account to be used; in these instances, the device provider implements their own user-authentication process.

When working with Android devices that have users sign in with a Google user account, you can request some information from the user profile. This is accomplished by leveraging the `AccountManager` class and adding a couple of permissions to your application.

Starting with the permissions, you will need to add the following to your application manifest XML:

```
<uses-permission android:name="android.permission.GET_ACCOUNTS"></uses-permission>
<uses-permission android:name="android.permission.AUTHENTICATE_ACCOUNTS">
</uses-permission>
```

With the permissions in place, you can now use the `AccountManager` to retrieve the accounts that are available on the device.

> **Note**
>
> The `AccountManager` gives you the ability to find all accounts on the device. This allows you to work with more than a Google account, and will also allow you to work with multiple Google accounts.

The following shows a snippet of code that uses the `AccountManager` to create an object that is then stored in a list and iterated over for a matching Google account:

```
AccountManager myAccountManager = (AccountManager)
  getSystemService(ACCOUNT_SERVICE);
Account[] list = myAccountManager.getAccounts();
String googleAccount = "No Google Account";

for(Account account: list) {
  if(account.type.equalsIgnoreCase("com.google")) {
    googleAccount = account.name;
    break;
  }
}
// set text view to googleAccount
TextView tv = (TextView) findViewById(R.id.myTextView);
tv.setText(googleAccount);
```

Note that for demonstration purposes, a `String` named `googleAccount` is created and is later populated during iteration through `list`. It is populated based on looking for a specific type of account (in this case, `com.google`). This means that any account that is connected to Google will be returned. Because this is just a sample snippet looking for a specific account, you should be aware that some users may have more than one account tied to their device.

> **Tip**
>
> If you're working with an Android emulator and are having trouble getting the snippet to work, make sure you are using an emulator that was built using a target that supports the Google APIs and is a minimum of API level 5.

You can also use the `getAccountsByType()` and `getAccountsByTypeAndFeatures()` methods to return objects that are more specific to what you need. If you are using an account for authentication purposes, remember to check that the account exists in the list of returned accounts. Failure to do so will result in the app requesting an authorization for an account that doesn't exist and will give an error of undefined.

Android Backup Service

The Android Backup Service is provided for applications that need to store a small amount of user data. This is a great solution for saving preferences, scores, notes, and similar resources that should be transferable between devices or during device restoration.

> **Note**
>
> The maximum storage you are allowed to use with the Android Backup Service is 1MB per account per application. The service is also not intended for use as a data-synchronization service, but instead as a means to restore application data.

To use Android Backup Services, you must register your application with Google to receive a Backup Service Key. At the time of writing, the URL for this is http://code.google.com/android/ backup/signup.html. Registration is a short process that requires you to read and agree to a terms of service agreement with Google. After you read and accept the terms, you are asked to provide the package name of your application. If you are developing multiple applications, you need to agree to the terms and enter the package name for each application.

After registering, you are given an XML element that you need to place in your application Manifest XML as a child of the `<application>` element. The following demonstrates what a generated key looks like:

```
<meta-data android:name="com.google.android.backup.api_key"
    android:value="ABcDe1FGHij2KlmN3oPQRs4TUvW5xYZ" />
```

While you are still working inside of the application manifest XML file, you need to add a parameter of `androidbackupAgent` to the `<application>` element. The value of this property should match the name you use for your backup agent. The following gives an example of using `MyBackupAgent` for the name of the backup agent:

```
<application android:label="MyApp" android:backupAgent="MyBackupAgent">
```

Take specific notice of the naming convention used on the backup agent. Rather than using camel-case to signify a variable, it uses upper-camel-case or PascalCase formatting. This is because you need to create a class of that name and extend the `BackupAgentHelper`. It should also implement an override for the `onCreate()` method. The following snippet shows a demonstration class:

```
import android.app.backup.BackupAgentHelper;
import android.app.backup.FileBackupHelper;

public class MyBackupAgent extends BackupAgentHelper {

  // set the name(s) of a preference file to backup
  static final String HIGH_SCORES_FILENAME = "scores";
  static final String INVENTORY_FILENAME = "inventory";

  // create a key to identify the backup data set
  static final String FILES_BACKUP_KEY = "mybackupfileskey";

  // allocate the helper and add it to the backup agent
  @Override
  void onCreate() {
    FileBackupHelper helper = new FileBackupHelper(this,
```

```
                HIGH_SCORES_FILENAME, INVENTORY_FILENAME);
        addHelper(FILES_BACKUP_KEY, helper);
    }
}
```

To back up multiple files, two strings are created and set to the filenames that need to be backed up. The strings are then passed as arguments to the `FileBackupHelper()` method. The `FILES_BACKUP_KEY` will be used when restoration is needed. Because the value is a "key," it does not have to be lower-, camel-, upper-, or mixed-case.

Files are not the only resources you can back up from your application. If you want to back up application preferences, you can use the `SharedPreferencesBackupHelper`. Using the `SharedPreferencesBackupHelper` is almost identical to using the `FileBackupHelper`. The following class demonstrates how preferences are backed up:

```
import android.app.backup.BackupAgentHelper;
import android.app.backup.SharedPreferencesBackupHelper;

public class MyBackupAgent extends BackupAgentHelper {
// set the names of the preferences to back up
// these should match values used in getSharedPreferences()

  static final String PREFS_OPTIONS = "optionsprefs";
  static final String PREFS_SCORES = "highscores";

// create a key to use with your preferences backup
  static final String PREFS_BACKUP_KEY = "myprefsbackupkey";

// allocate the helper and add it the backup agent
  void onCreate() {
    SharedPreferencesBackupHelper helper =
        new SharedPreferencesBackupHelper(this, PREFS_OPTIONS, PREFS_SCORES);
    addHelper(PREFS_BACKUP_KEY, helper);
  }
}
```

To begin a backup process, you need to use the `BackupManager` and the `dataChanged()` method to request a backup. After the request happens, the backup manager calls the `onBackup()` method and the backup will be performed. The following shows the snippet that is used to create the backup request:

```
public void requestBackup() {
  BackupManager bm = new BackupManager(this);
  bm.dataChanged();
}
```

Note that in the class where you place that, you also need to use `import android.app.backup.BackupManager`. You should also remember that the backup service is not run "on demand," but you should still call it whenever data is changed so that a user has a better chance at having the most up-to-date information saved.

Using Google Drive Android API

Many Android users have a device that is compatible with Google services that gives them access to Google Drive. Google Drive is a storage service that works with other Google services, including Google Play Services. This allows users to store many gigabytes of data for free with an option for them to buy more space if needed.

As apps have become more sophisticated, users have started to increase their dependency on being able to move and access data from wherever they are, on whatever device they have. To make things more complex, users expect to be able to not only read data, they expect to be able to write data and have that data be saved without having to worry about getting in an elevator, taking a subway, or going through a tunnel. In each of these scenarios there is a chance that connectivity will drop and a potential write or save operation will fail due to the sudden loss of connectivity.

The Google Drive Android API allows you to overcome these issues by offering access to user data through an Android native picker, giving users transparent offline synchronization for data to maintain write integrity, and by working with devices running Gingerbread and above.

To get started implementing the API into your app, you need to register your app in the Google Developers console. This is the console that allows access to Google Services and is separate from the Play Store console (https://console.developers.google.com).

If you are working with a new application that has not been registered in the Developers Console, you can register your application and the Developers Console walks you through creating and signing it.

If you have already registered your app, you can select it and use the APIs & Auth menu to select APIs and find Drive API in the list. This will then allow you to turn on access for your application. Note that you will need to generate and sign your .apk file. If you need to submit authorized requests, you have to add OAuth 2.0 credentials to your app and use the Developer Console to generate a client ID.

Once you have all of your credentials set up and access to the Drive API enabled, you are ready to create a client in your Android application to start accessing data. This is done by building a client in the `onCreate()` method of an Activity and connecting it in the `onStart()` Activity. If a user has never authenticated when using the application, the `onConnectionFailed()` callback method will be invoked. This allows the user to authorize access to their data from within the app. The following snippet demonstrates the creation using the Builder pattern, the connection of the client, and a snippet for the `onConnectionFailed()` callback method:

```
@Override
public void onCreate(Bundle savedInstanceState) {
  super.onCreate(savedInstance);
```

```
myGoogleApiClient = new GoogleApiClient.Builder(this)
    .addApi(Drive.API)
    .addScope(Drive.SCOPE_FILE)
    .addConnectionCallbacks(this)
    .addOnConnectionFailedListener(this)
    .build();
}


@Override
protected void onStart() {
  super.onStart();
  myGoogleApiClient.connect();
}


@override
public void onConnectionFailed(ConnectionResult connectionResult) {
  if (connectionResult.hasResolution()) {
    try {
      connectionResult
          .startResolutionForResult(this, RESOLVE_CONNECTION_REQUEST_CODE);
    } catch (IntentSender.SendIntentException e) {
      // The app cannot resolve the connection, add error logic here
    }
  } else {
    GooglePlayServicesUtil
        .getErrorDialog(connectionResult.getErrorCode(), this, 0).show();
  }
}
```

If the user is prompted to authenticate their app, then the onActivityResult() method for the activity will be called. This also passes back an argument that should be checked to match RESULT_OK; if it does, the client will need to be connected again. The following snippet shows an example of overriding the method to handle this scenario:

```
@Override
protected void onActivityResult(final int requestCode,
                                final int resultCode, final Intent data) {
  switch (requestCode) {
    // put your cases here
    case RESOLVE_CONNECTION_REQUEST_CODE:
        if (resultCode == RESULT_OK) {
          myGoogleApiClient.connect();
        }
        break;
    // put other cases or default here
  }
}
```

After your connection has been made and authenticated, you can use the `DriveFile` interface to read and write files. Due to the architecture of Drive, there are essentially two copies of every file you work with—one that is created locally and one that is stored out in Drive. Using the `DriveFile.open()` method allows you to check locally for a file and, if it's not found, attempt to retrieve it from the Drive service.

> ## Note
>
> If you intend to retrieve files only for reading, you can use an `InputStream`. If you intend to only save a file, you can use an `OutputStream`. If you intend to do both, you should use `ParcelFileDescriptor` because it can handle both reading and writing. You need to use a `ParcelFileDescriptor` when appending to a file because `WRITE_ONLY` truncates the file you are writing to.

When you retrieve a file from Drive, a resource called `DriveContents` will be available as a temporary copy of the file you are working with. This resource does require that you verify that it was able to get the file you want to work with. The following snippet shows a request made for a file as well as the process of verifying the contents of the `DriveContents` resource:

```
// either create a file object, or use Drive.DriveApi.getFile()
// MODE_READ_ONLY signifies working with an InputStream
file.open(myGoogleApiClient, DriveFile.MODE_READ_ONLY, null)
    .setResultCallback(contentsOpenedCallback);

ResultCallback<DriveContentsResult> contentsOpenedCallback =
    new ResultCallback<DriveContentsResult>() {
  @Override
  public void onResult(DriveContentsResult result) {
    if (!result.getStatus().isSuccess()) {
      // File cannot be opened, display appropriate message
      return;
    }
    // set contents to the binary return
    DriveContents contents = result.getDriveContents();
  }
};
```

To read the binary contents that were just opened, you need to create a `BufferedReader`, a `StringBuilder`, and a `String`. When you are finished working with the file, remember to close the file with either `DriveContents.commit` or `DriveContents.discard`. The following snippet shows how to convert the binary data into a `String` as well as how to close the file:

```
// add this snippet where you are working with the binary read
DriveContents contents = result.getDriveContents();
BufferedReader reader =
    new BufferedReader(new InputStreamReader(contents.getInputStream()));
StringBuilder builder = new StringBuilder();
```

```
String line;
while ((line = reader.readLine()) != null) {
    builder.append(line);
}
// Create a String to house the contents
String contentsAsString = builder.toString();
// Perform logic with the string

// The following will close the file
contents.commit(mGoogleApiClient, null)
    .setResultCallback(new ResultCallback<Status>() {
  @Override
  public void onResult(Status result) {
    // handle based on result status
  }
});
```

Writing to files is similar to reading from them in that you need to retrieve and open the file you want to write to, perform the write, and then close the file. Remember that you will need to use a `ParcelFileDescriptor` when you are appending to a file rather than using an `OutputStream`. The following snippet demonstrates opening a file to work with, appending a `String` message to the file and then closing the file:

```
// create a file object, use Drive.DriveApi.getFile(), or use DriveContents
file.open(mGoogleApiClient, DriveFile.MODE_WRITE_ONLY, null)
    .setResultCallback(new ResultCallback<DriveContentsResult>() {
  @Override
  public void onResult(DriveContentsResult result) {
    if (!result.getStatus().isSuccess()) {
      // File cannot be opened, display appropriate message
      return;
    }
    DriveContents contents = result.getDriveContents();
  }
});

// append a string to the file that was opened
try {
  ParcelFileDescriptor parcelFileDescriptor =
      contents.getParcelFileDescriptor();
  FileInputStream fileInputStream =
      new FileInputStream(parcelFileDescriptor.getFileDescriptor());
  // read to the end of the file
  fileInputStream.read(new byte[fileInputStream.available()]);

  // append to the file
  FileOutputStream fileOutputStream = new FileOutputStream(parcelFileDescriptor
```

```
      .getFileDescriptor());
   Writer writer = new OutputStreamWriter(fileOutputStream);
   writer.write("Howdy World!");
   writer.flush();
} catch (IOException e) {
   e.printStackTrace();
}

// close the file
contents.commit(mGoogleApiClient, null)
    .setResultCallback(new ResultCallback<Status>() {
   @Override
   public void onResult(Status result) {
        // handle based on response status
   }
});
```

Once a file has been closed, it will be flagged to synchronize with the Drive service. The synchronization service is run automatically and will perform connectivity checks to ensure that any files that need to be updated will complete when the network is available and that this operation performs successfully.

Using Google Play Games Services

Google Play Games is a service that allows game developers to create achievements, track login information, grant user permissions, and add a social aspect to gaming that allows you to provide smoother and more addictive gameplay to your users. There is a lot to learn and cover to implement all of the available services, and in this section we are going to focus on what has been the most troublesome aspect of handling user data.

There has long been an issue of figuring out how to provide a quality "save" experience for users who get a new device or have multiple devices. When users only have one device, saving game data is a manageable affair. As a developer, you could save to the local file system or database and you were done.

The problem with this strategy is that many users have more than one device. They may not actually "own" multiple devices, but within the life of your app they may upgrade or change devices. When this happens, a user does not want to spend more of their time doing what they had already done previously to get back to where they were in your game.

Developers have ended up using a variety of strategies to save, restore, and synchronize game data between devices. Any implementation is better than none, but to ease this particular burden, Google has provided a free service that can help you handle this process with Google Play Games Services.

To use Google Play Games Services, you will need to log in to the Google Play Developer Console and add your name to it. This includes a description of your game as well as the name of it. You also need to make sure you have credentials set up for your game. This usually includes creating an OAuth client and linking it to the console.

Google has written up a guide that you can follow, with detailed steps on how this initial setup is done. It is also the best place to go to for reference because it is updated to reflect what the Google Play Developer Console looks like and how it is used. Visit this guide at https://developers.google.com/games/services/console/enabling.

With your app registered in the console, you can now access all of the features of Google Play Games Services. For examples on all of the features you can use, you should visit the samples code repository that is hosted on GitHub at https://github.com/playgameservices/android-basic-samples.

Working with Saved Games

To add game saving through Google Play Games Services, you need to provide only two things:

- A binary blob of game data
- Metadata containing Google-provided data as well as data you provide, which includes an ID, name, description, last modified timestamp, time played, and a cover image

Note that you are given 3MB of data for the binary data blob, and 800KB for your cover image. The cover image is used to help the player visually understand what and where they were in your game. The cover image should be something to not only show your game but should be something to help entice the player to continue playing in case they haven't played the game in a while.

The data and cover image are stored in the Drive account for the user playing the game. This folder is hidden from them and contains the game blob and cover image. Due to the Drive service being used, when you create your Google Services API client, you will need to include Games and Drive as part of the client. The following shows an example of creating the API using the builder method that allows access to Google Plus, Google Games, and Google Drive:

```
@Override
public void onCreate(Bundle savedInstanceState) {
    // create Services API with Play, Games, and Drive access
    myGoogleApiClient = new GoogleApiClient.Builder(this)
        .addConnectionCallbacks(this)
        .addOnConnectionFailedListener(this)
        .addApi(Plus.API).addScope(Plus.SCOPE_PLUS_LOGIN)
        .addApi(Games.API).addScope(Games.SCOPE_GAMES)
        .addApi(Drive.API).addScope(Drive.SCOPE_APPFOLDER)
        .build();
}
```

In code, a game is referred to as a `Snapshot`. This is the combination of the required blob and metadata for the saved game. To save the `Snapshot`, you need to obtain a reference to it, use the `open()` and `writeBytes()` methods to write current game data, and then use the `commitAndClose()` method to save the `Snapshot`. The following snippet shows you how these methods are used to save a game:

```
private PendingResult<Snapshots.CommitSnapshotResult>
  writeSnapshot(Snapshot snapshot,
  byte[] data, Bitmap coverImage, String desc) {

  // get the contents of the snapshot and write it
  snapshot.getSnapshotContents().writeBytes(data);

  // set the metadata change
  SnapshotMetadataChange metadataChange = new SnapshotMetadataChange.Builder()
  .setCoverImage(coverImage)
  .setDescription(desc)
  .build();

  // commit the snapshot
  return Games.Snapshots.commitAndClose(myGoogleApiClient, snapshot, metadataChange);
}
```

To load a saved game, you should use an asynchronous method to move the process from the main thread. This can be done using `AsyncTask` with an override to the `doInBackground()` method. You can then call the `load()` method:

```
private byte[] mySaveGameData;

void loadFromSnapshot() {
  // Consider using a loading message or widget here

  AsyncTask<Void, Void, Integer> task -
      new AsyncTask<Void, Void, Integer>() {
    @Override
    protected Integer doInBackground(Void... params) {
      /*
       * Open the saved game using myCurrentSaveName
       * using "true" as the third argument of open()
       * will create a save game if one has not already been created
       */
      Snapshots.OpenSnapshotResult result = Games.Snapshots
          .open(myGoogleApiClient, myCurrentSaveName, true).await();

      // did the open method work?
      if (result.getStatus().isSuccess()) {
        Snapshot snapshot = result.getSnapshot();
        try {
          // read the byte content of the saved game.
          mySaveGameData = snapshot.getSnapshotContents().readFully();
```

```
        } catch (IOException e) {
          // Logging the IO error
          Log.e(TAG, "Error while reading Snapshot.", e);
        }
      } else {
        // Logging the status code error
        Log.e(TAG, "Error while loading: " +
            result.getStatus().getStatusCode());
      }
      return result.getStatus().getStatusCode();
    }

    @Override
    protected void onPostExecute(Integer status) {
      // Close the loading message or progress dialog if used
      // and update the UI
    }
  };
  task.execute();
}
```

If you do not want to implement your own design for handling game loading, you can use an out-of-the-box solution that is provided by the Google Play Games Services. This is launched by using two methods that call an Intent that displays any saved games the user has, and may allow the user to delete or create a new saved game based on arguments passed to the methods. The following snippet demonstrates how to show the Saved Games UI as well as how to use the onActivityResult() method to handle creating a new save or loading an existing one:

```
// display the Saved Games UI
// RC_SAVED_GAMES is set to an int to identify it
private static final int RC_SAVED_GAMES = 1003;

private void showSavedGamesUI() {
  // set number of saves to show
  int maxNumberOfSavedGamesToShow = 3;
  // args 3 and 4 represent allowAddButton and allowDelete
  Intent savedGamesIntent =
      Games.Snapshots.getSelectSnapshotIntent(myGoogleApiClient,
      "See Saved Games", true, true, maxNumberOfSavedGamesToShow);
  startActivityForResult(savedGamesIntent, RC_SAVED_GAMES);
}

// save a new game or load an existing one
// start by creating a temp snapshot
private String myCurrentSaveName = "snapshotTemp";
```

```
// this callback is triggered after startActivityForResult() is called
// from the showSavedGamesUI() method.

@Override
protected void onActivityResult(int requestCode, int resultCode,
    Intent intent) {

  if (intent != null) {
    if (intent.hasExtra(Snapshots.EXTRA_SNAPSHOT_METADATA)) {
      // load a snapshot
      SnapshotMetadata snapshotMetadata = (SnapshotMetadata)
      intent.getParcelableExtra(Snapshots.EXTRA_SNAPSHOT_METADATA);
      // avoid hardcoding names, use the name from the snapshot
      myCurrentSaveName = snapshotMetadata.getUniqueName();

      // continue logic here to load the game data from the Snapshot

    } else if (intent.hasExtra(Snapshots.EXTRA_SNAPSHOT_NEW)) {
      // Create a new snapshot, name it with a unique string
      String unique = new BigInteger(281, new Random()).toString(13);
      myCurrentSaveName = "snapshotTemp-" + unique;

      // continue the create the new snapshot logic
    }
  }
}
```

If you need further references on how to implement this logic into your game, visit the package docs at https://developers.google.com/android/reference/com/google/android/gms/games/snapshot/package-summary. You can also view the "SavedGames" code sample at https://github.com/playgameservices/android-basic-samples/tree/master/BasicSamples/SavedGames. This sample also includes how to migrate data from the old Cloud Save service to the Saved Games service that is part of the Google Play Games Services.

Summary

In this chapter, you learned the basics of working with account details by using the AccountManager. This was done by specifying a package name that matched some Google accounts, and a name for the user account was retrieved. You also learned that there may be multiple accounts on a device and that you should get them all and either return a list or allow the user to choose which one to use.

You also learned about the Android Backup Service. This service allows you to make small backups that will restore user settings when they have to wipe, hard-reset, or set up a new device. You learned that this is not a suitable service for data synchronization, but is a helpful and free solution for minor data restoration needs.

You learned about the Google Drive Android API that can be used to load files to and from a device using Google Drive. You learned about the benefits of using this service because it allows for a seamless integration for mobile users who are constantly moving in and out of data or network range. You also learned how to read and write files using this API.

Finally, you were shown a portion of the Google Play Games Services. These services offer a lot of methods and libraries to help make game development easier. You learned how to save games using a snapshot, how to load a game, and how to use the built-in UI solution for performing both saves and loading games to a device.

## 15

Google Play Services

Google Play services is a collection of APIs provided from Google that help developers take advantage of data, calculations, and methods to create better applications. This is done by allowing you to tap into the vast data sets and communication assets that Google has integrated into its many services.

In this chapter, you learn how to add Google Play Services to your application, create a client to communicate with the services, and gain exposure to some of the APIs that are bundled in Google Play Services.

Adding Google Play Services

If you have never used Google Play Services in an application before, you need to do some initial setup. You should start by opening the Android SDK manager and downloading the most current version of the Google Play Services. If you do not see this in the manager, you may need to scroll to the bottom of the list and expand the Tools section.

If you are inside of Android Studio 1.3+, when you use the icon to open the SDK Manager, the preferences window will open with Android SDK selected from the menu on the left. You will then need to click the SDK Tools tab and click the checkbox next to it. Note that you may receive a message that not all packages can be installed. When this happens, click the button to launch the standalone SDK Manager, and then you should be able to check the box and download the required packages.

> **Note**
>
> If you have already created an AVD to use for testing your application, make sure it supports the Google APIs. If you use an AVD that doesn't support the Google APIs, your application will not function properly and may cause an ANR or crash at runtime.

After you download Google Play Services, you are then ready to alter your application Gradle file. Open the `build.gradle` file for your application module. This is located in your project's

`ApplicationDirectory/app/build.gradle`. In the Dependencies section, add the following line:

```
dependencies {
  // other dependencies may be listed here
  compile 'com.google.android.gms:play-services:7.8.0'
}
```

Note that you should use the most current version available; in this example, the version 7.8.0 is used, but it will increment as newer versions of Google Play Services are released.

After you make the edit, you need to re-sync your Gradle build file. This can be done by clicking the Sync Project with Gradle Files message that appears at the top of the editor screen. If you do not see the banner, you can use the context menu and click Tools, Android, Sync Project with Gradle Files.

When the build finishes, you are ready to begin using Google Play Services in your application.

If you have a large project with many imports and/or heavy framework usage, you may receive an error when you attempt to compile. This is due to a limit of having only 65,536 methods in your application. You can selectively compile just the portions of Google Play Services by calling them as a dependency rather than using all of them, like so:

```
// use this
compile 'com.google.android.gms:play-services-fitness:7.8.0'
// instead of this
compile 'com.google.android.gms:play-services:7.8.0'
```

Table 15.1 lists the currently available services.

Table 15.1   **Available Google Play Services**

Google Play Service	Dependency
Google+	com.google.android.gms:play-services-plus:7.8.0
Google Account Login	com.google.android.gms:play-services-identity:7.8.0
Google Actions, Base Client Library	com.google.android.gms:play-services-base:7.8.0
Google App Indexing	com.google.android.gms:play-services-appindexing:7.8.0
Google App Invites	com.google.android.gms:play-services-appinvite:7.8.0
Google Analytics	com.google.android.gms:play-services-analytics:7.8.0
Google Cast	com.google.android.gms:play-services-cast:7.8.0
Google Cloud Messaging	com.google.android.gms:play-services-gcm:7.8.0
Google Drive	com.google.android.gms:play-services-drive:7.8.0
Google Fit	com.google.android.gms:play-services-fitness:7.8.0

Google Play Service	Dependency
Google Location, Activity Recognition, Places	com.google.android.gms:play-services-location:7.8.0
Google Maps	com.google.android.gms:play-services-maps:7.8.0
Google Mobile Ads	com.google.android.gms:play-services-ads:7.8.0
Mobile Vision	com.google.android.gms:play-services-vision:7.8.0
Google Nearby	com.google.android.gms:play-services-nearby:7.8.0
Google Panorama Viewer	com.google.android.gms:play-services-panorama:7.8.0
Google Play Game services	com.google.android.gms:play-services-games:7.8.0
SafetyNet	com.google.android.gms:play-services-safetynet:7.8.0
Google Wallet	com.google.android.gms:play-services-wallet:7.8.0
Android Wear	com.google.android.gms:play-services-wearable:7.8.0

Using Google API Client

The easiest way to connect to Google Play Services is to use the Google API Client. In previous chapters, the Google API Client was used to establish connections using the builder pattern. The builder pattern is preferred because it allows you to quickly add and remove services as well as optimize the creation of the connections and resources needed.

The following snippet is a refresher on how to use the builder pattern to create a `GoogleApiClient`:

```
GoogleApiClient myGoogleApiClient = new GoogleApiClient.Builder(this)
    .addApi(Drive.API)
    .addScope(Drive.SCOPE_FILE)
    .addConnectionCallbacks(this)
    .addOnConnectionFailListener(this)
    .build();
```

To complete a connection, not only must you add the API you want to use, but you must also implement a callback interface for `ConnectionCallbacks` and `OnConnectionFailedListener`. These are needed to protect the application from crashing when the services are unavailable or when the device running the app does not support using Google services.

There are three methods you can override in your Activity that allow you to place logic to deal with connection, suspension, and failure. Each method gives you an opportunity to place your logic and even recover from a potential error.

If you encounter an error that triggers the `onConnectionFailed()` method, attempt to resolve the error by calling the `hasResolution()` method on the `ConnectionResult` object. This allows you to have the user fix what is wrong and attempt the connection again. If a resolution is not available, use `GoogleApiAvailability.getErrorDialog()`, which gives information and a potential solution (such as updating Google Play Services on their device) to the connection error.

Listing 15.1 demonstrates using the `onConnected()`, `onConnectionSuspended`, and `onConnectionFailed` methods as well as building a dialog for the user to interact with when an error occurs.

Listing 15.1 Override Methods Used when Connecting to Google Play Services

```
// set up variables used when connection failure occurs
// requestCode to pass with activity - cannot be a negative number
private static final int REQUEST_RESOLVE_ERROR = 1331;
// tag for the error dialog fragment
private static final String DIALOG_ERROR = "dialog_error";
// set a boolean to track if error resolution is happening
private boolean myResolvingError = false;

@Override
public void onConnected(Bundle connectionHint) {
  // the connection is good, add logic for success here
}

@Override
public void onConnectionSuspended(int cause) {
  // there was a connection, but it has now failed
  // disable any components that rely on the connection working here
}

@Override
public void onConnectionFailed(ConnectionResult result) {
  // the connection has failed, this may be for one or more of the
  // APIs you are attempting to use with the GoogleApiClient
  // is an error currently being resolved?
  if (myResolvingError) {
    // an error is already in process
    return;
  } else if (result.hasResolution()) {
    try {
      myResolvingError = true;
      result.startResolutionForResult(this, REQUEST_RESOLVE_ERROR);
    } catch (SendIntentException e) {
    // problem connecting to resolution intent, try connecting again
      myGoogleApiClient.connect();
    }
  } else {
    // cannot use hasResolution(), call showErrorDialog() to build a dialog
```

```
      // and display contents of GoogleApiAvailability.getErrorDialog()
      showErrorDialog(result.getErrorCode());
      myResolvingError = true;
    }
}


private void showErrorDialog(int errorCode) {
  // create a fragment for the error dialog
  ErrorDialogFragment dialogFragment = new ErrorDialogFragment();
  // create a bundle to pass the error arguments
  Bundle args = new Bundle();
  args.putInt(DIALOG_ERROR, errorCode);
  // set the arguments into the dialogFragment and then show it
  dialogFragment.setArguments(args);
  dialogFragment.show(getSupportFragmentManager(), "errordialog");
}

// this is called from ErrorDialogFragment on dialog dismiss
public void onDialogDismissed() {
  myResolvingError = false;
}

// the dialog fragment to display the error
public static class ErrorDialogFragment extends DialogFragment {
  public ErrorDialogFragment() { }

  @Override
  public Dialog onCreateDialog(Bundle savedInstanceState) {
    // get error code and return the dialog
    int errorCode = this.getArguments().getInt(DIALOG_ERROR);
    return GoogleApiAvailability.getInstance().getErrorDialog(
      this.getActivity(), errorCode, REQUEST_RESOLVE_ERROR);
  }

  @Override
  public void onDismiss(DialogInterface dialog) {
    // on dismiss call onDialogDismissed to set myResolvingError to false
    ((MyActivity) getActivity()).onDialogDismissed();
  }
}

// user has resolved issue onActivityResult callback is then called
@Override
protected void onActivityResult(int requestCode, int resultCode,
    Intent data) {
  if (requestCode == REQUEST_RESOLVE_ERROR) {
```

```
      myResolvingError = false;
      // check if the error is now OK and that a connection has not
      // already been established or attempted
      if (resultCode == RESULT_OK) {
        if (!myGoogleApiClient.isConnecting() &&
            !myGoogleApiClient.isConnected()) {
          myGoogleApiClientConnect();
        }
      }
    }
  }
}
```

The listing should be fairly well documented with inline comments; however, you should take special note of the Boolean `myResolvingError` that is used to keep track of the connection state. It should also be noted that Google Play Services have an `ErrorDialogFragment` already defined so that you do not need to define it again.

It can be easy to forget that a user may decide to "pocket" his device or rotate his screen in the middle of a connection being established. When this happens, the Activity is restarted and any connections may be left in a connecting state. By saving the value of the Boolean inside of `onSaveInstanceState()`, you can overcome this particular issue.

The following shows how this can be saved in the `onSaveInstanceState()` method and restored during the `onCreate()` method:

```
private static final String STATE_RESOLVING_ERROR = "resolving_error";

@Override
protected void onSaveInstanceState(Bundle outState) {
  super.onSaveInstanceState(outState);
  outState.putBoolean(STATE_RESOLVING_ERROR, myResolvingError);
}

@Override
protected void onCreate(Bundle savedInstanceState) {
  super.onCreate(savedInstanceState);
  // the rest of your onCreate code should be here

  myResolvingError = savedInstanceState != null
    && savedInstanceState.getBoolean(STATE_RESOLVING_ERROR, false);
}
```

Now that you know how to create a connection using the `GoogleApiClient`, it is time to see some examples of using Google Play Services.

Google Fit

Google Fit is part of Google Play Services. It allows you to use the sensors in a device mixed with the computational heavy powers of Google to track the activity of a user. What makes Google Fit great is that it can use information from all of the devices a person may have and that are deemed the most accurate. This makes the only fitness "wearable" that a user needs the one they usually always have with them.

Note that Google Fit is actually a collection of APIs used to make the magic happen. The following is a list of these APIs and what they are used for with Google Fit:

- **Sensors API**: Gives access to raw sensor data from devices and companion devices
- **Recording API**: Allows data to be stored and recorded with subscriptions
- **History API**: Allows for batching fitness data by inserting, deleting, and reading it
- **Sessions API**: Allows data to be grouped into sessions via metadata
- **Bluetooth Low Energy API**: Allows compatibility with BLE devices, enabling data to be interpreted and read from various BLE devices
- **Config API**: Allows the use of custom data types and configuration settings used with Google Fit

Enable API and Authentication

Some of the Google Play Services provided require more setup than just creating a connection client. Using Google Fit requires that you log in to your Google Developer Console (https://console.developers.google.com) and either create a new project or choose one you have already added. After you have created or chosen a project, you then need to enable the Fitness API. This can be done by finding the APIs & Auth menu and then typing **Fitness** into the search box. This then shows you the Fitness API page, which gives a brief description of what it does. Clicking the Enable API button near the top of the page will turn the API on for your project.

Now that you have the API enabled, you need to manage the connection to it. This is done by generating an OAuth 2.0 client for your Android app. This is done by clicking the Credentials link that is under the APIs & Auth menu. This will then show you a page that allows you to add your OAuth credentials. Before you click the Add Credentials link, make sure your project is properly filled out for the OAuth Consent screen. Filling out this data can be done by using the tabs at the top of the page. The OAuth Consent screen is shown to users when they initially make a connection to your application with their data. This also gives you an opportunity to add branding, policies, terms of service, and a Google+ page for users to see that allows them to make sure they understand that the data really is going to the app they want and to know what you will be doing with the information.

After you fill out the information you want to provide, you can save your changes and then go back to the Credentials tab and click the Add Credentials button on the page. This activates a drop-down menu asking what type of credentials you would like to add. You should then choose the OAuth 2.0 Client ID option.

Next, you are asked to choose the application type. There are many options listed, but you should click the option for Android because you will be using the API in your Android app. When you click this option, the page shows options that pertain to creating a client for your app. You can give the client ID a name and then pass in a signing-certificate fingerprint. If you do not already have one, you will need to run the following command from your command line or terminal:

```
keytool -exportcert -alias androiddebugkey -keystore ~/.android/debug.keystore
  -list -v
```

Note that the entire sample should be on one line, but was broken into two lines here. You should also correct the path to where your keystore file is. If you need to use the `debug.keystore` file, it is at the following location:

- **OS X and Linux:** ~/.android/debug.keystore
- **Windows:** %USERPROFILE%\.android\debug.keystore

When the command is run, you are prompted for the password to your keystore (if you are using the `debug.keystore` file, the password is empty, so you may press the Enter key to continue when prompted for a password). You will then see the output of your certificate. This contains quite a bit of data about the certificate. The piece of information you require is in the Certificate Fingerprints section. You need to copy the values displayed in the SHA1 section.

After typing or pasting your fingerprint into the required field in the Developer Console, you need to add the package name for your application and then decide if you want to allow deep linking from Google+. Deep linking allows clicks and shares of your application to automatically launch or prompt for an install of your application based on the deep-link data.

When you have made your decision, you can then click the Create button to generate your OAuth 2.0 client. After a few moments, you should receive your OAuth 2.0 client ID.

App Configuration and Connection

Google Fit is part of Google Play Services. In the first section of the chapter you were shown that you need to add a dependency to your application's `build.gradle` file. As a reminder, you need to add the following to the `dependencies` section of the app `build.gradle` file:

```
dependencies {
  // other dependencies may be listed here
  compile 'com.google.android.gms:play-services:7.8.0'
}
```

You are now ready to create the `GoogleApiClient` and add the Fitness API as well as specify the scopes you need to access. A list maintained by Google can be found at https://developers. google.com/fit/android/authorization (note that the field names start with "FITNESS"). The following demonstrates an example of building a client and adding two scopes for access to user data:

```
myClient = new GoogleApiClient.Builder(this)
    .addApi(Fitness.API)
    .addScope(FitnessScopes.SCOPE_ACTIVITY_READ)
    .addScope(FitnessScopes.SCOPE_BODY_READ_WRITE)
    .addConnectionCallbacks(this)
    .addOnConnectionFailedListener(this)
    .build();
```

Once the client has been made, you can then start making the calls you need inside of the onConnected() method. This may include creating listeners so that you can display live data, display heart rate, and even allow the user to manage their weight.

Nearby Messages API

One of the newer services that is provided by Google Play Services is the Nearby API. The Nearby API allows devices on either the Android or iOS platform to exchange messages. This is done by creating a publish-subscribe service that allows for small amounts of binary data to go between the devices. Transmission is done through either Wi-Fi, Bluetooth, or even by an ultrasonic modem that uses the speaker and microphone to send and parse data.

This means that you can now control the range of messages sent. Messages are no longer limited by physical space and can reach as far as any device with an Internet connection, or as close as within 5 feet (1.5 meters) of each other.

Although offered as a Google service when using the messaging portion of the Nearby API, having a Google Account is not required for the users of your application. However, to provide unique-in-time pairing codes as well as maintain common tokens and API keys to authenticate the application token, as a developer you will need to add this API in the Google Developers Console and generate an SHA1 fingerprint of your certificate.

Enabling Nearby Messages

Open the Google Developer Console (https://console.developers.google.com) and either create a new application or choose the existing application you will be working with. Once the project has been created or selected, click the APIs & Auth menu and then the APIs link.

If you do not see the Nearby Messages API in the list of available APIs, use the search box and type **nearby messages**. A link to the API then appears. By clicking the API, you can use the Enable API button to allow your application access to the API.

Once the API has been enabled, you then need to get the SHA1 fingerprint of your keystore certificate. This can be done by using the keytool command in your command line or terminal. For precise instructions, refer to the section "Enable API and Authentication," earlier in the chapter.

After obtaining your SHA1 fingerprint, click the Credentials link that is under the APIs & Auth menu in the Google Developer Console. You should then click the Add Credentials button and choose API Key from the drop-down menu.

Of the options displayed, you should choose Android key, name the key, and then click the Add Package Name and Fingerprint button. Enter in your application package name and pass in the SHA1 fingerprint and then click the Create button. This processes and generates your API key.

After generating the API key is complete, you need to make some modifications to your Android application. The first thing you need to do is add a Google Play Services dependency to the application module of your project. Open up the `build.gradle` file of your app and make sure you add the call to the `dependencies` section as follows:

```
dependencies {
    // other files
    compile 'com.google.android.gms:play-services:7.8.0'
}
```

Next, you need to add a `meta-data` element that contains your generated API key to your application manifest XML. This element can be added anywhere inside of the `<application>` element. It should contain both a name and value property and look similar to the following:

```
<meta-data
  android:name="com.google.android.nearby.messages.API_KEY"
  android:value="GENERATED_API_KEY_GOES_HERE" />
```

The next thing you need to configure is your `GoogleApiClient`. This only requires that you add the Nearby Messages API. The following shows a sample client built using the builder method:

```
myGoogleApiClient = new GoogleApiClient.Builder(this)
    .addApi(Nearby.MESSAGES_API)
    .addConnectionCallbacks(this)
    .addOnConnectionFailedListener(this)
    .build();
```

Sending and Receiving Messages

The Nearby Messages API allows small payloads of data to be passed through a publisher and subscriber model. When a device wants to connect to another device, it sends out a small payload of data as a message using either Bluetooth or ultrasonic transmissions to any devices near it that are listening. This makes the sender the publisher and the listeners the subscribers. When tokens are received, they are then sent to the server for validation. If the validation is successful, a connection is created and the subscription process is complete.

Note

The Nearby Messages API really does live up to its name. Note that it is not called the Nearby Video Streaming or Nearby Photo Sharing service. Transmitting large media files is expensive in both time and battery cost and will only end up aggravating users. Keep to using it for data payloads that are 3KB or less.

To publish a message, you need to create a `message` object that contains a byte array and then pass it using the `Nearby.Messages.publish()` method. The following example shows a snippet of this being done:

```
message = new Message(myByteArray);
Nearby.Messages.publish(myGoogleApiClient, message)
    .setResultCallback(new ErrorCheckingCallback("publish()"));
```

From this snippet, notice that a callback method is used to pass back an error with a `String` value of `"publish()"` to let you know that something went wrong when you attempted to publish. The use of a `ResultCallback` is required so that you can keep a status on the success or failure of your broadcast. The following status codes may be passed to help you determine what happened if something goes wrong:

- **APP_NOT_OPTED_IN**: The user has not granted permission to use `Nearby.Messages`.
- **BLE_ADVERTISING_UNSUPPORTED**: The client made a request using `BLE_ONLY` and the device does not support BLE.
- **BLE_SCANNING_UNSUPPORTED**: The client made a scanning request using `BLE_ONLY` and the device does not support BLE.
- **BLUETOOTH_OFF**: The client made a request that requires Bluetooth and it is currently disabled.
- **TOO_MANY_PENDING_REQUESTS**: There are more than five `PendingIntents` triggered from the app to `Messages#subscribe`.

To subscribe to messages from a publisher, you need to create an instance of `MessageListener` and use `Nearby.Mesasges.subscribe()`. The following snippet shows an example of this:

```
messageListener = new MessageListener() {
  @Override
  public void onFound(final Message message) {
    // logic for handling the message payload
  }
};

Nearby.Messages.subscribe(myGoogleApiClient, messageListener)
    .setResultCallback(new ErrorCheckingCallback("subscribe()"));
```

Similar to when publishing messages, when subscribing to messages, you must use a `ResultCallback`. In the previous example, a string was passed to help identify where an error occurred. The same status codes may also be passed here that are passed when publishing.

Listing 15.2 shows a larger example of setting up a client, publishing, and subscribing using Nearby Messages.

Listing 15.2   Publishing and Subscribing in an Activity

```
@Override
protected void onStart() {
  // set up a connection to services unless already connected
  super.onStart();
  if (!myGoogleApiClient.isConnected()) {
    myGoogleApiClient.connect();
  }
}

@Override
protected void onStop() {
  if (myGoogleApiClient.isConnected()) {
    // save some battery by using unpublish/unsubscribe
    Nearby.Messages.unpublish(myGoogleApiClient, myMessage)
      .setResultCallback(new ErrorCheckingCallback("unpublish()"));
    Nearby.Messages.unsubscribe(myGoogleApiClient, myMessageListener)
      .setResultCallback(new ErrorCheckingCallback("unsubscribe()"));
  }
  myGoogleApiClient.disconnect();
  super.onStop();
}

// GoogleApiClient connection callback
@Override
public void onConnected(Bundle connectionHint) {
  Nearby.Messages.getPermissionStatus(myGoogleApiClient).setResultCallback(
    new ErrorCheckingCallback("getPermissionStatus", new Runnable() {
      @Override
      public void run() {
        publishAndSubscribe();
      }
    })
  );
}

// onActivityResult is called when a button tap occurs in the
// Nearby permission dialog
@Override
```

```java
protected void onActivityResult(int requestCode, int resultCode,
        Intent data) {
  super.onActivityResult(requestCode, resultCode, data);
  if (requestCode == REQUEST_RESOLVE_ERROR) {
    mResolvingError = false;
    if (resultCode == RESULT_OK) {
      // no errors, or permission issues, time to publish/subscribe
      publishAndSubscribe();
    } else {
      // either an error or permission denial happened, see resultCode
      showToast("Failed to resolve error with code " + resultCode);
    }
  }
}


private void publishAndSubscribe() {
  // when GoogleApiClient is connected subscription to nearby messages
  // happens automatically. However, this code may execute more than once
  // during the activity lifecycle, these requests to subscribe() that use
  // the same MessageListener will be ignored

  Nearby.Messages.publish(myGoogleApiClient, myMessage)
    .setResultCallback(new ErrorCheckingCallback("publish()"));
  Nearby.Messages.subscribe(myGoogleApiClient, myMessageListener)
    .setResultCallback(new ErrorCheckingCallback("subscribe()"));
}


// this ResultCallback displays a toast when errors occur
// it also displays the Nearby opt-in dialog when needed

private class ErrorCheckingCallback implements ResultCallback<Status> {
  private final String method;
  private final Runnable runOnSuccess;

  private ErrorCheckingCallback(String method) {
    this(method, null);
  }

  private ErrorCheckingCallback(String method, @Nullable Runnable runOnSuccess) {
    this.method = method;
    this.runOnSuccess = runOnSuccess;
  }

  @Override
  public void onResult(@NonNull Status status) {
    if (status.isSuccess()) {
```

```
        Log.i(TAG, method + " succeeded.");
        if (runOnSuccess != null) {
          runOnSuccess.run();
        }
      } else {
        // currently the only resolvable error is that the device is not opted
        // in to Nearby. Starting the resolution displays an opt-in dialog
        if (status.hasResolution()) {
          if (!mResolvingError) {
            try {
              status.startResolutionForResult(MainActivity.this,
                REQUEST_RESOLVE_ERROR);
              mResolvingError = true;
            } catch (IntentSender.SendIntentException e) {
              showToastAndLog(Log.ERROR, method +
                " failed with exception: " + e);
            }
          } else {
            // This is reached on init due to both publishing and
            // subscribing at the same time. Instead of informing the user
            // with a Toast, just log that it happened
            Log.i(TAG, method + " failed with status: " + status
              + " while resolving error.");
          }
        } else {
          showToastAndLog(Log.ERROR, method + " failed with : " + status
            + " resolving error: " + mResolvingError);
        }
      }
    }
  }
}
```

Remember that when publishing or subscribing communication actively, your device can use 2–3 times the normal battery rate. This makes it imperative that you call the unpublish() and unsubscribe() methods in the onPause() and/or onStop() methods of your app.

It is also recommended that you are clear to users about what data is going to be broadcast so that they don't feel like their privacy is being threatened and that malicious users may be intercepting data they deem sensitive.

Summary

In this chapter, you learned about Google Play Services. You learned how to create a client in your application to connect to the services as well as how to add the needed dependencies.

You also learned that some of these services require some setup within the Google Developer Console.

You learned that services can be included individually or as a complete bundle of all services. It may seem like including all of them is a good idea; however, you were informed that this will limit the number of methods you can use, including methods used in included libraries.

Finally, you were given examples of integrating with two of the many Google Play Services. You were shown how to enable the API in the Developer Console and connect to each service, and you were given some sample snippets of how to begin using these services in your application.

## 16

Android Wear

Android Wear was introduced in June 2014 as a way of changing how people use their mobile devices. Google initially advertised the platform as an extension of a user's mobile device, giving the user "glanceable" notifications that would inform without taking a person away from the experience they were currently involved in. In this chapter, you learn about the design and creation of notifications and applications for Android Wear.

Android Wear Basics

Android Wear is a fascinating extension of the Android family. Android Wear devices run a modified version of Android that works with many of the same classes, packages, and sensors that are in other Android devices. As a developer, there are some differences you should be aware of that will help you deliver quality apps. The following is a list of considerations you should keep in mind when creating your app:

- Wear devices have much smaller batteries than other Android devices.
- Leaving sensors in a data collection mode will impact battery life.
- Not all Wear devices have the same amount of pixels or pixel density.
- Not all users will have a watch with a square or round face.
- Not all Wear devices contain the same sensors.
- Tasks should be completed in 5 seconds or less.

Each of the items in this list is something that can have a profound impact on the user installing, keeping, or killing the app with a bad rating in the Play store.

> **Tip**
>
> As a general rule, whenever there is a Google service available, you should leverage it to mini-mize sensor collection impact and to increase battery life. For example, using the Google Fit API for pedometer data can save battery life by determining if data from a connected Android device (such as a mobile phone) is as accurate as or more accurate than a Wear device.

Android Wear devices were created to be slightly different to allow users to choose a device that matches their personal style and use case. As listed previously, some considerations need to be taken when you are working with these different styles.

To help you make better apps, the Wearable UI Library can be used in creating widgets, such as cards, as well as utility classes, such as WatchViewStub, to help you invoke the correct layout XML file. The Wearable UI Library should be included by default when creating a new Wear project with Android Studio, but if you are working with a legacy project or not using Android Studio, you can add the following to your gradle.build file in your wear module:

```
dependencies {
  // other dependencies
  compile 'com.google.android.support:wearable:+'
  compile 'com.google.android.gms:play-services-wearable:+'
}
```

Screen Considerations

What makes Android Wear different from standard Android devices is the device screen. Just like with other Android devices, you should refrain from using exact pixel numbers. This has everything to do with different manufacturers using different pixel densities as well as different resolutions for each device. You can, and should, use DP values because these will scale appro-priately using a calculated measurement.

Another difference between Wear devices and Android devices is that Wear devices are currently available in two basic shapes: round and square. Knowing this, you are given the opportunity to create two layouts for your application. It is not necessary to create two separate layouts; however, the user experience may be less than ideal because the layout of a square face will be cropped when viewed on a round watch face. This potential problem can be mitigated by using either the WatchViewStub class or a BoxInsetLayout.

The WatchViewStub class detects the watch face shape and inflates the correct layout. This class is automatically invoked at runtime and is able to inflate the correct layout based on the attributes and values placed in your main activity layout XML. The following shows a snippet of XML that will inflate different layouts based on the screen shape of the device:

```
<android.support.wearable.view.WatchViewStub
  xmlns:android="http://schemas.android.com/apk/res/android"
  xmlns:app="http://schemas.android.com/apk/res-auto"
  xmlns:tools="http://schemas.android.com/tools"
```

```
    android:id="@+id/watch_view_stub"
    android:layout_width="match_parent"
    android:layout_height="match_parent"
    app:rectLayout="@layout/activity_wear_rect"
    app:roundLayout="@layout/activity_wear_round">
</android.support.wearable.view.WatchViewStub>
```

This snippet of code uses two properties that contain values that help the application find and inflate the proper layout XML file. The first property is `app:rectLayout`, and it contains a value of `@layout/activity_wear_rect`. This means that when the screen is determined to be a square or rectangle, the file `res/layout/activity_wear_rect.xml` will be used for the UI layout.

Similarly, the `app:roundLayout` property contains a value of `@layout/activity_wear_round`, which will use the file `res/layout/activity_wear_round.xml` to render the UI layout for Wear devices that have a round face.

A drawback to using this particular method of screen layout handling is that you are unable to directly access your app view until the layout has been inflated. This can be overcome by using `setOnLayoutInflatedListener()` on the `WatchViewStub` object to create a listener that will execute code when the detection and layout inflation has been completed. The following snippet shows how this can be accomplished in the `onCreate()` method of your Activity:

```
@Override
protected void onCreate(Bundle savedInstanceState) {
  super.onCreate(savedInstanceState);
  setContentView(R.layout.activity_wear);

  WatchViewStub stub = (WatchViewStub) findViewById(R.id.watch_view_stub);
  stub.setOnLayoutInflatedListener(new WatchViewStub.OnLayoutInflatedListener() {
    @Override public void onLayoutInflated(WatchViewStub stub) {
      // the view has been inflated and can now be used
      TextView tv = (TextView) stub.findViewById(R.id.text);
      // rest of your code
    }
  });
}
```

If you decide that you do not want to work with the added complexity of maintaining two layouts, you can use a single layout that leverages `BoxInsetLayout`. Also note that starting a new Wear project in Android Studio will create a layout that includes this layout element by default.

The `BoxInsetLayout` class extends a `FrameLayout` that places the main layout area inside of the viewable area of the screen shape. `Gravity` is added to handle the placement of the included layout widgets. The following snippet demonstrates how this is achieved:

```
<android.support.wearable.view.BoxInsetLayout
  xmlns:android="http://schemas.android.com/apk/res/android"
  xmlns:app="http://schemas.android.com/apk/res-auto"
  android:background="@drawable/wear_background"
  android:layout_height="match_parent"
  android:layout_width="match_parent"
  android:padding="15dp">

  <FrameLayout
    android:layout_width="match_parent"
    android:layout_height="match_parent"
    android:padding="5dp"
    app:layout_box="all">

    <TextView
      android:gravity="center"
      android:layout_height="wrap_content"
      android:layout_width="match_parent"
      android:text="@string/hello_text"
      android:textColor="@color/black" />

    <ImageButton
      android:background="@null"
      android:layout_gravity="bottom|left"
      android:layout_height="50dp"
      android:layout_width="50dp"
      android:src="@drawable/btn_left" />

    <ImageButton
      android:background="@null"
      android:layout_gravity="bottom|right"
      android:layout_height="50dp"
      android:layout_width="50dp"
      android:src="@drawable/btn_right" />
  </FrameLayout>
</android.support.wearable.view.BoxInsetLayout>
```

In this snippet example, the `gravity` is set on the `TextView` and `ImageButton` elements in order to align them properly to the screen. You should also note that values are set in `dp` to allow them to scale based on the pixel density of the device rendering the layout.

To help with the visual layout of applications, Google provides a UI kit that can be downloaded in either PDF or Adobe Illustrator format from https://developer.android.com/design/downloads/index.html. Note that there are other design guidelines there, so look for the Wear section.

These design assets are crucial for making quality apps that will match the built-in styles that ship with Android Wear. They also provide the layout specifications used for button, image, text, and even card placement and padding.

Debugging

Just like when you create an Android app, being able to run, test, and debug your Wear application is essential. There are two ways to get this accomplished. You can use either an actual Wear device or an emulator.

Connecting to an Emulator

Developers who have access to physical devices will always have the edge when it comes to developing Wear apps. This is because they have greater access to device functionality, real-world use, and extra sensor data. However, not having a device does not automatically preclude you from developing Wear applications. Emulators are provided for both square- and round-faced devices.

To create a Wear emulator, you need to open the AVD Manager. If you are using Android Studio, you can either use the icon shortcut or click Tools, Android, AVD Manager.

When the AVD Manager opens, click Create Virtual Device; then, from the window that appears, choose the size, shape, resolution, and pixel density you would like to emulate. By default, some hardware profiles are available for selection. If you want, you can also choose to create your own by clicking the New Hardware Profile button.

Once you have either created a new profile or chosen an existing one, click the Next button. The next window allows you to choose the version of Android you want installed on the emulated Wear device.

> ### Note
> If you are missing a version that you believe is available, click the Cancel button and close the AVD Manager window. Then, open the SDK Manager and make sure you are up to date and have selected the SDK files for the version of Android Wear you want to develop with.

After choosing the version you want to work with, clicking the Next button takes you to a summary window that allows you to make any last-minute changes and to review the selected options for the emulator. If you are happy with the results, you can click the Finish button to create the Wear emulator.

Once it has been created, launching a Wear emulator is the same as launching an Android emulator. You can either run a Wear application from Android Studio and choose the Wear emulator device as the target, or you can launch the device from the AVD Manager window by clicking the Play action button.

Now at this point, you have an emulator that runs an application; however, it will not offer full functionality until you have paired the emulator with an Android device. To do this, you need to install the Android Wear app from the Google Play store on your Android device.

Next, you should connect your device through USB to your computer. Note that your Android device must have debugging enabled by having Developer Mode enabled. Once connected, you should then forward the communication port for your emulator to your Android device. This command must be run every time you connect your Android device to your computer; it is done by using the following `adb` command from a command line or terminal:

```
adb -d forward tcp:5601 tcp:5601
```

You then need to open the Android Wear app on your Android device and connect to the emulator. This is done by choosing to pair with a new watch and then using the menu in the upper-right corner to select Pair with Emulator.

When you are connected, you can then click the menu icon in the top right of the Android Wear application and select Try Out Watch Notifications. Note that the text in this menu may change, but there will be an option to view or test notifications. To confirm that the emulator and device are working, you can try sending a notification to the emulator. If everything is set up properly, you should see the notification on the emulator. Figure 16.1 shows a screenshot taken while testing a notification on a Wear emulator.

Figure 16.1   This sample notification was sent from a connected phone to the emulator.

Connecting to a Wear Device

The first step to debugging a Wear device is to enable debugging via the Developer Options on the device. This menu is initially hidden; however, it can be enabled by going to the Settings of the device and then opening the About option. This displays information about your device. In the same way that you unlock the Developer Options menu on Android tablets and phones, you need to tap on Build Number seven times. You can then swipe away the About screen, and you should see a new menu option below About called Developer Options.

You may then be able to toggle Debug over Bluetooth to true. If it is grayed out, you first need to enable ADB Debugging followed by enabling Debug over Bluetooth.

Similar to working with a Wear emulator, you need an Android device with debugging enabled that's connected to your computer through USB in order complete the debugging setup. The difference is that instead of first enabling debugging over Bluetooth in the Android Wear app and then using a port forward with the `adb` command, you open the Android Wear app and click the gear icon in the upper left to open the Settings menu.

On the Settings page, you need to scroll to the bottom and select your Wear device for the Device to Debug item in the Debugging over Bluetooth section as well as enable the slider for the Debugging over Bluetooth item. The text in the section should change to "Host: disconnected" and "Target: connected" if the Wear device is configured for Bluetooth debugging.

To connect the host, you need to run the following `adb` commands with your Android device connected via USB and with USB debugging enabled:

```
adb forward tcp:4444 localabstract:/adb-hub
adb connect localhost:4444
```

When the second command is executed, the text inside of the Debugging over Bluetooth section should now show "Host: connected." Figure 16.2 shows the settings window of an Android device connected to a Moto 360 Android Wear device with Bluetooth debugging enabled and connected.

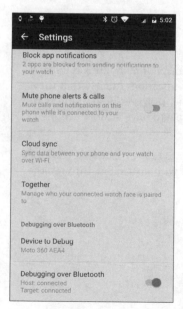

Figure 16.2 The Wear device is selected, and Bluetooth debugging is enabled and connected on both the Wear and Android devices.

Note that once the devices are connected, you need to allow debugging from the computer to your Wear device. The screen on your Wear device changes to give you the option to allow debugging, to cancel debugging, or to trust the device that is currently connected. Choosing to trust the connected device allows you to skip the dialog when you connect; however, you should still use caution when adding a permanent connection.

Communicating with Android Wear

Now that you are connected and can debug your app from either an emulator or device, you need to start sending information between the Wear device and your companion Android device. In order to provide the best experience possible, you may want to include the Android support library, Google Play Services, and the Wearable UI support library. These dependencies should be added to the `build.gradle` of the app module.

> **Note**
>
> If you are creating a client by using `GoogleApiClient` and adding the Wearable API along with other APIs, you may run into client connection errors on devices that do not have the Android Wear app installed. You can avoid these errors by using the `addApiIfAvailable()` method and passing the Wearable API so that the missing API can be gracefully handled by your client.

Notifications, actions, and data can be passed back and forth between a Wear device and an Android device. Much of this is handled by Google Play Services, and also requires the installation of the Android Wear application on the Android device. Let's look at how information can be displayed and how data is transferred between devices.

Notifications

By default, notifications are automatically bridged to Wear devices. For many, this is a major reason to use a Wear device because it allows users to receive notifications quickly that they may otherwise miss or be interrupted by when using their phone. However, something that makes notifications different for Wear devices is that they are able to have custom actions attached.

A standard notification needs to be built using an instance of `NotificationCompat.Builder`. The following snippet shows a notification being built and sent with an `Intent` through the `NotificationManager`:

```
int notificationId = 007;
Intent viewIntent = new Intent(this, ViewEventActivity.class);
viewIntent.putExtra(EXTRA_EVENT_ID, eventId);
PendingIntent viewPendingIntent =
    PendingIntent.getActivity(this, 0, viewIntent, 0);
```

```
// create notification using support library
NotificationCompat.Builder notificationBuilder =
    new NotificationCompat.Builder(this)
    .setSmallIcon(R.drawable.ic_event)
    .setContentTitle(eventTitle)
    .setContentText(eventLocation)
    .setContentIntent(viewPendingIntent);

// set up instance of NotificationManager service
NotificationManagerCompat notificationManager =
    NotificationManagerCompat.from(this);

// Use notify() to build the notification and send
notificationManager.notify(notificationId, notificationBuilder.build());
```

When this notification appears on the Wear device, the specified PendingIntent is triggered by the user swiping the notification to the left and then tapping the Open button. This will then open the PendingIntent used in the setContentIntent() that was added when the notification was built. However, this does not open the notification on the Wear device; instead, it opens it on the handheld device.

Just like with standard device notifications, you can specify another action by using the addAction() method to the NotificationBuilder. The addAction() method allows you to set an icon (drawable), a description (String), and an Intent to launch when tapped. By adding to the previous snippet, the notificationBuilder includes the following:

```
// use addAction() to add
NotificationCompat.Builder notificationBuilder =
    new NotificationCompat.Builder(this)
    .setSmallIcon(R.drawable.ic_event)
    .setContentTitle(eventTitle)
    .setContentText(eventLocation)
    .setContentIntent(viewPendingIntent);
    .addAction(R.drawable.ic_menu_share,
        getString(R.string.share), sharePendingIntent);
```

If you have an action that you only want visible on a Wear device, you need to create an Intent and an action to use, and then use the extend() method and pass WearableExtender with the action attached to it via the addAction() method. The following snippet demonstrates this in action:

```
// create the intent used for the reply action
Intent actionIntent = new Intent(this, ActionActivity.class);
PendingIntent actionPendingIntent =
    PendingIntent.getActivity(this, 0, actionIntent,
        PendingIntent.FLAG_UPDATE_CURRENT);
```

```
// create the action that will trigger on tap
NotificationCompat.Action action =
    new NotificationCompat.Action.Builder(R.drawable.ic_action,
        getString(R.string.label), actionPendingIntent)
    .build();

// create the notification, attach the action, and build
Notification notification =
    new NotificationCompat.Builder(mContext)
    .setSmallIcon(R.drawable.ic_message)
    .setContentTitle(getString(R.string.title))
    .setContentText(getString(R.string.content))
    .extend(new WearableExtender().addAction(action))
    .build();

// remember to send notifications via NotificationManagerCompat
```

This snippet of code completes the build of the notification object, so you do not have to do this when you call the `notify()` method to display the notification. With this snippet, you have created an action that only appears on a Wear device and not on the phone or other device to which it is connected.

Sending Data

To optimize the process of sending information between devices, the Wearable Data Layer API has several components that are used specifically for Wear devices. The following is a list of objects and services that are part of the API:

- **DataItem**: Object that stores data to be synced between handheld and wearable devices.

- **Asset**: Object that stores binary blob data; assets will be automatically cached to improve Bluetooth performance.

- **DataListener**: Used for determining when data layer events are in the foreground; note that it will only work when your app is in the foreground.

- **WearableListenerService**: When not working exclusively in the foreground, WearableListenerService should be extended, allowing the system to control the lifecycle and data binding.

- **ChannelApi**: This API is useful for transferring files that are large, such as movies, music, and other media files. Use of the ChannelApi allows you to transfer files without creating a container file first and then synchronizing the data.

- **MessageApi**: Small payload messages use the MessageApi. These are messages such as media player commands and one-way directives.

Like with other Google Play Services, you need to create a client to access the Wearable Data Layer. The following snippet demonstrates the minimum code needed to create and connect a client:

```
GoogleApiClient myGoogleApiClient = new GoogleApiClient.Builder(this)
    .addConnectionCallbacks(new ConnectionCallbacks() {
      @Override
      public void onConnected(Bundle connectionHint) {
        Log.d(TAG, "onConnected: " + connectionHint);
        // Data Layer ready for use
      }
      @Override
      public void onConnectionSuspended(int cause) {
        // log the cause of connection pause
        Log.d(TAG, "onConnectionSuspended: " + cause);
      }
    }).addOnConnectionFailedListener(new OnConnectionFailedListener() {
      @Override
      public void onConnectionFailed(ConnectionResult result) {
        // log reason for connection failure
        Log.d(TAG, "onConnectionFailed: " + result);
      }
    }).addApi(Wearable.API).build();
```

The process for building the client uses the builder pattern to create the client and includes the onConnected(), onConnectionSuspended(), and onConnectionFailed() methods. Depending on how you want your application to work and what messaging information you are planning to pass back and forth, you need to insert your code into the onConnected() method where the comment Data Layer ready for use is.

When sending messages with the MessageApi, you can choose a specific node or available connections between the Wear and connected device, or you can broadcast to all of them. Specifying the node and capabilities creates a more streamlined service, but will require extra implementation to handle the hand-off between different nodes (such as Bluetooth and Wi-Fi switching on and off).

The following snippet of code shows you how to find all available nodes and return them in a HashSet of Strings that can then be used for sending a message:

```
private Collection<String> getNodes() {
  HashSet<String> results = new HashSet<String>();
  NodeApi.GetConnectedNodesResult nodes =
      Wearable.NodeApi.getConnectedNodes(myGoogleApiClient).await();
  for (Node node : nodes.getNodes()) {
    results.add(node.getId());
  }
  return results;
}
```

For a full example of sending, receiving, and working with Android Wear, see the official sample code available at https://github.com/googlesamples/android-FindMyPhone/.

Summary

In this chapter, you learned about Android Wear and when Wear devices were introduced. You were also introduced to the concepts Google has set forward to create apps that match with the purpose of using a Wear device. You learned that similarly to Android devices, Wear devices come in different shapes and sizes, including watch face shapes. You learned how to provide different layout files to match the different shapes, as well as how to leverage the BoxInsetLayout to make your layout scale to be displayed on both shapes of watch faces.

You also learned how to create an emulator for Android Wear by using the AVD Manager as well as how to connect to the emulator and enable debugging to work with data from your actual Android device. You were then shown how to enable Bluetooth debugging through the Developer Options on the Wear device.

You also learned about extending notifications to Wear devices and how to customize the messages to only appear on the Wear device. You then were given a brief overview of the APIs and objects that can be used to synchronize and send data between the connected and Wear devices.

## 17

Google Analytics

As the mobile device market gains more developers, the need to analyze and formulate a plan for a successful app is more important than ever. Previously, testing and tuning an app relied heavily on direct user feedback, focus groups, and user reviews. As part of your developer tool belt, you can integrate Google Analytics and find out where your app falls down and where users are struggling.

Adding Google Analytics

Google Analytics is a service provided by Google that works on multiple platforms. Web developers use Google Analytics to monitor the visits and purchases made by users. Now mobile developers using Android or iOS can take advantage of Google Analytics in their apps.

Before we get too far into the process, you first need to enable Google Services for the app. This can be done by visiting https://developers.google.com/mobile/add and using the wizard to generate your configuration file.

If you have not already added your app to the Google Developer Console, you can use this wizard to create a new app and specify the Android package name for your app. While using the wizard, you will also be asked to choose or create a new analytics account to track and report data. When you are finished either choosing an account or creating one, make sure to generate your configuration file. This will download a file named google-services.json to your computer.

When the file has been generated and downloaded, you need to move or copy it into the app folder of your Android project. Because your installation of Android Studio and your project directory may vary, you need to locate the /app folder and place the google-services.json file in it.

Once you copy your configuration file, you need to make an edit to the top-level build.gradle file of your project. You need to add the following dependency:

```
classpath 'com.google.gms:google-services:1.4.0-beta3'
```

Note that this version is current as of this writing, and you need to update to the latest version to take advantage of any new features and functionality. You also need to make some additions to your app module `build.gradle` file, which consists of adding the following lines:

```
// other plugins
apply plugin: 'com.google.gms.google-services'


dependencies {
  // other dependencies
  compile 'com.google.android.gms:play-services-analytics:8.1.0'
}
```

Now that you have the build configured, you need to make some changes to your `AndroidManifest.xml` file. Because Google Analytics is an online service and you will be sending data, you need to add the INTERNET and ACCESS_NETWORK_STATE permissions to your `AndroidManifest.xml` file. The following shows a snippet of the required entries:

```
<manifest xmlns:android="http://schemas.android.com/apk/res/android"
    package="com.example.analytics">

  <uses-permission android:name="android.permission.INTERNET"/>
  <uses-permission android:name="android.permission.ACCESS_NETWORK_STATE"/>


  <application android:name="AnalyticsApplication">

    <!-- The rest of your application manifest -->

  </application>
</manifest>
```

With the configuration in place, Google recommends that you subclass Application to set up your tracking information. The following code snippet shows the code that Google recommends implementing:
```
/*
 * Copyright Google Inc. All Rights Reserved.
 *
 * Licensed under the Apache License, Version 2.0 (the "License");
 * you may not use this file except in compliance with the License.
 * You may obtain a copy of the License at
 *
 *     http://www.apache.org/licenses/LICENSE-2.0
 *
 * Unless required by applicable law or agreed to in writing, software
 * distributed under the License is distributed on an "AS IS" BASIS,
 * WITHOUT WARRANTIES OR CONDITIONS OF ANY KIND, either express or implied.
 * See the License for the specific language governing permissions and
 * limitations under the License.
 */
```

```
package com.google.samples.quickstart.analytics;

import android.app.Application;

import com.google.android.gms.analytics.GoogleAnalytics;
import com.google.android.gms.analytics.Logger;
import com.google.android.gms.analytics.Tracker;

/**
 * This is a subclass of {@link Application} used to provide shared objects for
 * this app, such as the {@link Tracker}.
 */
public class AnalyticsApplication extends Application {
  private Tracker mTracker;

  /**
   * Gets the default {@link Tracker} for this {@link Application}.
   * @return tracker
   */
  synchronized public Tracker getDefaultTracker() {
    if (mTracker == null) {
      GoogleAnalytics analytics = GoogleAnalytics.getInstance(this);
      // To enable debug logging use: adb shell setprop log.tag.GAv4 DEBUG
      mTracker = analytics.newTracker(R.xml.global_tracker);
    }
    return mTracker;
  }
}
```

You can now get an instance of the tracker and start tracking inside of an Activity by adding the following code to the appropriate methods:

```
@Override
protected void onCreate(Bundle savedInstanceState) {
  super.onCreate(savedInstanceState);
  setContentView(R.layout.activity_main);

  // set up the shared Tracker
  AnalyticsApplication application = (AnalyticsApplication) getApplication();
  mTracker = application.getDefaultTracker();
}

@Override
public void onResume() {
  super.onResume();  // Always call the superclass method first
```

```
// add log to make sure that GA is being called...
Log.i(TAG, "Setting screen name: " + name);
mTracker.setScreenName("Image~" + name);
// send the "hit" to GA
mTracker.send(new HitBuilders.ScreenViewBuilder().build());
}
```

Note that instead of using the onResume() method, you could use another Activity or ViewPager. For any View, Fragment, or Activity for which you want tracking information, you need to add the tracking code as well as send the Hit by using the HitBuilders class.

You can find a demo application on GitHub that shows a slightly different configuration but is a great starting point for your Android project for adding Google Analytics to your app. It can be found at https://github.com/googleanalytics/hello-world-android-app.

Google Analytics Basics

Web developers have enjoyed the Google Analytics service for several years. It enables them to set up marketing campaigns, test different versions of web pages, and, most importantly, find where the gaps are in their online offerings.

As an app developer, the prospect of being able to determine where users are struggling and even see the amount of time they spend on a view inside of your application can help you to create and fine-tune an application that will be used more and shared with others.

By default, Google Analytics provides the following information when integrated into an app:

- User and session count
- Session duration
- Operating system information
- Device model
- Geographic location

In addition to the included statistics, you can use and create the following to enhance your app analytics:

- Events
- Goals
- Ecommerce
- Custom timings
- Custom dimensions
- Custom metrics

Each of these additional features gives you greater insight into your application and can work together to help you get the most out of your app. Let's take a closer look at what each of these features is and how it would be used.

Events

An event is an action or objective that a user performs that can be quantified. For example, you can create an event that will track how many times a user taps the Help button, or even how many views the Support section of your app is getting.

Events are made up from four components:

- Category
- Action
- Label (optional)
- Value (optional)

The category is a custom name or organizational group you can add to your actions. Because you may want to track more than one action, you may find that grouping actions together will help you process the return data. It is important that you plan for how you will be reporting data before you decide on a concrete category name. If you were to use a generic category, such as Visits or Views, you may end up with a lot of information that really isn't quantifiable for a particular page. Instead, "Visit – Help" and "View – High Score" would be better category names if you are wanting to capture those specific events. If your app happens to be a game, you could consider using the level the player is on as the category name.

The action is separate from the category, but is still part of the event. You can name an action based on what a user is doing, or what task they have initiated or completed. For example, you could name an action "abandonment," "paused," or "saving." Note that because actions are separate from categories, you can use the same named action inside of two different event calls with different categories. This flexibility allows you to have an action that happens in two different categories and also gives you the ability to have unique actions that only happen in one category.

A label is an optional component that is used for additional information you want tracked with the category and action. This label could be used to pass system information, download information, or even create a note on why the event was triggered.

Value is also an optional component, and unlike the other components it's a positive integer value. This value can be tied to just about any integer value you want. For example, you could use it as a counter value, a time-to-render value, or even a value to track how long a user has been on a certain screen, view, or level.

The following code snippet demonstrates tracking an event in a game:

```
// Event to track coin gathering
mTracker.send(new HitBuilders.EventBuilder()
  .setCategory("Brackety Bricks")
  .setAction("Collect")
  .setLabel("coin")
  .setValue(1)
  .build());
```

Goals

Goals determine if objectives are being met in your app. The objectives are defined by you and may consist of page visits, purchases, or even collecting user information. Goals are closely tied to conversion, which is the term for a completion of a goal or objective.

Goals can fall into one of the following types:

- **Destination**: A user has loaded or visited a specific location.
- **Duration**: A user has spent a minimum amount of time in a session.
- **Pages/Screens per session**: A user has visited or viewed a specific number of pages or screens.
- **Event**: A specific event was triggered.

Goals also work with funnels for tracking how users reach goals. Funnels show you the shape of user traffic and flow through a site or app. At the beginning, all users start at the top of the funnel and then they filter out as they fail to achieve a particular goal or objective. This leaves you with a smaller sample and gives not only a "funnel" shape to your report, but also shows how the traffic is funneled, through conversion to goal completion.

For more information on how to work with custom funnels in Google Analytics, visit https://support.google.com/analytics/answer/6180923?hl=en.

When you are working with an ecommerce or monetary goal, you can assign a dollar amount. This can be helpful when making forecasts or when working on a commerce plan. The generated reports take the amount you assign per goal and give you an estimate on whether you are on track to meet your financial goals or if you need to adjust your app or objectives.

Think carefully about how to want to create goals, because you are only allotted 20 goals in total. You can create goal sets of five goals each if the goals you have created are related to each other. Once you create a goal, you cannot delete it. You can, however, repurpose it. Keep in mind that because you are modifying an existing goal, it may make the reports you run confusing because it will appear that the "new" goal existed in the past and with numbers that may not make sense in the "new" context.

Ecommerce

Enhanced ecommerce allows you to track impressions, promotions, checkout process, refunds, transactions, and other purchase-related activities. Ecommerce works closely with goals and events, because to report ecommerce data you must send it with an existing hit.

To track a product purchase made in your application, you must first create a product and assign a name and price to it. You can then set up a `ProductAction` and assign a transaction ID. Following that, you build the tracking event and send it to Google Analytics. The following code snippet demonstrates this:

```
// create the Product
Product product = new Product()
  .setName("Rocket Fuel")
  .setPrice(10.00);

// set the ProductAction
ProductAction productAction = new ProductAction(ProductAction.ACTION_PURCHASE)
  .setTransactionId("T01701");

// add the transaction to an Event
HitBuilders.EventBuilder builder = new HitBuilders.EventBuilder()
  .setCategory("In-Game Store")
  .setAction("Purchase")
  .addProduct(product)
  .setProductAction(productAction);

// send the transaction data with the event
mTracker.send(builder.build());
```

Custom Timings

A custom timing is used when you want to measure the length of time it takes to complete a particular task in your app. Custom timings are similar to events in that they are created in almost the same manner; however, custom timings are different in that they are time based.

The following snippet shows an example of how to create a custom timing for how long it takes a user to complete a task in a game:

```
// build and send a custom timing
mTracker.send(new HitBuilders.TimingBuilder()
  .setCategory("Brackety Bricks")
  .setValue(42000)  // 42 seconds
  .setVariable("First Stage")
  .setLabel("Race")
  .build());
```

Similar to setting up an event, you use a category, value, and label. The difference is that instead of an action, a variable is used instead. The integer value component is used to send timing information.

Custom Dimensions

Custom dimensions allow you to create reports that track users with a particular trait, attribute, or matching metadata set. This can be useful for determining a player's skill level, the difficulty level the majority of players select, or even the type of device most players are using to play your game.

Setting up a custom dimension requires some setup inside of the Google Analytics web interface. Note that similar to working with goals, you only have 20 available slots for setting up custom dimensions.

The following is a snippet used to add data that shows the currently selected skill level for the level Brackety Bricks:

```
// set a custom dimension to track level and difficulty
mTracker.setScreen("BracketyBricks");
mTracker.send(new HitBuilders.ScreenViewBuilder()
  .setCustomDimension(3, "Brackety Bricks")
  .build()
);
```

Custom Metrics

Custom metrics are similar to custom dimensions, in that they are allowed to use different scopes. A custom metric is best used when you need to create a report that covers data that may be difficult to track elsewhere without creating excess and erroneous data.

Creating a custom metric is done inside of the Admin settings, under the Property section and as an option listed in Custom Definitions of the Google Analytics web interface. A custom metric requires the following:

- A name
- A scope set to either Hit or Product
- A formatting type of Integer, Currency, or Time

Optionally, you can opt to set up a minimum value as well as a maximum value for your custom metric.

The following snippet shows reporting a view to a hint screen during a level of Brackety Bricks as a custom metric:

```
mTracker.setScreen("BracketyBricks");
mTracker.send(new HitBuilders.ScreenViewBuilder()
  .setCustomMetric(1, "Hint Page")
  .build()
);
```

Summary

In this chapter, you learned how to add Google Analytics to your Android project. You learned about the features of Google Analytics that you can use to gain a greater understanding of your application and how users are using your app.

You learned about tracking user interaction through events. You were shown how to create events to track specific tasks or objectives in your app.

You also learned about goals and how they work with events and ecommerce tracking to create funnel reports. You learned that the funnel is important because it allows you to fine-tune your app to meet the needs of your users and increase your revenue stream. You also learned that you are limited to having 20 goals that can be reused but not deleted.

You learned about ecommerce tracking and how data is sent with other events. You learned that ecommerce is used with creating products and tracking the transaction and sale of products.

You also learned about using custom timings with Google Analytics. Custom timings are similar to events; however, the value passed is used to track how long a user takes to complete an objective rather than be used as a counter or other numeric value.

You then learned about custom dimensions. Custom dimensions require extra setup, but allow you to track custom values such as the skill or difficulty setting selected for a particular level. Similarly to goals, you are limited to having 20 custom dimensions in total, but they can be reused when needed.

Finally, you learned about custom metrics, which are similar to custom dimensions in reporting useful data back to you. You learned the requirements for using a custom metric as well as how to implement the code for reporting the metric back to Google Analytics.

18

Optimization

Creating a well-balanced app goes beyond creating network connections, adding data storage, and using eye-popping visuals. A well-crafted app takes into consideration the limitations of the device and uses various techniques to maximize the experience for the end user. In this chapter, you learn about extending the `Application` class, setting up custom logging for your app, changing the configuration based on the version of your app, and managing device memory.

Application Optimization

When you're creating your app, the odds are high that you have spent a considerable amount of time going over the critical `onCreate()` method, adding a proper amount of unit testing, and using the `Log` class to fine-tune the expected objects and values being used in your application. These are all excellent steps in creating a solid high-performance app. However, each of these steps can be modified to give you even finer control over your application and to enhance the experience you are offering to your users.

When it comes to an overall schematic of your application, every optimization counts and every bit of performance you can squeeze out of the app will make a difference. The following recommendations and tips will help you create an app that runs leaner and longer.

Application First

When looking back on the Activity lifecycle of Android, the first thing you learn is that code in the `onCreate()` method will always be executed first. This is true when speaking directly of the lifecycle of your app; however, any `ContentProviders` will execute their `onCreate()` method and any code inside of it will initialize and run before the `onCreate()` in your Activity.

There is a step you can add between the `ContentProvider.onCreate()` and the `onCreate()` of your app. This is done by extending the `Application` object. The following demonstrates this in action:

```
package mypackage;
public class MyApplication extends Application {
  // custom subclass

  public void onCreate() {
    // this onCreate() will run before any others
  }
}
```

In order to use this subclass, you need to add it to your application manifest. This is done by setting the `android:name` property in the `<application>` element. You can also list your Activity, the services needed, and any receivers your app needs. The following code demonstrates how to do this in your application manifest XML:

```
<?xml version="1.0" encoding="utf-8"?>
<manifest
    xmlns:android="http://schemas.android.com/apk/res/android"
    package="mypackage.MyApplication">
  <application
    android:name="mypackage.MyApplication"
    android:allowBackup="true"
    android:icon="@drawable/ic_launcher"
    android:label="@string/app_name"
    android:theme="@style/AppTheme">

    <activity android:name="MyActivity"> <intent-filter>

      <action android:name="android.intent.action.MAIN" /> </intent-filter>

    </activity>

    <!-- the rest of your services, receivers, etc -->

  </application>
</manifest>
```

Given a cursory glance, using this application setup might not seem to be that great of an enhancement; however, by using this in your app, you can now perform the following tasks:

- Initialize the SDKs and libraries your app needs.
- Register any dynamic broadcast receivers your app uses.

- Create and manage any services your app needs.

- Manage the actual starting point of your app by having it be the absolute entry point because it is called first.

Most of these benefits may be done in a regular Activity; however, a standard app may be called in a variety of ways. This could be through a service, an explicit or implicit Intent, or other broadcast receivers. The ability to control the actual flow so that you can manage state is a boon for making sure your app is able to respond appropriately at any stage of being invoked.

> **Note**
>
> Running various library initializations and doing some setup work will help your application get up to speed and working quickly; however, you should never do any blocking work (such as creating network connection) inside of `Application.onCreate()`. Adding anything that will block will cause your app to create an ANR or crash immediately on launch, thus rendering your app useless.

Application Logging

While you are working on extending the application, you may want to implement a different form of logging. The Log class gives you the ability to throw specific log messages and types in your application. One of the biggest problems with logging inside of an app is unit testing. The Log class tends to throw a `RuntimeException` when used in local unit tests. Another problem is that if you are creating libraries that will be used in other Android projects, you must make sure to remove your log messages or else others will run into the same errors and exceptions when running their own unit tests.

To get around this potential problem, you can create a class that extends `Handler` that routes your custom messages to LogCat and registers it to run at app launch. You can then create a method that gets the handler, sets a logging level, and displays the message to LogCat. The following shows a sample method that could be called from the `onCreate()` method of your main Activity:

```
private void initLogging() {
  // set package name
  final String pkg = getClass().getPackage().getName();
  // set handler for the package
  final AndroidLogHandler alh = new AndroidLogHandler(pkg);
  // create the logger
  Logger logger = Logger.getLogger(pkg);
  logger.addHandler(alh);
  logger.setUseParentHandlers(false);
  // set default log level here
  logger.setLevel(Level.FINEST);
  logger.info("Logging initialized with default level " + logger.getLevel());
}
```

Another benefit of this type of logging is that you can create logic checks to determine if logging should be sent. You can check the currently logging level, and if it's not at the level you want, nothing will be logged. The following shows an example of this in action:

```
private void nameCheck(String name) {
  if (LOGGER.isLoggable(Level.WARNING)) {
    LOGGER.warning("checking name: " + name);
  }
}
```

For a full example of both extending `Application` and implementing this logging example, a sample app that can be imported into Android Studio has been created by Doug Stevenson, one of the Android team members. This sample application can be found at https://github.com/AnDevDoug/devtricks.

Application Configuration

One of the best features that the Gradle build system brings to Android is the ability to create custom configurations for your Android Studio project. You should consider versioning your configuration for a variety of reasons, including the following:

- To change credentials for API and database authentication
- To change ports or endpoints for various services
- To toggle testing and debugging output
- To use modified constants, variables, and resources
- To create a white label app

The values or constants you want to use as defaults should be stored inside of an XML file in your `res/values` directory. The files you wish to alternate between can then be versioned into a new folder; to keep things easy, you could create a new directory in the `res` directory, leaving you with a folder path of `res/values-1`.

This should leave you with the following structure in your project:

```
res/values/config.xml // original config file path
res/values-1/config.xml // dev config file path
```

This particular method of storing information does not leverage the power of the Gradle build system, but does allow you load the constants you need and keep them in properly versioned files. In order to leverage the power of the Gradle system, you can inject values that are contained inside of the `ProductFlavors` section of the `gradle.build` file in your app module.

The values placed are stored in a `resValue` entry that then lists the `type`, `key`, and `value`. The following shows a sample entry from the app module's `gradle.build` file that sets up a configuration based on the same version of the app, but in different folders:

```
apply plugin: 'com.android.application'

android {
  // set compile options and other resources

  defaultConfig {
    // you can inject resources here in addition to others you may have set
  }

  buildTypes {
    // you can inject resources here in addition to others you may have set
  }

  productFlavors {
    // set up production resource injection
    prod {
      versionName '1.0'
      resValue 'string', 'my_api_key', 'HARKNESS'
    }

    // set up development resource injection
    dev {
      versionName '1.0-dev'
      resValue 'string', 'my_api_key', 'BADWOLF'
    }
  }
}

dependencies {
  // add your dependencies
}
```

When the app is built, you can then gain access to the values by either calling them in the onCreate() method of your application or by loading them into the object model. Depending on the route you take, you can access the values via the getResources() method. To load the values from the preceding sample snippet, you would use the following:

```
getResources().getString(R.string.my_api_key)
```

Memory Management

Changing the way you load configuration files and how your app is initialized is great for making sure your app gets off on the right foot; however, none of that will matter if your app is constantly running out of memory and throwing an OutOfMemoryError that confuses users and leaves them uninstalling your app and using a different one.

When developing your application, it is important that you are doing what you can to maximize the efficiency of your code base. This means that you should take great care in how objects are created, what types you are using, and that you are not blocking the natural garbage collection process.

You can minimize how often garbage collection runs by minimizing the amount of objects you create. This even applies to temporary objects. If you can create a single object and repurpose the value of it, you will better off than creating new objects. Garbage collection is a wonderful thing, but it is still a drain on system resources.

Take advantage of the getMemoryClass() function. This function checks the size of the memory heap (in MB) that is available for your app. If you attempt to go beyond this limit, your app will throw an OutOfMemoryError exception. Note that getMemoryClass() is a method on ActivityManager. This can be used as follows:

```
int memoryClass = activityManager.getMemoryClass();
```

When creating threads for your app, you should be aware that each thread is a garbage collection root. Devices in the market before Android Lollipop was released use the Dalvik Virtual Machine and will keep references to these threads open so that garbage collection does not occur automatically on them. This makes it an absolute necessity for you to close threads when you are finished with them. Failure to do so will lock the memory allocated to them, which will not be released until the process (your app) is terminated by the system. You can avoid spinning up new threads by using a Loader for a short asynchronous operation within an Activity lifecycle; a Service should be used when you need to report back to an Activity by means of a BroadcastReceiver, or you could use an AsyncTask for other short-term operations.

When using a Service, make sure it only runs for the amount of time you need it. Creating an IntentService allows you to create a Service that will finish when it is finished handling an Intent. Services may be necessary for your app to work correctly; however, they expose your app as a potential bottleneck for memory and battery problems for users. A user who believes your app is a problem will not hesitate to remove it from their device. If you need to have a long-running Service, you should consider setting the android:process property in your Service in the AndroidManifest.xml file. Make sure that when you do this you avoid allowing the Service to make changes or influence the UI in any way. If it does, you may more than double the amount of memory your Service uses.

Using Proguard is not just a recommended step for code obfuscation: It also optimizes your code by finding unused code and removing it. The returned code is compacted and should reduce the amount of RAM required to run the code. You can combine using Proguard with zipalign to make sure that the uncompressible resources in your apk file are aligned correctly within the archive. This in turn saves on the amount of RAM needed to run your app. The zipalign tool can be run by using the following code in your terminal (provided that the Android SDK is in your system path):

```
zipalign 4 infile.apk outfile.apk
```

Note that you can pass an argument of -f to force overwriting the outfile.apk file should it already exist. Using an argument of -v will show the verbose output of the utility. If you believe that your apk file is already aligned but would like to verify it, you can run the following:

```
zipalign -c -v 4 outfile.apk
```

The argument of -c will "confirm" the alignment of the file. The -v argument is still used as a verbose output of the utility running.

Garbage Collection Monitoring

When viewing the log from LogCat or from DDMS, you'll see several messages related directly to garbage collection. The following list explains the messages that you will find and what they mean:

- **GC [reason]**: The reason that garbage collection was run. Here are some possible reasons:

  - **GC_CONCURRENT**: Garbage collection that frees up memory as the memory heap fills up.

  - **GC_FOR_ALLOC**: Garbage collection that occurs because the app has attempted to allocate memory when the memory heap was already full, causing the system to stop the app and reclaim memory.

  - **GC_HPROF_DUMP_HEAP**: Garbage collection that occurs due to the creation of an HPROF file for further analysis of the memory heap.

  - **GC_EXPLICIT**: An explicitly called garbage collection. If you are seeing this, you or one of your included libraries may have a problem as garbage collection is being forced to run manually.

- **Amount freed**: The amount of memory freed or reclaimed from garbage collection.

- **Heap stats**: The percentage free and the (number of live objects) / (total heap size).

- **External memory stats**: The external allocated memory on API level 10 and lower, shown as (amount of allocated memory) / (limit at which collection will occur).

- **Pause time**: The larger the heap, the longer the pause time. Concurrent pause times will show two pauses: One at the beginning of the collection and another near the end.

Checking Memory Usage

Besides using the DDMS or LogCat tool to view memory usage in Android Studio, you may want to use an adb command-line tool to view the status of memory management. Remember that when using adb you need to have your device in debugging mode and connected to your computer. To make sure your device is connected and that your computer can see your device, you can run the following command:

```
adb devices
```

Note that Linux and OS X terminal windows may need to use ./adb to execute the command. You may also see the following message:

```
*daemon not running. starting it now on port 5037 *
```

If the next line tells you that the daemon was started successfully, you should check your device to see if it has connected or is ready to exchange SSH keys with the computer. Once you have verified that your phone is set up correctly, you can run the adb devices command again to see the devices that are connected to your computer.

If you are not using a physical device, you can start an Android emulator and run the command to make sure the emulator is connected properly to your system. If it is properly attached, you should see it listed similar to the following:

```
List of devices attached
emulator-5554    device
```

With a device listed, you can now use adb to collect the memory information for a specific package. The following command displays the results from the com.android.phone package:

```
adb shell dumpsys meminfo com.android.phone
```

Figure 18.1 shows the command being run and the output that is returned in a terminal window.

The returned values are a snapshot of how the com.android.phone package is behaving on the device. You can see if the package has increased in memory size since launch, the size of the memory heap as well as space available for it, the number of objects that have been created, and database information.

Note that the package com.android.phone is just an example. When testing your app, make sure to be testing package(s) you use to get results that are relative to your app.

Although all the information presented is important, pay particularly close attention to the Pss Total and the Private Dirty columns. The Pss Total column represents all connections to the main device memory thread, whereas the Private Dirty column keeps track of the actual amount of RAM your application is using on the heap since the app was started.

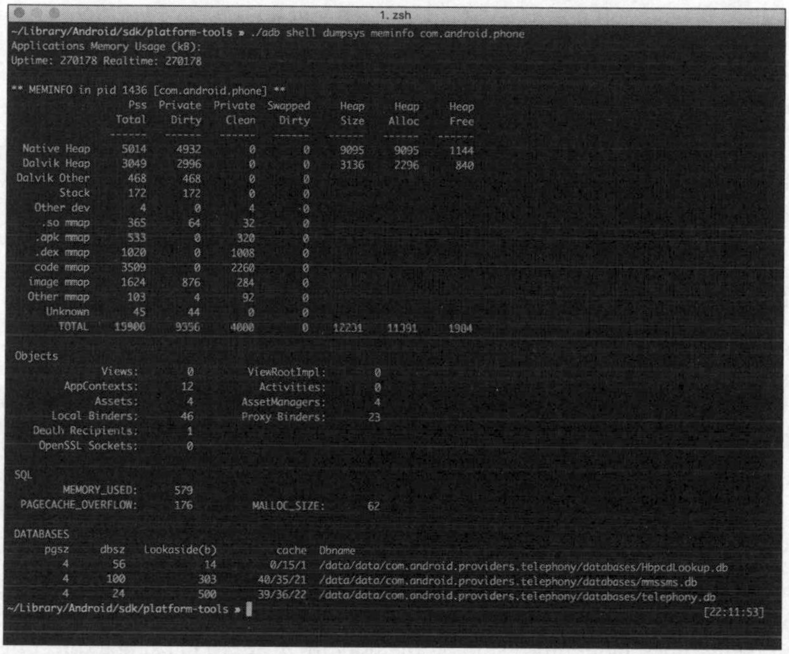

Figure 18.1   You can discover a considerable amount of memory information about the packages on your device.

Performance

You can do a few things inside your code that can help optimize not only the memory in use, but also the speed at which the system will run your code on a device. Many optimizations may be overlooked due to timelines, or even just because the code you use is the way you are familiar with coding and is something you have always done. That doesn't mean that your app will not work; however, it does mean that some devices may not be able to run your app at the speed you expect, making some users frustrated with the bad performance they perceive.

Working with Objects

It was previously mentioned that garbage collection for your application will run based on the number of objects you create. You can minimize object creation by not using temporary objects and working directly on an existing object.

When you use a method that returns a `String` that will be appended to a `StringBuffer` object, there is no need to create a new object to contain the return `String` and then add the temp object to the `StringBuffer` object. Instead, you should try to work directly with the `StringBuffer` object, skipping the temporary object all together.

You should also consider using StringBuilder when you do not have multiple threads accessing it at the same time. StringBuilder does not have every method marked for synchronization like StringBuffer does and will give a considerable performance boost when working with Strings.

If you do not need to modify the state of an object, you should make your methods static. This increases the initial time needed for your method, and grants the additional bonus of you knowing that your method will not be changing the state of the object.

Static Methods and Variables

In addition to making your methods static, you should also make any constants static final. Adding this to a variable you will be using as constant, the system knows that it will not need to store your object into a field that will need to be referenced every time you want to use the variable.

You should also avoid the use of enum. In standard Java, an enum provides an incredibly useful way of handling constants; however, when using one, you double the amount of memory allocated for it. If you can get by without using an enum, you should do it.

When getting values for your variables, you should avoid using getters. Android is faster when working directly with an object instead through a method call. This is due to the virtual method call being much more processor and memory intensive than using a direct field lookup. The exception to this rule is when you are working with interfaces where using getters is an acceptable practice because the field cannot be directly accessed.

Enhanced for Loops

When you find yourself needing to iterate over a value, how you choose to build your for loop matters. You should be acquainted with for loops, so the following code should be familiar:

```
int total = 0;
for (int i = 0; i < myArray.length; ++i) {
  total += myArray[i].myItem;
}
```

In this example, an int is set up to contain a total count and then the for loop is executed to get the number of myItems that are stored in the myArray to be stored in the total variable. This loop is functional, but it is not optimized. Even though the variable i is defined, the length of myArray must be looked up on every single iteration. To speed this up, you can use the enhanced for loop syntax that was introduced in Java 1.5:

```
int total = 0;
for (<type> a : myArray) {
  total += a.myItem;
}
```

By using this syntax, the compiler is already aware of the length of the `myArray` object and avoids having to perform a lookup every time the loop runs. Note that `<type>` should be changed to the type (`int`, `String`, etc) that you are expecting to work with.

float, double, and int

Even though a `double` will take up two times the space in memory that a `float` will take, try to use a `double` if possible.

An interesting performance note is that a `float` will be two times slower than an `int` to process. If you do not need the extra precision of a `float` or `double`, you should opt for an `int` or an `Integer` if you need to handle potential `null` values or need a wrapper.

Optimized Data Containers

Android has included several data containers you can leverage that yield a more memory-performant app. Instead of using a `HashMap`, consider using one of the following, depending on the data your `HashMap` would store:

- `SparseArray` instead of `HashMap <Integer, Object>`
- `SparseBooleanArray` instead of `HashMap <Integer, Boolean>`
- `SparseIntArray` instead of `HashMap <Integer, Integer>`
- `SparseLongArray` instead of `HashMap <Integer, Long>`
- `LongSparseArray` instead of `HashMap <Long, Object>`

Using these built-in types is faster and they are optimized for Android to work with. They are allocation-free and do not auto-box keys. `SparseArrays` are also more memory efficient because they do not require as much overhead as a `HashMap`.

You should use a plain or raw array (`int []`) instead of a `HashMap` when you can. This helps with performance because a wrapper is not needed to perform field lookups.

Summary

In this chapter, you learned some new methods for enhancing the performance as well as the organization of your app. You learned that you can control the entry point of your app and optimize the resources it will need to use by extending the `Application` class.

You also learned that by creating your own logging implementation in conjunction with extending the `Application` class, you can create a log that works with unit testing instead of throwing errors.

You learned that you can also create different configurations that you can use based on the version of your app. This is incredibly useful when working with different credentials for services, APIs, and database access across different environments.

You learned about streamlining your app for maximum memory usage by incorporating various tactics, such as minimizing object creation, being aware of how much memory is available for your app, and using command-line tools in conjunction with the `adb` command to view memory usage.

Finally, you learned about increasing performance by writing code that is optimized for Android. This includes using `static final` variables, being careful with primitive types, and not using a `HashMap`, because many other data containers are available that will yield similar results with better performance.

## 19

Android TV

There have been many attempts to create an experience that a group of people can take part in and share while staying in the comfort of their own home. Many homes have at least one TV, and it is generally located in an area with lots of space where can be viewed by many people. Android TV takes advantage of this space by allowing you to create applications that can be used and enjoyed in this environment. In this chapter, you learn the basics of creating an Android TV application and some of what the Android TV SDK offers to help you get your app to the big screen.

The Big Picture

Phones, tablets, and other Android devices are wonderful for taking your life with you, but when it comes to enjoying content with friends, family, and others, it can get a little crowded around a small screen.

Some content doesn't do as well in the small screen space and needs more space in order to be fully enjoyed. Apps that stream video and music or even deliver a multiplayer experience can be used and enjoyed easier on a TV.

Google has stepped into the TV domain before and had many early successes with partners using the Google TV platform. This platform was an early attempt to provide many of Google's services to the masses using the biggest screen in the house. In June 2014, it was announced at Google I/O that Android TV would be the successor to Google TV.

Android TV focuses on providing the following services:

- Cinematic access to your personalized Google goods
- Voice search
- App and content recommendations based on content consumption
- Games and apps

Android TV may not appear to be too different from a standard Android device in basic capability; in this respect, almost any app can be ported to Android TV for users to start enjoying. This comes with a few caveats, however: Because of the form-factor of the TV, some considerations need to be made to make the app work correctly and be useable on an Android TV–capable device.

Ten-Foot View

When working with Android TV, you will often hear about the "ten-foot view," which is the typical viewing distance from user to screen. This means that the amount of detail that goes into an app changes. Whereas precision and detail are massive factors to consider on a small-screen device, many of those details can now become lost or difficult to pick out when viewed from a distance.

When designing a user interface, you should use a grid or similar system so that items are large, easy to read, and easy to navigate with a remote. You should also build your app to be presented in landscape rather than portrait orientation.

Apps built for Android TV should use Fragments to help you manage sections of the screen rather than a single View that is stretched or scaled to fit. Because of the landscape orientation of TVs, you should also implement GridViews rather than ListViews, because a GridView will take advantage of the available horizontal screen space.

To help you with your visual layout, consider using the Leanback support library. Leanback is required by Android TV; however, this support library includes a theme that will give you many of the recommended styles your app should be using as well as a head start on getting your app visually ready. The following shows how this theme can be applied by adding it to the <activity> element of your application manifest XML:

```
<activity
    android:name="com.example.android.TvActivity"
    android:label="@string/app_name"
    android:theme="@style/Theme.Leanback">
```

If you do not want to use this particular theme, at least implement the following, because Android TV apps should not show a title bar:

```
<activity
    android:name="com.example.android.TvActivity"
    android:label="@string/app_name"
    android:theme="@android:style/Theme.NoTitleBar">
```

Many resources are sharable between a standard Android app and an Android TV app; however, you should never share layout resources. Always make sure to create separate ones. You should not be using an ActionBar in the Android TV because it is difficult for a user to navigate with using a remote.

If your app integrates with advertisement services, note the following:

- The user should be able to dismiss full-screen non-video ads immediately using the remote control.

- It is recommended that you use video ads that can be dismissed within 30 seconds.

- If an ad is not full screen, the user should be able to interact and click it using a remote.

- Ads should not attempt to open a web browser or link to a web URL.

- Ads should not be able to link to other apps that are not available for TV devices.

If, for any reason, you require loading or using web resources, you must use a `WebView`, *not* a browser. A full browser implementation is not currently supported on Android TV. This is especially important when you are creating multiplatform (Android and Android TV) apps.

Controls are also different on a TV. Because users are away from the screen, you need to think about how navigation should work with a remote. Remotes should have a two-axis directional pad. This provides movement along the X and Y planes and, depending on your app, you should add a visual clue to where the cursor is so that the user can quickly make directional changes. You should also take care to ensure that every element in your app is accessible via a controller.

Your app should be built without any reliance on the user having to press the Menu key on a remote. This doesn't mean you can't wire the key in, but it does mean that you should have a Settings or Options area with all of the menu items available.

To help a user visually understand the interface, there are four states an item such as a button can be in to show visual styles:

- **Focused**: `android:state_focused="true"`

- **Hovered**: `android:state_hovered="true"`

- **Pressed**: `android:state_pressed="true"`

- **Default**: No property required for the default state

The following code snippet will alter the assigned drawable resource based on these states:

```
<?xml version="1.0" encoding="utf-8"?>
<selector xmlns:android="http://schemas.android.com/apk/res/android">
  <!-- focused -->
  <item android:state_focused="true"
      android:drawable="@drawable/button_focused" />
  <!-- hovered -->
  <item android:state_hovered="true"
      android:drawable="@drawable/button_focused" />
  <!-- pressed -->
  <item android:state_pressed="true"
      android:drawable="@drawable/button_pressed" />
```

```
<!-- default -->
<item android:drawable="@drawable/button_normal" />
</selector>
```

Along with visual indicators, you should also add audio cues. These cues can help a user determine that input was received, and they are of particular help when reaching the end of a scrollable list.

TV Capabilities

TVs come in different sizes and shapes, and not all TVs even contain the same aspect ratio. Many TVs may contain an aspect ratio of 16:9, whereas others may have a 4:3 or even a 21:9 aspect ratio. Despite these current differences in aspect ratio, Google recommends that you build your visual assets for a 1920×1080 screen (HD). In addition to this size, you should add 5% to the size to account for motion as part of the interface. This gives you a working space of 2016×1134px.

Another issue that some TV screens present is "overscan," which used to refer to the margin of space that falls outside the bezel or display range when the image is projected on the TV screen. Today, this applies to the zoom level a TV may have enabled. You can get around this issue by making sure that your critical content has at least 48px of space from the left and right sides of the screen as well 27px of space between the top and bottom. If you are working at a different size, you should be safe by using a margin of 10% for the width and height of the screen. This area is known as the "action-safe area."

The following shows a `LinearLayout` that takes into consideration the margin values to make sure the content shown will be inside of the action-safe area:

```xml
<?xml version="1.0" encoding="utf-8"?>
<LinearLayout xmlns:android="http://schemas.android.com/apk/res/android"
  android:id="@+id/base_layout"
  android:layout_width="match_parent"
  android:layout_height="match_parent"
  android:orientation="vertical"
  android:layout_marginTop="27dp"
  android:layout_marginLeft="48dp"
  android:layout_marginRight="48dp"
  android:layout_marginBottom="27dp" >
</LinearLayout>
```

> **Tip**
>
> As a reminder to those new to using the `android:orientation` property, it contains a value of `vertical`, which does not mean that the layout will be in portrait. Instead, views will be stacked rather than placed side-by-side.

To recap, when working with a screen, you should plan on the following:

- Background assets should be 2016×1134px.

- Designs should fit within 1920×1080px.

- The action-safe area is inside of 1728×972px.

Many TVs also differ in included functionality. To address these issues, the following feature descriptors are unavailable to Android TV:

- `android.hardware.touchscreen`

- `android.hardware.faketouch`

- `android.hardware.telephony`

- `android.hardware.camera`

- `android.hardware.bluetooth`

- `android.hardware.nfc`

- `android.hardware.location.gps`

- `android.hardware.microphone`

- `android.hardware.sensor`

Note that even though `android.hardware.microphone` is listed here, this does not apply to the microphone input of a remote or controller.

If you have created a cross-platform application that does use one or more of these features on other devices but will continue to function without them, you can add `android:required="false"` to any element. This way, users can enjoy all of the features or enhancements of your app on their phone or tablet, and still have some functionality on their Android TV.

Text, Color, and Bitmaps

Text sizes, colors, and bitmaps all important when you are working with Android TV. The variety in the technology, size, and shape of a TV adds a new layer of complexity and fragmentation to deal with. To provide the best experience, make sure you implement the following guidelines:

- Text should have a minimum size of 12sp (scale-independent).

- Text by default should have a size of 18sp.

- Card titles should be sized at 16sp in Roboto Condensed.

- Card subtext should be sized at 12sp in Roboto Condensed.

- Browse screen titles should be 44sp in Roboto Regular.

- Browse category titles should be 20sp in Roboto Condensed.

- Details content titles should be 34sp in Roboto Regular.

- Details subtext should be 14sp in Roboto Regular.

- Make your text concise and easy to read in chunks rather than in long paragraphs and sentences.

- Use light-colored text on dark-colored backgrounds.

- Sans-serif and anti-aliased fonts are the easiest to read on TV screens.

- Use dp and sp units rather than absolute pixels.

Using sp units over dp (density-independent) units is suggested with Android TV, as it will scale based on user font-size preferences. A dp value may or may not be accurate based on the device and TV in use.

It is important to follow these guidelines so that when users are using their Android TV your app looks same on the Browse screen and when viewing the Details sceen and the Cards of recently used or viewed items, thus giving the user a consistent and enjoyable experience.

You should always avoid using "light" or "thin" fonts and styles because this may give your fonts an aliased or jagged appearance on some TV screens.

When working with color, keep the following guidelines in mind:

- Colors will not render the same on TV screens as they do on monitors, phones, and tablets.

- Some TVs apply smoothing, sharpening, saturation, and other filters that may distort or change color.

- Environmental differences may change color hue, brightness, and saturation.

- Some TV are unable to show perfect gradients and will instead provide color bands.

- Be careful when using pure or highly saturated colors for large areas of the screen; these may be displayed at an overly intense level compared to the rest of your colors.

- Avoid filling the screen with pure white.

- Add high contrast to elements that are different from each other so that the images and sections do not appear muddy and are easy to visually recognize as different areas.

- Always make sure that text and backgrounds have a high level of contrast; otherwise, text may become impossible to read.

Your app should have an app banner that can be displayed on the home screen of the Android TV device. This banner should be 320×180px (xhdpi resource). There should be legible text in the image rather than just a picture. Note that if you offer a multilingual app, you must include an app banner for every language you support. This app banner is configured by adding the following property to your application manifest XML:

```
<application
  ...
  android:banner="@drawable/banner">
  <!-- other manifest elements go here -->
</application>
```

The home screen of Android TV displays recommendations based on user activity. These recommendations consist of a few components:

- Large icon
- Small icon
- Content title
- Content text
- Background (optional)

Figure 19.1 shows a wireframe of the card that displays these components for apps.

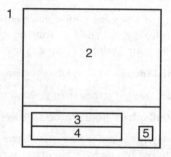

Figure 19.1   (1) Background image, (2) large icon, (3) content title, (4) content text, (5) small icon

Follow these guidelines for the large icon:

- Cannot be a transparent image.
- Minimum height of 176dp.
- Minimum width of 2/3 the height (if 176dp tall, the minimum width should be 117dp).
- Maximum width of 4/3 the height (if 176dp tall, the maximum width should be 234dp).

The small icon should follow these guidelines:

- Flat image.
- Will be displayed at 100% opacity when the card is selected and at 50% when the card is not selected.

- Icon should be imposed over the colored background for the title and content section.

- The icon should have a size of 16×16dp with a white icon on a transparent background saved in a monocolor PNG format.

As a reminder, the text on these cards should follow these guidelines:

- Card titles should be sized at 16sp in Roboto Condensed.

- Card subtext should be sized at 12sp in Roboto Condensed.

The background image will be shown as a full-screen background when your card is selected. It should not be just a larger or expanded image of the large icon, but should show another image of your app or content that enhances the experience. It should follow these guidelines:

- Must be 2016×1134 (otherwise, the system will scale).

- Must not be transparent.

Widgets are provided in the Leanback support library that add support for these background images as well as update them as items gain and lose focus.

When you're working with bitmaps, the same performance enhancements apply that are recommended with standard Android apps. The following list contains the recommendations for working with large bitmaps in your Android TV app:

- Use the `recycle()` method on any `Bitmap` objects when they are no longer needed.

- Load images when they are needed rather than preloading them.

- Use an `AsyncTask` or a similar background process to get images from the network.

- Either work with appropriately sized images or resize the images when you download them rather than trying to put too large of an image in place.

Building an App

The quickest way to get started building an Android TV app is to use Android Studio and start a new project. When you are in the New Project Wizard, uncheck the Phone and Tablet option and check the TV option. After you choose this option, you can set a target SDK level. Similar to when you work with phone and tablet apps, choose a minimum level rather than a maximum level. Note that Android TV requires a minimum level of Lollipop (API level 21).

> **Note**
>
> If you cannot choose the TV option because it is grayed out, launch the Android SDK Manager and update your SDK packages.

After finishing the New Project Wizard, you will have a project with three layout files:

- `activity_details.xml`
- `activity_main.xml`
- `playback_controls.xml`

As mentioned earlier, it is good practice to create Android TV apps using Fragments. Each of these files contains a Fragment that will handle a different portion of your app.

Another file you should be aware of is `res/values/themes.xml`. This file is included automatically when you create a new Android TV project and includes the theme for Leanback. It also sets up the styles of several items. The following shows the file's content:

```xml
<resources>
  <style name="Theme.Example.Leanback" parent="Theme.Leanback">
    <item name="android:windowEnterTransition">@android:transition/fade</item>
    <item name="android:windowExitTransition">@android:transition/fade</item>
    <item name="android:windowSharedElementExitTransition">
      @android:transition/move
    </item>
    <item name="android:windowSharedElementEnterTransition">
      @android:transition/move
    </item>
    <item name="android:windowAllowReturnTransitionOverlap">true</item>
    <item name="android:windowAllowEnterTransitionOverlap">true</item>
    <item name="android:windowContentTransitions">true</item>
    <item name="android:colorPrimary">@color/search_opaque</item>

  </style>
</resources>
```

The next file you should examine is the application manifest XML. This file contains several important elements, including Leanback declarations as well as setting up your project activities. The following shows the contents of the `AndoridManifest.xml` file:

```xml
<?xml version="1.0" encoding="utf-8"?>
<manifest xmlns:android="http://schemas.android.com/apk/res/android"
  package="com.dutsonpa.helloatv" >

  <uses-permission android:name="android.permission.INTERNET" />
  <uses-permission android:name="android.permission.RECORD_AUDIO" />

  <uses-feature
    android:name="android.hardware.touchscreen"
    android:required="false" />
```

```
<uses-feature
  android:name="android.software.leanback"
  android:required="true" />

<application
  android:allowBackup="true"
  android:icon="@mipmap/ic_launcher"
  android:label="@string/app_name"
  android:supportsRtl="true"
  android:theme="@style/Theme.Leanback" >
  <activity
    android:name=".MainActivity"
    android:banner="@drawable/app_icon_your_company"
    android:icon="@drawable/app_icon_your_company"
    android:label="@string/app_name"
    android:logo="@drawable/app_icon_your_company"
    android:screenOrientation="landscape" >
    <intent-filter>
      <action android:name="android.intent.action.MAIN" />

      <category android:name="android.intent.category.LEANBACK_LAUNCHER" />
    </intent-filter>
  </activity>
  <activity android:name=".DetailsActivity" />
  <activity android:name=".PlaybackOverlayActivity" />
  <activity android:name=".BrowseErrorActivity" />
</application>
</manifest>
```

It is worth taking particular notice of the element `<category android:name="android.
intent.category.LEANBACK_LAUNCHER" />`. If you do not include this filter, your app will
not be visible to users running the Google Play Store on their Android TV device. Beyond that,
it will not even be visible when loading your app through developer tools. This filter should
always be in place when creating Android TV apps.

As previously mentioned, not all hardware features of Android are supported on Android TV.
To make sure that app knows that a touchscreen is not required, it has been included along
with the property `android:required="false"`. This allows the system to function even
though a touchscreen is not detected, as well as to display your app in the Play Store on the
Android TV device.

The last file you should check is the `gradle.build` file in the app module. This file contains
some support libraries that you will want to include to make your app function correctly. Note
the following dependencies that should be included:

```
dependencies {
  compile fileTree(dir: 'libs', include: ['*.jar'])
  compile 'com.android.support:recyclerview-v7:23.0.1'
```

```
    compile 'com.android.support:leanback-v17:23.0.1'
    compile 'com.android.support:appcompat-v7:23.0.1'
    compile 'com.github.bumptech.glide:glide:3.4.+'
}
```

Each of these dependencies offers methods that your app will need. Here's a list of them and what they do:

- **recyclerview**: This provides the needed classes for displaying long lists and is required by the Leanback library.

- **leanback**: This provides the widgets, themes, and media playback support essential for proper Android TV app functionality.

- **appcompat**: This provides compatible dialogs, activities, and other classes that allow your app to work with different base versions of Android.

- **glide**: This is not a required dependency; however, it provides a visual media service that efficiently retrieves and processes visual media files. You can learn more about glide by visiting https://github.com/bumptech/glide.

- **cardview**: This dependency is not included in the example; however, consider using it for displaying media files as well as descriptions on cards.

Now that you have a sample project ready to go, it is time to look at how you debug and view it.

Emulation and Testing

If you own an Android TV device, you may be able to use it to debug over USB. The process to enable Developer Mode is similar to a standard Android device. In short, you need to perform the following steps:

1. Navigate to the system settings.

2. Find the Device row and select **About**.

3. Scroll down to Build and click or press the **Enter** key on your remote repeatedly until a message appears saying "You are now a developer."

4. Navigate to the Preferences row and select **Developer options**.

5. Select **USB Debugging** and select **On**.

6. Connect a USB cable between your Android TV device and your computer.

When you connect the USB cable to your computer, you may see an "Allow USB Debugging" message appear; you can then select to always allow or just for this time. Once you have done that, running the adb command from a console or terminal window should show the Android

TV device. Once it appears in the list, you can then use Android Studio or the adb command to start working with and debugging your app.

If you do not have an Android TV device, you can still create an emulator using the AVD Manager. Either you can create a manual emulator, or you can follow the wizard by following these steps:

- Select "TV" for the Category type.

- Select a TV size and resolution that you wish to emulate and then click Next.

- Select the version of Android TV that wish to run on the emulator as well as the CPU type. (Note that on most systems, selecting an x86 will yield a faster running emulator.) Click Next.

- Confirm the device settings, or use the buttons and fields to make changes. (Note that changing the Android TV to run in Portrait orientation is possible, but not recommended). Click Next.

- Wait for the emulator to be built, select the emulator, and then click the launch icon to start the AVD.

Note that when you are emulating a TV, either you need a monitor with a higher resolution than the AVD or you need to scale the AVD.

There are two ways you can scale the AVD:

- You can open the AVD Manager and click the Edit button (the icon that looks like a pencil) for your Android TV AVD and then change the Scale setting to scale to make the AVD appear larger or smaller on your monitor.

- You can change your launch configuration to scale from inside of Android Studio. This can be done by clicking Run in the File menu and then clicking Edit Configurations. In the window that appears, find the Target Device section and click the Emulator radio button and choose your AVD. Now scroll back up and click the Emulator tab. In this section, there is a line labeled Additional Command Line options. In this field, enter the percent you want the emulator to scale to. For example, if you want the emulator to appear at 70% of normal size, type **-scale 0.70**.

Remember, testing with an emulator is not nearly as good as using an actual device to test with. If you have the ability to get actual hardware, you should do so. This will allow you to test with remotes, controllers, as well as other Bluetooth peripherals and devices.

For simple testing with your emulator, you can use the arrow, Esc (for back), and Enter keys to navigate your application.

Summary

In this chapter, you learned about Android TV and the various components that make up differences between standard Android and Android TV applications.

You learned that dealing with larger screens requires you to think differently to support the features and size of a TV screen versus the smaller screen of phones and tablets. You learned that the layout used on Android TV apps is focused on grids and Fragments.

You also learned about the importance of visual styling. Because TVs are bigger and have a variety of screen technologies in use, text, colors, and images are displayed differently. Therefore, care should be taken to make sure your app is legible and clearly visible.

You learned about the base components required to make an app work on Android TV, including declarations for Leanback support. Leanback not only provides widgets, themes, and utilities, but is necessary for your app to appear in the Google Play Store that is accessible from the Android TV device. You also learned about other dependencies that the Leanback library needs as well as some optional ones that will help you create better Android TV apps.

Finally, you learned about testing your Android TV app on a physical device and an emulator. You were informed about how to unlock developer mode on an actual Android TV device and how to connect to it from your computer. You were then instructed on how to create an emulator using the AVD Manager and how to scale it using two different methods to make sure you can see your app on your computer regardless of the resolution of your monitor or computer screen.

## 20

Application Deployment

Once you have crafted the perfect app, you will need to deploy it. Application deployment is the final step in releasing your app to users. This generally consists of cleaning your project and creating an Android application package (APK). In this chapter, you learn about how to deploy your app from Android Studio as well as preparing the necessary assets needed for a successful launch in the Google Play Store.

Preparing for Deployment

Many developers only think of deploying as a means of taking code and releasing a package or APK file that can be uploaded to Google Play and distributed through the Google Play Store. Although this is definitely a major path for app release, there are other reasons to create and distribute APK files.

You may want to create an APK for the following:

- A privateor contract app release
- App testing with a remote group of users
- Enterprise app management
- Distribution in third-party app stores such as Amazon

When you are ready to deploy, you need to create a production build of your app. You should also make sure you have any external resources ready for use. Depending on the complexity and the intended distribution method of your app, this process may require additional setup and finalization before you can create your APK file.

Production Checklist

Creating a checklist for production allows you to quickly and effectively publish your application. This procedure is great to follow, whether you are a single developer or are working with a team where each member can take a portion of the list and complete it.

Not every item will be needed, and some steps may need to be added or expanded depending on your publishing target. For example, if you are building an enterprise app that will be distributed internally without the need to publish it in an app store, you will probably want to skip creating excess application marketing images and videos and a website; you may, however, opt to spend some time on training materials instead.

Regardless of your intended publication route, the following items will get you started in the correct direction.

Certificate Keys

Certificates are used as cryptographic keys that ensure an application is authentic by means of confirming that the publisher is using an authentic version of the app in their store. You are required to generate a pair of keys and sign your app with them. This ensures that you control the updates for the app and that you are the sole publisher to that app.

Keeping your key in a safe and secure location is paramount because you will be unable to update any apps you have created if you happen to lose your key. Keeping it in a secure location prevents anyone else from using your key to forge and force an update to your users.

Note that if you plan on distributing your app in the Google Play Store, your key must expire after October 22, 2033. Any certificates expiring before that date will cause your app to be rejected from being submitted.

When you publish your app, you can opt to either include your own key in the build process or use Android Studio to sign your application. Both have advantages and disadvantages. Adding the key information to your build process may be a good idea if your publishing setup is mostly automated with regular build cycles. Using Android Studio may be better if you work with limited releases or do not have an automated system for building your app.

Contact Email

A contact email is a requirement for publishing an application on the Google Play Store, and is also a good idea to include because users may need to ask you a question, request support, or in some cases need to be walked through using your app to avoid a refund request.

A contact email may be different from a support email, so you may be interested in providing both. If you do not provide a support email, try to return any emails as soon as you get them to avoid negative user experiences and reviews. When providing a support email, it would be good to include an automatic reply that confirms you have received the original email and that it is being assigned to a support team.

App Website

Creating a website for your application is a good idea, not only because you can host your policies, frequently asked questions, and contact information, but because you can leverage search engines to pick up your app and distribute it. Depending on the app you are creating, you can show in-depth videos and other marketing materials. It also gives you the option to cross-sell or up-sell the user on different products or services that work with or in conjunction with your app.

Some of the most successful apps succeed due to offering cross-platform solutions with a website that demonstrates how each piece works seamlessly with others to provide a service that works no matter what device the user has.

The app website can also be another social touch point that can give users more information on sharing your app with their friends as well as any special contests or events that your app may provide.

External Services or Servers

Making sure that your production servers are ready to go on launch day is an important part of the release process. It may not seem like a big deal, but if you (or your marketing team) have done your job building hype for your app, then it can be the make-or-break experience for many of your users. Few things are worse than a rush on launch day and seeing your app servers crash due to demand and then watching the negative reviews pour in and seeing another app welcome these users with open (and working) arms.

External servers may be used for application resource sharing, handling user requests, messaging, and keeping user information. You can mitigate some of the damage by building web applications that scale, but you may also want to take advantage of the on-boarding process that the Google Play Store offers. This allows you to roll out your application slowly, allowing you to keep a watchful eye on your server logs and processes.

Application Icon

Depending on the structure of your development team, you may have opted to start developing immediately with the default launcher icon rather than wait for a finished design icon. This is perfectly fine, but requires that you remember to insert the production icon before you publish your app.

As a reminder, you should provide a launch icon in the following sizes:

- **LDPI**: 36×36px
- **MDPI**: 48×48px
- **HDPI**: 72×72px

- **XHDPI**: 96×96px
- **XXHDPI**: 144×144px
- **XXXHDPI**: 192×192px

Licensing

Some applications require the user to agree to licensing terms in order to use the app. This agreement allows both sides to come to an understanding of the policies and practices that you have in place as a company or provider. This also gives you protection should a user decide to pursue any legal claims that involve your app.

License agreements are usually offered as an End User License Agreement (EULA) when you are accessing, moving, using, or otherwise working with the personal data of a user. Many users are comfortable giving you access to their data provided that you are not doing so maliciously and that your app offers them a useful interface for their data. A EULA must be offered to the user when they first launch your app, and if they refuse the agreement, the app must close.

A EULA is not a requirement; however, some licensing should be offered with your app. This protects your app from being taken and integrated or distributed without your knowledge and potential gain. In the same vein, if you want your app to be taken and used by others, you can offer a license that allows other developers and companies that ability.

The following is a short list of open-source licenses you may want to use if you are open-sourcing your app:

- **MIT**: http://www.opensource.org/licenses/mit-license.php
- **GPL 2.0**:http://www.gnu.org/licenses/gpl-2.0.html
- **GPL 3.0**: http://www.gnu.org/licenses/gpl-3.0.en.html
- **LGPL 3.0**: http://www.gnu.org/licenses/lgpl-3.0.html
- **Apache License 2.0**:http://www.apache.org/licenses/LICENSE-2.0
- **BSD 3-Clause**:http://opensource.org/licenses/BSD-3-Clause
- **Creative Commons**:https://creativecommons.org/choose/

Appropriate Package Name

The package name of your app is important for more than just the development of your app. Android uses your package name as an actual location on the filesystem to store data and information relative to your application. It also loads your package name into memory and allocates resources based on your package name. You cannot use a package name that another developer has chosen in order to protect applications from clashing and causing the system to be unstable.

For the previously mentioned reasons, it is a good idea to choose a package name based on your company or website name. Because package names are very similar to domain names, you could use a modified version as your package name. This also gives any users who see your package name a clue as to whom a process or file system record belongs.

As an example, if you owned the website www.dutsonpa.com and wanted to create an Android app called Office Warfare, you might consider a package name of com.dutsonpa.officewarfare. This name describes who created the app and what it is called. Depending on your application deployment strategy, you could even modify it slightly to add version or platform information. For example, if there were multiple platform versions, you mightconsider using com.dutsonpa.android.officewarfare to show what platform this package was specifically built for.

Note that once you publish an app to the Google Play Store, you cannot change the package name. Changing the package name registers an "updated" app as a "new" app instead. This leaves fragmented apps behind and may confuse users who suddenly stop receiving app updates and then notice two apps in the App Store with the same name.

Verifying Permissions and Requirements

Before you send your app into the wild, you should make sure you are sending it out with the correct permissions, hardware requirements, and supported API level.

The permissions your application states before installation are important because some users will refuse to install your app if it even hints at potentially using personal data in a way that they do not understand. Taking a few moments to make sure you know what permissions your app requires can go a long way in making your app successful in the marketplace.

You should take the time to check if you are requiring or restricting your app based on hardware requirements. If you are, then now is an ideal time to double-check that you have all of the permissions you need and have not left any out. Ratings slide quickly when users can see and install your app but watch it constantly close without any explanation.

The minimum API level of your application is important because it dictates which users can install it based on the version of Android on their device. Setting the minimum API level low is good for making sure that the maximum number of users can download your app.However, you need to make sure the features you are using support that API level. This may be done with some clever programming, or by including a support library.

If you are not sure what level you should be targeting, you can view the official dashboard at https://developer.android.com/about/dashboards/index.html. This dashboard lists the current distribution of active Android devices. Note that this list is generated by users who have the Google Play Store installed.

Log and Debug Removal

In Chapter 18, "Optimization," you learned about memory usage and ways to make your app run in a cleaner and more efficient manner. In continuing the optimization of your application, you should remove all the debugging and logging from your final production application. This saves the Android system from writing out excess logs that will never be read, and it saves on embarrassing notices, toasts, messages, and other forms of debug values appearing inside of the application.

You will want to remove any calls to the `Log` class as well as remove the `android:debuggable` property from the `<application>` element in your application's manifest XML file. Other debugging methods, such as `startMethodTracing()` and `stopMethodTracing()`, should also be removed.

Removal of Excess Unused Assets

It is not uncommon to have extra assets collect in a project over time. These may include assets that were cut during a release cycle, or ones that were used as placeholders until final art or assets could be approved and integrated into the app.

You should do your best to remove any test libraries, frameworks, extra JAR files that are not needed, unused layouts, strings, and other files. Pay special attention to anything in your `/res/raw` and `/assets` directories because files stored there may take up large amounts of space. These files may also need to be updated to the latest version and may require you to remove files that will no longer be used.

Because every byte of data matters, it is in your best interest to remove as much excess data as possible before you compile and publish your app. Because the space of a single APK file is limited and a user has to download that entire file before they can use your app, you need to be as thorough as possible in cleaning out your app before publishing.

Preparing for Google Play

When distributing your app through the Google Play Store, you have a few more requirements in order to successfully upload and launch your app. As the Google Play Store has matured, it has provided requirements that it has found increase user adoption and that help you feature and promote your app.

If you have not already created a Developer Account with Google, start by visiting https://play.google.com/apps/publish/signup/ and signing in with your Google Account. After you sign up, you need to accept a distributor agreement and pay a one-time fee of $25.

Once you are a registered developer, you can log into your Google Play Developer Account by visiting https://play.google.com/apps/publish/. After logging in, you can either add a new application or work with existing ones. By using the Add New Application button, you are prompted to name your application and either upload an APK or prepare the store listing of your app.

Note that both of these options must be completed before your app will be listed in the Google Play Store.

Application Screenshots

You are allowed to place eight images per form-factor on which your app will run. This means that you can place eight images for the following:

- Phone
- Tablet
- Android TV
- Android Wear

You must provide at least two images in either JPEG or PNG format without any transparency. Images must have a dimension of 320px and a maximum dimension of 3840px, with the maximum being no larger than twice as long as the minimum dimension. It is best to use images that show the functionality of your app and to use actual screenshots of your app in use rather than just promotion or marketing materials.

Note that if you want your application to be featured in the "Designed for Tablets" section of the Google Play Store, you will need to provide tablet-sized images.

You should also be aware that images for Android TV will only appear in the Google Play Store that is used on Android TV devices and not in the same store that tablets and phones use.

Promo Video

You may consider placing a video for your app that highlights the features and shows the app in action. This may also be a trailer or gameplay video that shows your app off in a produced manner. This way, a user can see what your app is like in actual use without having to download and install it first.

Videos must be hosted on YouTube and must not be restricted by age in order to be viewed. You must also make sure the YouTube link you use for your listing is a direct link to your video and not to a playlist or profile page.

When you use a promotional video, it will be shown on the app page as the first viewable graphic asset. This means that if you have uploaded eight other screenshots, the video will appear before these to encourage users to view the video content.

High-Res Icon

The high-res icon is both similar and different from the launch icon you included in your app. The high-res icon is displayed on the Google Play Store in the cards that display apps as well as on the listing page at the top. Because of this, it should be very close if not identical to the launch icon.

The high-res icon should be a 32-bit PNG (with alpha) sized at 512×512px with a maximum file size of 1MB.

Feature Graphic

The feature graphic is used on the listing page of your app and may be used on other pages or sections of the Google Play Store to highlight and show off your app. This image should highlight the creativity of your app, along with easy-to-read text showing the name of your app.

Note that you should avoid text other than the name of your app, and assets should be centered in the image. You should also avoid adding your launch or high-res icon in the image. This is a promotional standalone image that should complement your other assets rather than repeat them.

If you have added a promotional video to your app listing, then a Play button will be placed in the center of the feature graphic allowing users to view your promotional video when tapped or clicked.

The feature graphic should be either a JPEG or a 24-bit PNG (no transparency) with dimensions of 1024×500px.

Promo Graphic

The promo graphic is no longer a required asset and has been replaced by the feature graphic, which is an image that is used in versions of the Google Play Store or Android Market on devices running on Android earlier than 4.0.

The promo graphic should be treated in the same manner as the feature graphic; however, it does have a smaller dimension. It should be a JPEG or 24-bit PNG (no transparency) with dimensions of 180×120px.

Banner for Android TV

The banner is similar to the high-res icon, only it is displayed on Android TV devices only rather than being displayed on phones and tablets. Even though it is called a banner, it has relatively small dimensions.

The banner image should be a JPEG or 24-bit PNG (no transparency) with dimensions of 320×180px.

Getting Paid

If you are planning on charging for your app, you will need to link your Google Play Developer Account to the Google Payments Merchant Center. The Google Payments Merchant Center is where your business information will be stored and will require your legal business name, address, phone number, and the name that will appear on creditcard statements when a transaction is made.

If you already have a Google Play Developer Account and a Google Payments Merchant Center Account, you can link them together by logging into your Google Play Developer Account and clicking the Reports link and then choosing the Financial Reports option. This displays a message prompting you to set up your merchant account.

APK Generation

APK files are generated when the build process runs on your app. That said, the APK generated is usually signed with a debugging key that renders the APK useful for testing, but not usable for distribution. There are ways to sign an already generated APK, but the easiest way to make sure your application is signed and generated correctly is to use the built-in tooling of Android Studio.

Using Android Studio, the signing and APK generation of your app goes as follows:

1. Open your project in Android Studio.

2. Click the Build menu item and then click Generate Signed APK.

3. In the window that appears, select the app module of your app in the Module Selection box and click Next.

4. Select the `keystore` (certificate container with an extension of .jks) you want to use to sign the app. If you do not have one, you can generate one at this step by clicking the Create New... button, choosing a secure place to store the generated `keystore` file, and entering the information requested.

5. After you have either created a `keystore` or selected one and typed in the required passwords, click the Next button to continue.

6. Choose where to store the generated APK file as well as the "release" for the build type. Note that if you have multiple Gradle build configurations, you will have an option to select the one you want to use. Click the Finish button after you make your selection to start building the APK for your app.

When the process has completed, you can take the generated APK file and upload it to the Google Play Developer Console. If you are not planning on distributing your app through the Google Play Store, you can now use the generated APK file through other means of distribution.

If you plan on giving the APK file to other users, note that they will need to configure their Android device to install from "unknown sources." This is done through the device settings under Settings, Security. The user sees a message informing them that trusting unknown sources may make their device and personal data vulnerable to attack and that they agree to be solely responsible for any damage, loss, or theft that occurs from installing unknown apps.

After enabling Unknown Sources, the user can select an APK file through a file manager or similar utility and then launch it. Android recognizes the file and prompts the user to install the app, showing them a list of requested permissions and giving them an opportunity to decline the installation. Once approved, the app will be installed and is accessible in the app drawer.

Summary

In this chapter, you learned about the process of publishing an app. This began with a suggested checklist you should look over to make sure you are ready to publish and distribute your app. You learned about the importance of including these items and were given information on why each item on the list should be included or at least considered.

You learned about the assets required by the Google Play Store in order to make your app launch more successful, and even some extra assets such as promotional videos that will help you sell users on trying out and using your app.

Finally, you learned about using Android Studio to generate a signed APK file with a step-by-step guide for either selecting or creating a keystore for signing your app and creating the APK file. You were also informed of the potential problem of distributing your app outside of the Google Play Store and how users will need to enable or "opt into" allowing apps to be installed from unknown sources.

Index

B

Q-R

S

REGISTER YOUR PRODUCT at informit.com/register
Access Additional Benefits and SAVE 35% on Your Next Purchase

- Download available product updates.

- Access bonus material when applicable.

- Receive exclusive offers on new editions and related products.
  (Just check the box to hear from us when setting up your account.)

- Get a coupon for 35% for your next purchase, valid for 30 days. Your code will
  be available in your InformIT cart. (You will also find it in the Manage Codes
  section of your account page.)

Registration benefits vary by product. Benefits will be listed on your account page
under Registered Products.

InformIT.com—The Trusted Technology Learning Source

InformIT is the online home of information technology brands at Pearson, the world's foremost
education company. At InformIT.com you can
- Shop our books, eBooks, software, and video training.
- Take advantage of our special offers and promotions (informit.com/promotions).
- Sign up for special offers and content newsletters (informit.com/newsletters).
- Read free articles and blogs by information technology experts.
- Access thousands of free chapters and video lessons.

Connect with InformIT—Visit informit.com/community

Learn about InformIT community events and programs.

the trusted technology learning source

Addison-Wesley • Cisco Press • IBM Press • Microsoft Press • Pearson IT Certification • Prentice Hall • Que • Sams • VMware Press